SOLUTION-BASED CASEWORK

MODERN APPLICATIONS OF SOCIAL WORK

An Aldine de Gruyter Series of Texts and Monographs

Series Editor: James K. Whittaker

Paul Adams and Kristine Nelson (eds.), **Reinventing Human Services: Community- and Family-Centered Practice**

Ralph E. Anderson and Irl Carter, with Gary Lowe, **Human Behavior in the Social Environment: A Social Systems Approach** (Fifth Edition)

Richard P. Barth, Mark Courtney, Jill Duerr Berrick, and Vicky Albert, **From Child Abuse to Permanency Planning: Child Welfare Services Pathways and Placements**

Dana N. Christensen, Jeffrey Todahl, and William C. Barrett, **Solution-Based Casework: An Introduction to Clinical and Case Management Skills in Casework Practice**

Marie Connolly, with Margaret McKenzie, **Effective Participatory Practice: Family Group Conferencing in Child Protection**

Kathleen Ell and Helen Northen, **Families and Health Care: Psychosocial Practice**

Marian F. Fatout, **Models for Change in Social Group Work**

Mark W. Fraser, Peter J. Pecora, and David A. Haapala, **Families in Crisis: The Impact of Intensive Family Preservation Services**

James Garbarino, **Children and Families in the Social Environment** (Second Edition)

James Garbarino, and Associates, **Special Children—Special Risks: The Maltreatment of Children with Disabilities**

Roberta R. Greene, **Human Behavior Theory: A Diversity Framework**

Roberta R. Greene, **Human Behavior Theory and Social Work Practice** (Second Edition)

Roberta R. Greene, **Social Work with the Aged and Their Families**

Roberta R. Greene and Marie Watkins (eds.), **Serving Diverse Constituencies: Applying the Ecological Perspective**

André M. Ivanoff, Betty J. Blythe, and Tony Tripodi, **Involuntary Clients in Social Work Practice: A Research-Based Approach**

Jill Kinney, David A. Haapala, and Charlotte Booth, **Keeping Families Together: The Homebuilders Model**

Robert M. Moroney and Judy Krysik, **Social Policy and Social Work: Critical Essays on the Welfare State** (Second Edition)

Peter J. Pecora, Mark W. Fraser, Kristine Nelson, Jacqueline McCroskey, and William Meezan, **Evaluating Family-Based Services**

Peter J. Pecora, James K. Whittaker, Anthony N. Maluccio, Richard P. Barth, and Robert D. Plotnick, **The Child Welfare Challenge: Policy, Practice, and Research**

John R. Schuerman, Tina L. Rzepnicki, and Julia H. Littell, **Putting Families First: An Experiment in Family Preservation**

Madeleine R. Stoner, **The Civil Rights of Homeless People: Law, Social Policy, and Social Work Practice**

Albert E. Trieschman, James K. Whittaker, and Larry K. Brendtro, **The Other 23 Hours: Child-Care Work with Emotionally Disturbed Children in a Therapeutic Milieu**

Harry H. Vorrath and Larry K. Brendtro, **Positive Peer Culture** (Second Edition)

Betsy S. Vourlekis and Roberta R. Green (eds.), **Social Work Case Management**

James K. Whittaker, and Associates, **Reaching High-Risk Families: Intensive Family Preservation in Human Services**

SOLUTION-BASED CASEWORK

An Introduction to Clinical and Case Management
Skills in Casework Practice

Dana N. Christensen
Jeffrey Todahl
William C. Barrett

ALDINE DE GRUYTER
New York

About the Authors

Dana N. Christensen is Professor and Director of the Center for Family Resource Development, Kent School of Social Work, University of Louisville.

Jeffrey Todahl is Assistant Professor, specialization in Marriage and Family Therapy, College of Education, University of Oregon.

William C. Barrett is in private practice, Family Interventions of Kentucky, Frankfort, Kentucky.

ALDINE DE GRUYTER
A division of Walter de Gruyter, Inc.
200 Saw Mill River Road
Hawthorne, New York 10532

This publication is printed on acid free paper ∞

Library of Congress Cataloging-in-Publication Data
Christensen, Dana N., 1950–
    Solution-based casework : an introduction to clinical and case management skills in casework practice / Dana N. Christensen, Jeffrey Todahl, and William C. Barrett.
      p.   cm.
    Includes bibliographical references and index.
    ISBN 0-202-36117-9 (cloth : alk. paper). — ISBN 0-202-36118-7 (paper : alk. paper)
    1. Social case work. 2. Family social work. 3. Solution-focused therapy. I. Todahl, Jeffrey, 1963– . II. Barrett, William C., 1948– . II. Title.
HV43.C516 1999
361.3'2—dc21   99-22992
                                                  CIP

Manufacured in the United States of America

10 9 8 7 6 5 4 3 2 1

Contents

Introduction   xi

I. HISTORICAL CONTEXT

1   The Foundations of Solution-Based Casework   3

    Family-Centered Practice   3
    Ecological Perspective   4
    Competence-Centered Perspective   7
    Family Life Cycle Theory   9
    Postmodern Family Casework   11
    Solution-Focused Family Therapy   13
    Relapse Prevention Theory   15
    Integrating Solution-Focused and
       Problem-Centered Models   17

2   Searching for Solutions in the Postmodern
    World   21

    The Evolution of Casework Practice   22
    Current Challenges to Casework   25
    Rising Pressure from the Welfare to Work
       Movement   28
    Emerging Responses to the Crisis in
       Casework   29

II. ASSESSMENT

3   Anchoring Casework in Everyday Life Events   37

    "Sorting Things Out" Together   37

Partnership Changes the Meaning of
  Assessment   38
Keeping Ourselves Focused on Everyday
  Life   38
Routines Are at the Heart of Family Life   39
The Problem with Solutions   40
Overview of Family Development   41
Beginning Couple   42
Infant Preschool Family   43
School-Age Family   44
Adolescent Family   45
Launching Family   46
Postparental Family   47
Divorce and Remarriage   47
Keeping Your Finger on the Pulse of Family
  Life   48
Everyday Life and Patterns of
  Discouragement   49

4   Recognizing Patterns   51

Assessing Patterns in Everyday Life   51
Creating a Partnership to Find Solutions   52
Techniques for Building Partnerships   53
Recognizing Dominant Patterns in
  Everyday Life   56
Helping the Family Describe the Problem in
  Everyday Life Terms   57
Decision-Making in Assessment   62

5   Assessing Problem Detail   65

Relapse Prevention Requires Specific Skills   65
What Skills Should Be Targeted for
  Outcome?   65
Steps to Promoting Prevention Skills   68
Step 1: Recognizing Patterns in High-Risk
  Situations   68
Step 2: Learning the Details of High-Risk
  Patterns   69

Step 3: Practicing Small Steps toward
    Change   73
Step 4: Creating a Plan That Stays Focused
    on Solutions   76
Reinforcing Client Progress During
    Assessment   79
Summary   80

6   Building a Consensus for a Prevention Plan   83

Co-Constructing Measurable Goals with
    Your Clients   83
Searching for Solutions   83
Strategies That Work in Gaining Goal
    Consensus   86
Helping Clients Establish an Initial Safety
    Plan   94
Thinking Long-Term While Taking Short-
    Term Steps   95
What Goes into a Good Initial Safety Plan?   96
Considerations on Implementing a Safety
    Plan   96
Summary of the Role of Assessment in Case
    Planning   97
Appendix   99

III. MANAGEMENT ISSUES

7   The Process of Writing Objectives and Tasks   105

The Advantages of Being Specific and
    Measurable   105
When Case Plans Become Court Documents   107
Writing a Case Plan That Is Focused on
    Solutions   108
Uniting Around a Family Goal   109

Breaking Down the Goal into Family
   Objectives   109
Going from Family-Level Objectives to
   Individual-Level Objectives   110
The Primacy of Risk-Related Objectives   112
Breaking Down Objectives into Manageable
   Tasks   112
Writing Action Plans to Prevent Relapse   118

8   Solution-Based Case Management   125

The Challenge of Staying the Course   125
A Reminder about Targeting Outcome
   Skills   126
Challenge 1: Making the Transition from
   Intake to Ongoing   127
Challenge 2: Making the Transition from
   Casework to Treatment   132
Challenge 3: Integrating Welfare to Work
   Objectives   136
Challenge 4: Making the Most of Setbacks   136
Supervisor's Role in Case Management   140
Taking the Time to Supervise   141
Maintaining a Partnership   142
Maintaining a Focus on Specific Situations
   in Family Life   143
Summary   146

9   Treatment Providers' Role in Case
    Management   149

Introduction   149
Gathering Basic Information about the
   Referral   152
What Happened?   152
What Is the Safety Plan?   153
How Has the Problem Been Defined with
   the Family?   154

Sample Dialogue at the Time of Referral   155
Offering Services to Mirror Family
     Developmental Needs   159
Overview of Steps to Prevention   163
Helping Clients Learn the Details of Their
     Patterns   164
Helping Clients Practice Small Steps of
     Change   166
Helping Clients Develop Relapse
     Prevention Plans   168
Summary of Solution-Based Interviewing
     Techniques   169
Strategies for Collaboration   170

10   Solution-Based Interviewing Techniques   175

Techniques That Build a Consensus about
     the Problem   176
Normalizing   177
Externalizing the Problem   178
Searching for Exceptions to the Pattern   179
Tracking the Problem Pattern   180
Techniques for Creating Interest in Signs of
     Change   184
Between Session Observation   185
Old versus New T-Charts   186
Scaling Questions   187
Time-Oriented Questions   189
Anchoring Change in the New Self   191
Expanding the Audience for Change   192
Reinforcing Progress through Credentialing   194
Celebrating Rites of Passage   195
Reference Reading Specifically for
     Technique   197

11   How Staff Experience Change   199

Frustration and Old Models   199
Advantages to Solution-Based Casework   203
Challenges Inherent in Changing Habits   207
Success Stories   209

Implementing Solution-Based Casework:
   Training Considerations   213

References   219

Index   225

Introduction

Solution-based casework is an approach to assessment, case planning, and case management that combines what we know from clinical social work with what we value about sound social work practice. This text is a broad-based introduction to the concepts, skills, and practices that are considered important to case work practice in the postmodern world. Solution-based casework is grounded in family-centered social work and draws from clinical approaches within social work and mental health. The model further combines the best of problem-focused, relapse prevention approaches, which evolved from work with addiction and violence (Marlatt & Gordon, 1985; Pithers, 1990), with solution-focused models, which evolved from family systems therapy (Berg, 1994; de Shazer, 1988). By integrating problem- and solution-focused approaches from the clinical and social work traditions, treatment partnerships are more easily formed between family, caseworker, and service provider. Although treatment partnerships have always been effective, they are increasingly critical in a postmodern world of limited resources and increasing demand. A solution-based casework approach to social services builds a partnership that pragmatically focuses on the necessary skills that will account for safety and restore family pride in their own competence.

The approach was developed through consultation with workers, their supervisors, and their treatment providers, who were attempting to remedy problems viewed as contributing to recurrence of abuse and neglect (Christensen & Todahl, 1999). Problems identified included the following:

- Casework relationships in high-risk cases were frequently adversarial, with significant barriers to information necessary for assessing risk.
- Case plans were often written with outcome goals designating attendance in counseling versus the acquisition of specific skills.
- At-risk cases were red-flagged after a recurrence of abuse or neglect, rather than much earlier (e.g., after a lapse into high-risk behavior).
- Assessments and case plans were often based solely on the caretaker's (typically the mother's) degree of protectiveness, with no individual goals delineated for the offending family member.

- The original everyday developmental tasks that the family was having difficulty with (e.g., toilet training) got lost in the case after a while, and compliance issues replaced them as the central concern.
- Caseworkers had one thing in mind (which was too often vaguely defined) and the treatment provider/clinician had something else entirely different in mind (also too vaguely defined).
- Because no outcome skills were defined, caseworkers often deferred to treatment providers to tell them (based solely on clinical judgment) whether or not clients were now safe.
- Courts were often provided facts about a case without an organized attempt to specifically identify which skills clients had to demonstrate.

Clinicians and caseworkers wanted to work more closely together on agreed-upon outcomes. Lacking a common conceptual map was considered a significant barrier to improving their partnership with each other and with families.

Solution-based casework has been shown to serve as a common conceptual framework for integrating disparate segments of a response network. Because the model provides for specific outcome skills necessary for relapse prevention, and embraces family competency, all members of a therapeutic system (defined broadly) can work toward common goals. Because the model utilizes a partnership model based on what is successful, the family members are in a position to share good news about their progress in one area with providers who are working on another related aspect of the problem. Moreover, solution-based casework provides a method for tapping a family's areas of competence without diminishing the significance of everyone's concern for safety. We believe that developing partnerships that lead to identifiable family solutions is the best way to prevent future relapse.

Solution-Based Casework: An Introduction to Clinical and Case Management Skill in Casework Practice has been written to provide practitioners with a critical set of perspectives and skills that will guide them in meeting the challenges they face in modern social work practice. Although the text includes many useful specifics regarding assessment, case planning, case management, and treatment collaboration, students of social work practice will clearly need to know other useful and necessary areas of knowledge that go beyond the scope of this text, for instance, information on culture and gender, the scope of social practice, and specific assessment tools. This text has been written to provide specific information on basic casework skills that ought to be an integral part of every practitioner's preparation.

The text is divided into three sections. In Section I, which includes Chapters 1 and 2, the conceptual history and theoretical foundations of solution-based casework are presented so that the reader can place this approach to casework within the ongoing professional conversation about what constitutes sound practice. Chapter 1 discusses the significant influence of family-centered practice approaches as well as the more clinical influences of solution-focused therapy and relapse prevention theory. Chapter 2 traces the evolution of casework practice and attempts to build a case for adapting our approaches to the needs of emerging crises in the postmodern world.

Section II addresses issues of assessment and case planning. Chapter 3 discusses the need to anchor assessment in the everyday life of the family so that the family views the casework relationship as a useful partnership rather than a judgmental requirement or imposition. Chapter 4 introduces the importance of tracking specific patterns in the everyday life of families that lead to high-risk situations. Chapter 5 continues to discuss patterns of behavior and their importance to identifying relevant skills that will be needed to prevent future recurrence of the presenting problems. Chapter 6 assists the reader in taking the assessment information and using it to build a consensus with the family regarding a prevention plan. The chapter includes information on how to co-construct measurable goals with the family, strategies for gaining goal consensus, and techniques for establishing an initial safety plan.

Section III focuses on case management issues and how treatment team members experience a solution-based casework approach. Chapter 7 discusses the relevance of writing objectives and tasks that will guide case management when constructing a case plan. Chapter 8 presents the real-world challenges that sound case management faces in a segmented service delivery system. Specific suggestions are offered regarding how to meet those challenges and maintain the treatment team's focus on critical prevention skills that will reduce risk to family members. Chapter 9 looks at case management form the treatment provider's position. The chapter is written specifically for clinicians who work closely with caseworkers as well as for caseworkers who want to understand how a treatment provider thinks about their collaborative work. Chapter 10 concludes this section by reviewing the major interviewing techniques useful in solution-based casework. Although interviewing techniques are discussed throughout the book, all of the interviewing techniques are pulled together in this chapter so that their differences and similarities can be studied and practiced.

Because solution-based casework offers such a different working experience for many social workers, Chapter 11 discusses how staff react to the experience of working from a solution-based model. In their own words, workers, supervisors, and treatment providers discuss their frustrations with deficit models, advantages to changing their approaches, challenges to overcome, and finally their success stories. The text concludes with a brief description of several training considerations for a solution-based approach to casework.

Part I

Historical Context

Chapter 1

The Foundations of Solution-Based Casework

The concepts underlying solution-based casework are strongly influenced by social work theory and practice (Adams & Nelson, 1995; Germain & Gitterman, 1996; Hartman & Laird, 1983; Kemp, Whittaker, & Tracy, 1997; Pecora, Whittaker, Maluccio, Barth, & Plotnick, 1992), family developmental theory (Carter & McGoldrick, 1980; Duvall, 1957, 1971), solution-focused therapy (Berg, 1994; de Shazer, 1985, 1988, 1991; O'Hanlon & Weiner-Davis, 1989), and relapse prevention theory (Lane, 1991; Pithers, Marques, Gilbat, & Marlatt, 1983).

Informed by that rich body of literature, solution-based casework assumes that human problems can only be accurately understood in light of the context in which they occur and that case planning must take into consideration environmental factors, client competencies, family development, and relapse prevention strategies. Each of these factors is important in the effort to form enduring worker-client partnerships and in developing case plans that (1) are tied to everyday life events, (2) are measurable, (3) are accountable, (4) specifically target high-risk behaviors, and (5) plan for relapse prevention. Solution-based casework is a conceptual and skills-based practice model that we believe complements the social work and casework literature (e.g., Kemp et al., 1997). This chapter describes the major assumptions of solution-based casework and their relevance to social service professionals.

FAMILY-CENTERED PRACTICE

Solution-based casework is a family-centered model of casework practice. We agree with Nunnally, Chilman, and Cox (1988), who define family as "two or more people in a committed relationship from which they derive a sense of identity as a family," thereby including "nontraditional family forms that are outside the traditional legal perspective, . . .

3

families not related by blood, marriage, or adoption" (p. 11). Solution-based casework assumes that casework and human service delivery "should address the interface between human beings and their imping-ing environments" (Pecora et al., 1992). Further, as described by Germain (1979), practice should be "directed toward improving the transactions between people and environments in order to enhance adap-tive capacities and improve environments for all who function within them" (p. 8).

Given these assumptions, solution-based casework emphasizes ecolog-ical variables (Germain, 1979), community and community resources (Adams & Nelson, 1995), individual and family resources (Hartman & Laird, 1983), developmental theory (Carter & McGoldrick, 1980), and client competencies (Maluccio, 1981). Further, the permanency planning orientation, which argues that "all children are entitled to live in perma-nent families . . . preferably his or her own biological family" (Pecora et al., 1992, pp. 43–44), is endorsed. Casework should have as its primary objective the prevention and reduction of destructive behaviors. This is most apt to be achieved with a casework model that integrates (1) an ecological perspective, (2) an emphasis on communities and families as resources, (3) a respect for client competence, (4) a postmodern value base, and (5) planning that is rooted in relapse prevention. This orienta-tion promotes partnerships between professionals and service recipients that are focused on the prevention and reduction of destructive behavior.

ECOLOGICAL PERSPECTIVE

The ecological perspective suggests that individuals and families influ-ence and are influenced by their social context. "Ecology," therefore, is a metaphor that urges social scientists to understand behavior in light of the surrounding environment (Hartman & Laird, 1983). For instance, ma-rine biologists readily acknowledge that to understand the rapid extinc-tion of a particular species of sea life it is often necessary to study certain contextual variables, e.g., weather patterns, pollutants, and disease. Like-wise, social scientists who adopt an ecological perspective assume that individual behavior is multi-influenced by context. This stands in stark contrast to historical clinical paradigms, which assume that the contents of one's psyche adequately explain one's behavior. Seen in the light of ecology, behavior is multifactorial, i.e., influenced by one's beliefs, social values, socioeconomics, and a host of other variables. As described by Hartman and Laird (1983), "a human being can be considered variously as a psychological system, a chemical system, a biological system, or as a subsystem of many social systems" (p. 63). Individuals and families are therefore not seen as isolates, but as participants in a dynamic, living environment. To adequately understand individuals and relationships, one must also understand their "surround" (von Bertalanffy, 1968).

Given its affinity for context, the ecological perspective demands a panoramic view of assessment. Rather than attempting to understand behavior through the narrow lens of any single explanation, e.g., psyche, ego, or psychopathology, an ecological perspective investigates numerous micro and macro explanations. As a result, factors that are considered potentially relevant to problems in living are significantly expanded. This extension of assessment data is literally reflected in assessment questioning. For instance, rather than a primary interest in client mood, deficits, and beliefs, questions also are raised about community beliefs, community resources, potential acculturation issues, etc. It is not immediately assumed that clients live and breathe in an impenetrable shell that separates them from their environment. Instead, environmental factors are seen as completely relevant in assessing needs and in planning. Indeed, given the living, dynamic, and mutually influencing nature of individuals and society, changes in the environment are noteworthy. The correlation between the closing of an industrial plant, rising unemployment, and rising domestic assault should be considered relevant to the social service professional. Although one may not be able to change capitalist tides, one can assist clients in recognizing how their employment-related stressors contribute to their overall ability to manage their anger and factor that knowledge into relapse prevention planning. In that regard, traditional psychological explanations of problematic behavior are assumed to be inordinately narrow and, taken by themselves, inadequate.

When assessing problematic behavior, the ecological perspective holds that competent assessment must attend to micro (e.g., personality) and macro (e.g., socioeconomic) factors. However, given the abundance of potential contributing factors, this can be a daunting, even overwhelming task. Indeed, many ecologically sensitive assessment models have been promoted. Lee (1994) advocates "fifocal vision," an approach to assessment that fosters client empowerment by placing problematic behavior in an historical, class structure, and gender context. With this perspective, assessment moves well beyond a search for individual psychopathology. Instead, one wonders for instance how racism, social policy, gender discrimination, ethnocentrism, and classism may contribute to presenting issues. It is not immediately assumed, therefore, that stress is only self-induced or that stressors reside exclusively within the individual. Fifocal vision, argues Lee, is empowering and has direct implications for intervention. "These principles can guide us in thinking about situations of oppression . . . and in empowerment, including the development of criti-cal thinking, praxis, and raised consciousness" (p. 27).

Ecological assessment also considers environmental "fit," or the degree to which the environment provides adequate resources and, in turn, the degree to which residents meet their own needs in light of those re-sources. In this sense, dangerous behaviors are often associated with one's "mis-fit" with his or her environment. Consider the father who forcibly restrained and assaulted his adolescent son because, as described by the father, "The boy is bad. He is a bad boy." The temptation is to readily conclude that any father who assaults his child is destructive, unhealthy, and requires intervention to manage his impulses. Upon fur-ther inspection, however, it is discovered that fourteen months prior to the violent incident this family moved to the United States from Nigeria. Further, this was the first incident of physical violence between any mem-bers in the family; the disagreements between the adolescent and his parents were around curfew, clothing choices, and "the way he talks to us now"; and the parents stated, "We don't know how to handle this . . . he's never been a bad boy . . . usually this can be discussed with the elders." This information, which places the father's abusive behavior in context, suggests that he and this family are, not surprisingly, stressed by their new environment and their struggle to "fit."

Given this, assessment should include an interest in how clients seem to be coping with and adapting to their environment (Dubois, 1968; Ger-main & Gitterman, 1996). Indeed, problematic behavior at times may be less about one's character and more about cumulative discouragement as he/she struggles to adequately cope with and adapt to environmental demands. It is assumed that behaviors are significantly influenced by environmental demands. It is sometimes argued, however, that contex-tual explanations dismiss individual responsibility. Contextual explana-tions and individual responsibility, we believe, are not incompatible. This father is absolutely responsible for his choice to assault his son. The contextual perspective is a partial and accurate explanation that is palat-able, reduces defenses, and is essential in the effort to minimize relapse. An ecological perspective is distinguished by its refusal to immediately assume that destructive behavior is fully explained by individual pathol-ogy. A host of assessment variables, such as environmental fit and the enculturation process (as experienced by this family) are deemed com-pletely relevant (Falicov, 1988).

An ecological, panoramic view of assessment can be daunting. Solution-based casework provides a manageable assessment road map by merging macro considerations with more focused and tangible assess
ment questions rooted in everyday living. Chapters 3–6 will focus specifi-cally on the skills of solution-based casework assessment for case planning.

COMPETENCE-CENTERED PERSPECTIVE

In the latter half of this century, casework practice has been heavily influenced by physical and mental health treatment models that place primary emphasis on dysfunction (McDaniel, Hepworth, & Doherty, 1992). These models suggest that accurate diagnoses ought to instruct caseworkers and clinicians, i.e., certain diagnoses lead directly to pre-scribed, corresponding interventions. With this approach, individuals and families have been viewed as service recipients rather than capable, active partners in the change process. Indeed, the social service profession has been criticized as aloof, assuming an objective posture and emphasizing client deficits and pathology (Minuchin & Nichols, 1993). Further, clients who do not accept professionals' perceptions and recommendations are often labeled "resistant" and their contribution to the change process is minimized (Berg, 1994).

More recently, however, models that emphasize collaboration, client competence, individual and environmental change, and solutions (versus cures), and a mutually engaging relationship between clients and professionals are enjoying rising acceptance (Berg, 1994; de Shazer, 1991; Kinney, Haapala, Booth, & Leavitt, 1990; Maluccio, 1981; Pecora et al., 1992; Smale, 1995; Wood & Middleman, 1989). This shift in the professional relationship reduces contentiousness and facilitates working partnerships. Middleman and Wood (1990) provided the movement with critically useful descriptions of direct practice skills that structurally support a collaborative model.

Solution-based casework endorses this trend. It is assumed that the family and individuals within the family have attempted to resolve conflict, have too frequently been unsuccessful in those efforts, and are consequently discouraged. Emphasis, therefore, should be placed on detailing attempted solutions, identifying moments of success, and en-couraging the use of underutilized resources. This, however, is not to suggest that failed attempted solutions and deficits should be dismissed. Instead, they are seen as one aspect of a larger question. Namely, how can this family more completely meet the needs of its members at this particular moment in their life cycle? Accentuating client capabilities, we believe, is essential in effectively responding to that question.

At any given moment, social service professionals have the opportunity to emphasize clients' failure or clients' assets. It is indeed a choice between highlighting resilient forces or further perpetuation of discouraged processes. Bandler (1963) argued that social service professionals ought to emphasize interventions that mobilize clients and support their desire to relieve environmental pressures. He described the tension between progressive and regressive tendencies in the following manner.

> Two major tendencies in all people from birth to death . . . are ceaselessly in opposition. These [are] the progressive and regressive trends in nature. Other things being equal, progressive forces are stronger. . . . We must identify the progressive forces with which we can ally ourselves and which, at the appropriate time, we can help mobilize. (pp. 42–43)

Burke (1997) argued that punctuating client competence is perhaps the most salient ingredient in facilitating therapeutic change. "An active belief in clients' competencies is so essential that it alone can encourage 'spontaneous' change . . . a genuine conviction in the client's native capacities can be relayed without minimizing emotional pain." These assumptions "bank on the idea that individuals are often better able to modify their own reality than they realize and encourage clients to investigate positive solutions" (p. 2).

Client Resources Are Underutilized

It is not assumed that clients—even those with chronic histories of abusive and neglectful behavior—are void of the skills necessary to avert destructive behavior. To assume otherwise is to dismiss them of responsibility and support the problem-perpetuating belief of "I can't help it, I don't even notice when it's about to happen" (Jenkins, 1990). Instead, it is assumed that client skills are underutilized (Aponte, 1976). Indeed, a search for exceptions to maladaptive behavior will uncover problem-averting behaviors that the client has employed in the past, even if on only one occasion.

Clients Are More Than Their Symptoms

Clinical referrals and diagnostic categories typically use definitive and narrow descriptors. That is, a client is depressed, is a perpetrator, is obsessive-compulsive, is a crack addict, is the survivor of childhood sexual assault. Although these descriptors may be accurate for a given client, they are also seen as incomplete. That is, clients are more than the few sentences or paragraphs found in a case file. One is not only depressed, a perpetrator, obsessive-compulsive, etc. Further, case files reflect clients at their worst moment. Accepting this narrow definition reduces the perception of client capabilities and potentially undermines expectations. That is, a client who is obsessive-compulsive is not capable of removing the trash and the stench from his/her home. And, if he/she were to remove it, it would only prove temporary given his/her obsessive-compulsive condition. Accepting narrow definitions, therefore, too easily dismisses clients from their responsibilities and creates an atmosphere in which one too easily throws in the towel.

Protective Services Clients Tend to Expect Criticism

Clients who have been referred to protective services are, not surprisingly, often guarded and defensive when caseworkers, therapists, and other social service professionals intervene in their lives. This can be due to several factors, such as embarrassment; the client may have something to hide; anticipation of criticism by the professional; a belief that he/she has been misunderstood, wrongly accused, or discriminated against; a belief that personal life is no one else's business; and guilt associated with the harmful behavior.

Assuming client competence, as reflected in the worker's line of questioning, e.g., "Describe a moment when you were close to hitting him but didn't. What did you do?" reduces defenses and is important in developing a working partnership and in pointing out client ability and potential for mastery. Clients tend to anticipate that they will be criticized by professionals. They also do not tend to anticipate being asked what their personal goals are or how they believe they can be achieved, or for the worker to assume a collaborative posture. When this environment is created, and particularly when capability is assumed, the seeds for change-oriented work are planted.

FAMILY LIFE CYCLE THEORY

Although variation occurs in light of cultural diversity and family configuration (e.g., blended families, interracial marriage, gay and lesbian couples), family developmental theory suggests that families experience fairly predictable life stages and associated tasks (Carter & McGoldrick, 1980; Duvall, 1957, 1971). The developmental stages and their associated tasks are widely documented (Carter & McGoldrick, 1980). According to Carter and McGoldrick (1980), common family developmental stages are the beginning couple, infant/preschool years, school-age, the adolescent stage, launching, postparental, and considerations regarding divorce and remarriage. These developmental stages, their associated tasks, and their usefulness in casework practice will be discussed in more detail in Chapter 3.

Developmental theory is quite valuable as a way to (1) organize the complexity of case material, (2) normalize the challenges the family faces, and (3) develop partnerships based on a shared reality. Caseworkers, therapists, and other social service professionals are faced with the dizzying task of collecting data, developing rapport, determining objectives, and a host of management responsibilities (e.g., determining imminent risk, contacting collaterals, preparing legal documents, consulting with supervisors). Given this breadth of responsibility, case planning is often hurried and only vaguely attends to the specificity of the tasks the family is facing. However, anchoring case plans in the developmental tasks of everyday life, where the danger occurs, is instrumental in developing a clear, pertinent and tailored case plan.

Case Example

A young mother (Ms. Smith) who physically harmed her child comes to the attention of social services. The caseworker learns that Ms. Smith has a significant temper problem when she feels that her son is being verbally or physically aggressive toward her. She gets angry at other times but reports being able to manage her anger then (exceptions). When the caseworker asks her about the sequence of events (destructive pattern) that led up to the incident in question, they (the partnership) learn that the mother is more at risk when she is exhausted due to lack of sleep (she has an infant daughter), or has been discouraged about finances (near the end of the month) such as when the father of her four-year-old son has not sent his child support payment. She agreed with the worker that the morning is her most difficult time, particularly when she is tired, financially stressed, and/or has been drinking the night before.

This family is dealing with numerous stressors, including the normal tasks associated with single-parenting preschool children, e.g., financial burden and harried morning routines. Given these developmental stressors—and given that this parent has identified she is most at risk to abuse under these conditions, case planning[1] ought to precisely target those particular moments. Essential, developmentally minded assessment questions include (1) What everyday life task(s) is the family having difficulty with? (2) What are the details of the family interaction when they try to accomplish these tasks? (3) What individuals in the family are unable to maintain enough self-control to tolerate tension in meeting the tasks in question?

Several assumptions based on developmental theory are noteworthy. It is assumed that (1) families encounter common developmental challenges, (2) dangerous behavior occurs within the context of those common developmental challenges,[2] (3) understanding which moments a particular family or family member is at risk to abuse is essential to case planning, and (4) organizing case plans around those high-risk moments maximizes efforts to reduce relapse of destructive behavior.

Indeed, whether one is a third-generation welfare recipient or a supervisor of social services, one can appreciate the mundane struggles around curfew, disagreements with extended family, and sibling rivalry. Acknowledgment of the relative universality of life tasks reminds client and provider alike that it is within the drama of daily life that we all live and deal with individual needs and idiosyncrasies. That is to say, in an attempt to do something ordinary, something extraordinary can occur, i.e., destructive action. When carefully dissected, a given individual's maladaptive behavior typically occurs at certain moments, under certain conditions, and with certain other individuals. Therefore, case planning ought to target how individuals and families can manage those everyday developmental tasks in a manner that ensures safety. When case planning is organized around ordinary life events, the benefits include (1) a clear, manageable focal point, a means by which the complexity of case planning and interactional dynamics can be organized; (2) a tangible, readily applicable plan that all involved can visualize and relate to; (3) a plan that, due to its emphasis on details within events, enhances safety by alerting individuals to early signals of increasing danger; and (4) a plan that can be measured, where progress can be easily recognized and punctuated. Finally, when behavior is placed in a developmental frame, e.g., "morning routines are rough for nearly all single parents with young children," the individual and his/her intent is depathologized. This developmental frame increases clients' receptivity to explore alternative ways of behaving.

Indeed, individuals often are defensive, even before professionals have had an opportunity to begin fostering a working relationship. This is particularly true for families who have had previous involvement with protective services. This contentiousness can be reduced by depicting problems as part of the struggle of negotiating through life cycle stages. Destructive behavior, obviously, must not be condoned and individual culpability is essential, yet at the same time professionals must demonstrate understanding of the pressure of life and common developmental tasks of families. As such, all case plans should have goals and objectives at both the family and individual level. Family goals are based on family-level developmental tasks associated with dangerous situations, whereas individual goals emphasize skills necessary to successfully participate in tasks without harming anyone involved.

POSTMODERN FAMILY CASEWORK

With the advent of technologies (e.g., television, rapid transportation, internet) that connect diverse societies in manners never before possible, social scientists and many others have begun to recognize that healthy or adaptive living must be broadly defined. That is, even at a glance, it is apparent there are many ways to live, that relationships can be fulfilling and stable in a host of configurations, and that historical assumptions about healthy living are often narrowly defined and often ethnocentric. This awareness creates complexity. Indeed, it is more difficult to point to one way of living and deem it correct, and point to another and label it incorrect. One wonders what are the criteria for healthy living?

In this environment of increasing complexity, many historical casework assumptions likewise are being questioned. In particular, the ability of social scientists and social service professionals (e.g., social workers, family therapists, psychologists, psychiatrists) to be definitive authorities on healthy living is in doubt. Historically, social service and mental health providers were believed to be privy to special truths, to be containers of privileged knowledge about humanity and the psyche. Their role, therefore, has been that of disseminator of special truths to a naive client population. Given the complexity of contemporary life, however, one must wonder which truth, whose truth, and why?

Constructivism has emerged as a particular theoretical response to the increasing complexity of contemporary life. Constructivism, broadly defined, is the notion that although a truth may exist, it cannot be fully known, and therefore, is constructed, i.e., created by individuals, communities, and society (Maturana & Varela, 1980; Dell, 1985). Perceptions themselves are simply ideas; they do not represent "true" external reality. Given this, who is to say for instance that social service professionals' perceptions of clients' needs are correct? Can we be confident that our pronouncements, diagnoses, and interventions are correct? Can any one social service professional, or even any one professional discipline, account for the complexity of life? How often have social service professionals been adamant about their view only to find that it was in conflict with another professional's impression? How can we know? Can service professionals be certain that individuals must be "individuated" to be healthy (Bowen, 1978), that diffuse boundaries are troubling (Minuchin, 1974), and that neurosis is the manifestation of unconscious conflict that most certainly requires a lengthy therapy where transference can occur (Fairbairn, 1954)? Constructivism and related constructs have broadly influenced the social sciences, including a "postmodern" family therapy movement (Parry & Doan, 1994; White, 1986). Postmodern models embrace the assumptions of constructivism and have many applied implications (Brown & Christensen, 1999). Therapists and caseworkers, for instance, do not assume a privileged and more accurate understanding of clients' problems than their clients. This does not mean that professionals do not have a useful point of view. Instead, their knowledge is only a point of view, a perspective among many possible perspectives. Professionals, however, need not abandon their protective mission or their legal mandates (e.g., a parent who physically harms his/her child has violated the law and has behaved abusively). Instead, constructivism demands that professionals scrutinize their own beliefs, remain open to the beliefs of others, and develop the skills to facilitate a conversation wherein diverse views can merge in a manner that promotes safe living and reduces relapse of dangerous behavior. This removes the professional from the heretofore elevated, hierarchical position of objective disseminator of clinical truth. Instead, the professional is placed in a collaborative position with his/her client. The client is also credited with wanting to prevent abuse but for some reason, on at least one occasion, was unable to. Together, in partnership, they work to create a new way to cope with the client's presenting problem. The social worker is more interested in the client's ascribed meaning to the problem and his/her ideas about solutions than diagnostic categories and rote intervention schemes. Solutions that are created by clients and professionals in partnership are thus uniquely tailored to each client system, and are therefore much more likely to account for diversity and achieve relevance. In this way, the client's view of the problem and its solution are elevated. Client view is central, actively solicited, and taken seriously. There are many useful questions that elicit client meaning, such as: What do you believe contributes to the problem? What will contribute to the solution? What do you need to overcome the problem? How do you explain the problem to others? The simple act of demonstrating interest in the client's view of the problem can be instrumental in forming a partnership and planting seeds of meaningful change. When asked, "What do you think is the problem here?" one client who had been involved with protective services on several occasions over a period of several years, said, "You are the first person who has ever asked me that." The client, who had been previously described as defensive and resistant to change, actively engaged with this worker and later attributed her willingness to think about things and make some changes to "the way you kept asking me what I think and how I see it." This stands in stark contrast to other models where the client's view is seen as naive, rarely useful, even part of the problem. In the same way, the professional's point of view is legitimate. The difference is that the professional's view is not the only valid view worthy of serious consideration.

SOLUTION-FOCUSED FAMILY THERAPY

Solution-focused therapy (Berg, 1994, de Shazer, 1985, 1988, 1991; O'Hanlon & Weiner-Davis, 1989) is perhaps the most vividly described clinical application of constructivism. Other applications, such as the narrative therapies (White, 1986, 1988; White & Epston, 1990; Parry & Doan, 1994), which emphasize language, collaboration, and change-inducing conversations, also emerged out of the constructivist movement. Solution-focused therapy is in part a profession's reaction to the traditional therapy approaches, which were based on a disease model.

In disease-oriented therapies, diagnosis and labeling of the disease are cornerstones of the therapy process. Determining causation and gaining insight as to why the disease has occurred are central. It is assumed that if the disease can be located and understood, it can then be released (catharsis) or removed through an assortment of interventions (e.g., medication, cognitive restructuring, behavioral modification). Common to these therapies is an emphasis on disease and dysfunction. However, Berg (1994), de Shazer (1991), and O'Hanlon & Weiner-Davis (1989) argue that deemphasizing causality and pathology and instead punctuating solutions is more efficient, pragmatic, empowering, and effective. They assume that clients desire change, that change is a constant, evolving process, and that resistance is more about misguided therapist behaviors than client stubbornness. Further, symptomatic behavior is not viewed as mysterious or insidious, but as predominantly a response to the natural challenges of dealing with daily life and developmental stressors.

Searching for Exceptions to Everyday Life

The cornerstone of a solution-focused approach is the vigilant solicitation of exceptions to problematic behavior. This is very consistent with the philosophy underlying competency-based models (Adams & Nelson, 1995; Lee, 1994), but adds unique, specific strategies for identifying client competencies. It is assumed that clients have in fact attempted to solve their conflict but have been largely unsuccessful. Symptomatic behavior, therefore, is in part a manifestation of frustrated and failed efforts to cope with daily life. However, it is also assumed that they have not always failed. That is, at least on occasion, efforts have proven successful. It is these moments, these small successes or exceptions to the problem, to which solution-focused approaches devote their attention.

Discouraged individuals who have repeatedly experienced a sense of failure typically find it difficult to recognize moments when family members successfully manage conflict. In their discouragement, they may say, "My son never tells the truth" or "My daughter has always been trouble." Such expressions clearly do not reflect the entire situation. Professionals can assist individuals and families toward solutions by accepting their rather one-sided view of the problem, while at the same time helping them search for and identify any exceptions to the pattern. Identifying moments when someone didn't lie, didn't create conflict, and handled anger safely gives everyone an opportunity to explore how the exception became possible. What unique characteristics of that moment allowed the maladaptive pattern to be averted? The premise is simple. Since an exception to maladaptive behavior occurred at least once, it can occur again when similar conditions are recreated. Queries about exceptions are in themselves an intervention and directly suggest that clients have managed to deal effectively with problematic behavior at least on occasion and, by implication, can choose to duplicate their own previously exercised skills. Detailed illustrations of the skills necessary to elicit exceptions are addressed in Chapters 4 and 10.

Creating a Partnership

Solution-focused and constructivist assumptions, since they anticipate change, emphasize collaboration, and acknowledge client competence, naturally facilitate rapport between clients and professionals. For instance, although bravado may disguise their discouragement, clients often are indeed discouraged by their too frequently failed attempted solutions. Not surprisingly, many of these individuals and families eventually become convinced they lack the resources to conquer conflict (White & Epston, 1990). This entrenched and discouraging view of themselves tends to obscure their awareness of their existing potential solutions (de Shazer, 1988). They may be only vaguely aware of their historical successes. Therefore, being asked to describe "an incident where you nearly struck your spouse but instead did not touch her in any way" directly suggests that exceptions can and do occur. It also conveys that the professional (1) believes the client possesses essential skills, (2) believes the client can utilize them, and (3) since success has occurred historically, expects that the client can choose to develop and routinely implement them. When clients expect to be criticized by professionals but instead are questioned in this manner, productive partnerships often emerge. Further, emphasizing exceptions to maladaptive behavior reduces defenses and consequently serves as another facilitator of rapport. A detailed description of solution-focused techniques, including scaling questions and time-oriented questions, is included in later chapters.

RELAPSE PREVENTION THEORY

Caseworkers routinely encounter individuals who repeatedly behave violently and / or repeatedly neglect the needs of vulnerable children and the elderly. The phenomenon of opening, closing, and reopening files, sometimes over a period of years and even across generations, is widely known. Given this, it is extremely important that case planning earnestly target (1) the very moments when a given person is most apt to harm, and (2) skills that prevent the recurrence of abusive and neglectful behavior.

Relapse prevention theory has demonstrated usefulness in preventing relapse in several specialization disciplines, e.g., addiction counseling, sexual offender counseling, and aggression management (Lane, 1991; Marlatt & Gordon, 1985; Pithers et al., 1983). Likewise, relapse prevention theory is useful for casework since it offers a road map for focusing case plans on specific outcome skills that are known to increase the likelihood of prevention. Relapse prevention includes four basic steps: (1) recognition of patterns; (2) learning the details of high-risk patterns; (3) practicing small steps toward change; and (4) creating a relapse prevention plan. Each of these steps is important in constructing a case plan that is tailored to the idiosyncrasies of individuals and families (and therefore is particularly relevant), is measurable (and therefore creates accountability), and pinpoints risky behavior (thereby reducing the likelihood of relapse). Further, each of these steps moves clients along in their efforts to master skills that will ensure safety.

Relapse prevention assumes that individuals are often only vaguely aware of the intrapersonal and interpersonal nature of their responses to daily developmental stressors. As reflected in comments such as "and then we start all over again" or "I was afraid I was doing it again," members are cognizant that a pattern exists, but are often not confident of their ability to readily recognize the pattern, avoid the pattern, interrupt it once it starts, or when necessary, escape it before harm occurs. Given this, solution-based casework requires case planning to detail how individuals and families can manage their high-risk moments differently and ensure safety. Indeed, an individual may react violently in certain situations, while at other times he/she easily manages events. Individuals must recognize their vulnerability and develop skills that ensure safety. Casework assessment and planning, therefore, should identify (1) when individuals are at risk, (2) individual and contextual early warning signals, and (3) skills in avoiding, interrupting, and escaping risky situations.

Given the investigative responsibilities of protective service agencies, assessment tends to center around whether neglect, abuse, or maladaptive behavior has occurred. Relapse prevention, however, depends on an expanded assessment lens. As such, assessment must routinely include how the destructive behavior occurred. If assessment is focused primarily on whether or not there is evidence of pathology and destructive behavior, it becomes difficult to locate the problem within developmental and intrapersonal challenges and to identify problematic interactions. As such, case plans are at risk of simply listing the pathologies identified and assigning a rote treatment package (e.g., child abuse = parenting classes; presence of alcohol = alcohol counseling; past sexual abuse = victim counseling; domestic violence = perpetrator group). For instance, if a father strikes a child and leaves bruises, caseworkers need to know more than whether or not it occurred, the size and configuration of the bruise, or the father's frequency of attendance in court-mandated counseling in order to be reasonably confident of the child's safety. Identification of developmental tasks (e.g., the father struck the adolescent child during a disagreement about proper peers), details regarding how all involved respond to the tasks, and—most importantly—the specifics around how the father lost self-control are essential components in planning relapse prevention. Therefore, emphasis is placed on how individuals think, feel, and behave in high-risk situations. This information is central in constructing a uniquely tailored relapse prevention plan. Plans of this nature are rooted in skills tied to successful outcomes, e.g., the recognition of high-risk situations and a plan to avoid those situations whenever reasonably possible is a skill that contributes to the central desired outcome: the absence of harmful behavior. The procedures to create a relapse prevention plan are thoroughly detailed in Chapters 6 and 7.

INTEGRATING SOLUTION-FOCUSED AND PROBLEM-CENTERED MODELS

Creating a relapse prevention plan demands a detailed description of problem behavior and relevant surrounding events. Zeroing in on high-risk problem patterns is essential. A detailed description of the problem is imperative. Indeed, a reliable relapse prevention plan cannot be created without rigorous attention to the problem. Caseworkers must assess, for instance, when the problem occurs, who is involved, who is not involved, who does what and when, what typically occurs prior to the problem, what those involved think before, during, and after the event, and how dangerous behavior is explained and justified (Christensen & Todahl, 1999). In this sense solution-based casework shares assumptions with problem-focused models (Haley, 1987; Watzlawick, Weakland, & Fisch, 1974). Particularly relevant problem-focused assumptions include the following.

Service Recipients Are More Than Their Diagnostic Labels. Indeed, diagnostic labels distort and misrepresent uniqueness, variation, and individual idiosyncrasies. Therefore, case plans ought to be rooted in detailed descriptions of problematic behavior, i.e., a visual description of who does what under which circumstances. In this way, case plan objectives are precise and tailor-made. Skill development, then, is targeted and relevant, addresses high-risk behavior, and is therefore more apt to reduce recidivism.

The Problem Must Be Defined Clearly.   For instance, a problem that is described as "neglectful behavior" or "depression" is much too vaguely defined. Relapse prevention demands a cognitive and behavioral description of the problem. Social workers and treatment providers must know, for instance, what about the depression is harmful, what it looks like, how it manifests itself, and how it literally contributes to harm. A clear visual image of the problem is needed—a frame-by-frame accounting that tracks clients' interactions, emotions, behavior, and thinking.

Case Plan Goals Must Be Achievable, Measurable, and Behaviorally Defined.   The steps to achieving those goals should be skill based and intimately tied to high-risk behaviors. Harmful behavior is adaptive. Abusive and neglectful behavior is an adaptation: a way of dealing with the stressors of every day life. Case planning targets destructive adaptations and assists clients in creating and relying on safe, behaviorally defined alternative behaviors.

Clients Possess Many Competencies.   Given this, their ideas about the problem and problem resolution are highly regarded. The social worker and client should actively work together in partnership to define the problem and create solutions.

Exceptions to the Problem Are Keys to the Solutions.   An interest in exceptions to high-risk behavior, i.e., exceptions to the problem, is the hallmark of solution-focused models (de Shazer, 1985; Brown & Christensen, 1999). Solution-based casework assumes that an emphasis on the problem and exceptions to the problem are complementary. Emphasizing high-risk problem behavior, as stated, roots casework planning in the processes where danger occurs. Targeting planning in this manner enhances safety. Similarly, emphasizing exceptions to high-risk behavior provides clues to skills that the client has—but underutilizes—to avert danger. Therefore, pairing problem-focused and solution-focused models helps clients and professionals to clearly understand the processes surrounding harmful behavior and draw from clients' existing skills. In this context, clients are apt to be more receptive to expanding their skills and experimenting with new skills, since acknowledgment of their competence (by punctuating exceptions to the problem) reduces defenses.

Further, solution-based models have been criticized as being overly optimistic, as too quick to move to solutions and, in so doing, dismissive of serious problem behavior. Merging problem- and solution-focused models addresses these criticisms and significantly assists in meaningful case planning. Other advantages of merging these models include the following:

- Gathering details surrounding the problem makes it more difficult to dismiss the problem or deny it exists. When social workers facilitate a conversation that creates a visual frame-by-frame picture of harmful behavior, that behavior is more tangible. It is difficult to minimize such imagery.
- A detailed vision of client successes (exceptions to the problem) creates hopefulness and increases investment in efforts to enhance skills.
- A detailed, visual description of the problem and its exceptions leads to a clear plan. This clarity increases accountability.

NOTES

1. In common practice, case planning might have called for the mother to attend generic "parenting classes" as a condition of her court order. But the parent is not unskilled in parenting; in fact, she views herself as a much better parent than those in her family of origin or her peer group. She needs help with the specific challenges that she faces.

2. One important exception to this assumption is those acts of violence and abuse that are primarily personal pattern related (e.g., battering or sexual abuse).

Chapter 2

Searching for Solutions in the Postmodern World

Casework practice has a rich and varied tradition. Countless pioneering minds and earnest and competent individuals have shaped, and continue to shape, casework and the larger social service delivery system. At the same time, many assert that the human service delivery system, i.e., the interaction between government, caseworkers, therapists, health care professionals, educators, the legal system, the ministry, and others, is in a state of crisis (Adams & Nelson, 1995). The underachieving state of social services can be attributed to a host of factors, such as inadequate funding, the sheer magnitude of social problems, rapid social change (e.g., work force shifts, mounting socioeconomic disparity), and the complexity of modern life. Minuchin, in the foreword to *Reinventing Human Services: Community and Family-Centered Practice* (1995), depicts the dizzying "postmodern" world as one in which even reality is difficult to grasp: "Once upon a time, in a better world, people knew their reality. A table was called a table, a house a house. Poverty was poverty, and lack of food, hunger. People, rich and poor, knew their reality because they heard everyone using the same words" (p. vii). This complexity, wherein previously held "objective realities" are now questioned and scrutinized, is perplexing and has stretched and strained social service delivery. The notion that reality is subjective (constructivism, postmodernism) rather than objective (positivism, modernism) has directly influenced the sciences. Nichols and Schwartz (1995) described this transformation in the following manner:

Skepticism (re. objectivity) has been building in our culture this century. Einstein's relativity undermined our faith in the solid certainties of Newtonian physics. Marx challenged the right of one class to dominate another. . . . The feminist movement challenged patriarchal assumptions about gender, which had been considered laws of nature. As the world shrank and we were increasingly exposed to people of different cultures, we had to reexamine our assumptions regarding their "primitive" or "exotic" beliefs. Instead, we had to look at our own reality as only one of many ways people see the world. (p. 119)

The change from a modern to a postmodern worldview has many implications for casework and the human service system. It raises questions about how we, as service providers, see our clients, see ourselves, and define our role, and the manner in which we scrutinize ourselves and the services we provide. A postmodern perspective challenges professionals to (1) question established lexicon, (2) deconstruct established social beliefs, e.g., gender scripts, (3) question the utility of regarding professionals as astute and clients as naive, (4) to care less about diagnostic categories and more about clients' perceptions and descriptions of relevant events, and (5) to wonder more about diversity and pluralism and less about identifying universal social patterns.

This chapter will discuss the historical development of casework, the influence of modernism, and particularly modernism's contribution to the current challenges in social service delivery. Further, this chapter will contrast modernism- and postmodernism-based social service delivery, and will introduce how solution-based casework (Christensen & Todahl, 1999) can complement efforts to establish collaborative community and family-based human services.

THE EVOLUTION OF CASEWORK PRACTICE

Originating in England, *parens patriae* is a legal principle that contributed to "statutory authorization for Child Protective Services in the United States" (Pecora et al., 1992, p. 230). This principle holds that governmental bodies are justified in intervening in private matters, e.g., family life, when it is believed that protection of children is needed. *Parens patriae* is thought to have first been exercised in England in 1696 (Areen, 1975). In the United States, evidence of governmental and community intervention on behalf of abused and neglected children can be identified as early as the seventeenth century:

> Reported criminal cases involving child abuse date back to 1655. . . . The state of Massachusetts extended the provisions of the colonial poor laws to ensure that all persons under the age of 21 years live "under some orderly family government" (Axinn & Levin, 1982, p. 32). The city of Boston in 1735 received legislative approval for the care of neglected children. . . . Beginning in 1825, states began to legislate the right of social welfare agencies to remove children. . . . New York was the first state to pass legislation to protect and safeguard the rights of children as part of the Protective Ser-

vices Act and the Cruelty to Children Act, passed in 1874. (Pecora et al., 1992, pp. 230–231)

Countless individuals, agencies, societies, and governmental bodies contributed to the development of protective services in the United States. The Society for the Prevention of Cruelty to Children (established in 1875), the Society for the Protection of Cruelty to Animals, and the National Federation for Child Rescue Agencies (established in 1835), for instance, were all actively involved in pioneering efforts. The mission of these organizations was on "investigating complaints of neglect, exploitation, or cruelty" to children (Pecora et al., 1992). Abusive and neglectful behavior toward children, although prosecuted as early as 1655 in England (Bremner, 1970) and 1840 in Tennessee (Watkins, 1990), was rarely enforced (Thomas, 1972).

According to the American Humane Association (AHA, 1992), during the first half of the twentieth century the protection of children was largely "initiated through the efforts of local, private, non-profit societies" (p. 3). In the 1920s, for instance, there were at least 250 such societies throughout the country. Gradually, state-operated social service agencies coordinated and provided protective care. Rapid changes occurred in the 1960s: by 1966, reporting laws had been adopted in 49 states. These laws, which institutionalized protective services, "obligated professionals who work with children as well as ordinary citizens to report child abuse or neglect to local departments of social services" (ibid.). Complementary federal laws, such as the Child Abuse Prevention and Treatment Act (Public Law 93-247, passed in 1974), were adopted in the 1970s and 1980s. This tied federal funds to states' efforts around "creating systems of identification, reporting and response to child abuse and neglect" (ibid., p. 4). The central organizing purpose of the Child Abuse Prevention and Treatment Act was as follows:

- A broad and uniform definition of child abuse and neglect
- Nationwide coordination of efforts to identify, treat and prevent child abuse and neglect
- Research leading to new knowledge and demonstration of effective ways to identify, teat, and prevent child maltreatment
- Compilation of existing knowledge and dissemination of information about successful methods and programs
- Training of professionals, paraprofessionals and volunteers
- Encouragement of states, as well as private agencies and organizations, to improve their services for identifying, treating, and preventing child maltreatment
- A complete and full study of the national incidence of child abuse and neglect. (U.S. DHEW, 1975, as cited in Daro, 1988, pp. 15–16)

Despite casework's mission of assisting families in their ability to protect and manage their own lives, many argue that a contentious relationship between casework and families emerged early in the nineteenth century (Adams & Nelson, 1995). Hartman and Laird (1983) described the relationship as ambivalent: "Although social workers have always thought of themselves and have been seen by others as professionals who 'work with families,' a study of their involvement with the family reveals considerable inconsistency and ambivalence in attending to a family focus" (p. 11). Indeed, since their inception, rather than emphasizing preservation of the family and reunification, child welfare agencies have frequently separated children from their families and placed them in institutions and foster care (McGowan & Meezan, 1983). Mary Richmond (1917), regarded by many as the founder and designer of casework practice, argued that effective practice requires an emphasis on the family as the central organizing unit of attention. Richmond (1917) defined "cases" as "families" and asserted that the benefits of "individual treatment would crumble away" if caseworkers dismissed family variables (p. 134). Richmond (1930) asserted. "[T]he family itself continues to be the pivotal institution around which our human destinies revolve" (p. 262). Her advocacy for family-focused casework was further evidenced by her "theory of the wider self" and the notion that "a man really is the company he keeps plus the company that his ancestors kept" (Richmond, 1917, p. 134).

Hartman and Laird (1983) suggest that the "mental hygiene movement, psychoanalytic psychology and an 'inner-outer' split" moved casework away from its stated family-oriented mission and Richmond's pioneering ideals (p. 12). Richmond's *Social Diagnosis* (1917), which promoted family-centered practice, was published just as psychology, psychiatry, and individually oriented therapies began their ascendance. As described by Hartman and Laird (1983), E. E. Southard directly criticized Richmond's *Social Diagnosis* and, at the 1918 National Conference of Charities and Corrections, promoted a "psychiatric model." Southard (1918) indicated that individual analysis ought to "demolish what seems to be an erroneous pet view of social workers. That is to say, I want to replace the family as the unit of social inquiry with the individual as the unit of social inquiry" (p. 337). Others, such as Mary Jarrett (1919), further promoted a psychological, individual orientation. Jarrett argued that "the adaptation of an individual to the environment, in the last analysis, depends upon mental makeup" (p. 587). The individual orientation of social casework became more fully entrenched with the introduction of Virginia Robinson's (1930) *A Changing Psychology of Social Case Work*. Robinson defined social casework as "individual therapy through a treatment relationship" (p. 187). The unit of study, she asserted, "has shifted to the individual" (p. 95). Bertha Reynolds (1932), in reviewing this text, predicted that, because of its emphasis on individual and intrapsychic needs, casework "will never be the same again" (p. 109).

Despite more current social work and casework literature that promotes partnership, empowerment, and family-focused care (e.g., Adams & Nelson, 1995; Hartman & Laird, 1983; Lee, 1994), casework practice even to this day frequently emphasizes an individual, deficit orientation and, in so doing, too readily ostracizes family members. Although individual culpability must not be minimized, an exclusive, individual orientation places workers and families at odds, i.e., children are too readily regarded as needing to be *rescue* from their families. Indeed, although intended as a statement of endorsement of families, a current guiding casework philosophy is "rescue [italics added] the family for the child" (AHA, 1992, p. 3). The assumption that families need to be rescued from themselves—and that service providers are capable of accomplishing that feat—in practice too frequently damns families and sets in place a contentious relationship wherein the wise (professionals) instruct the naive (individuals and families). Several decades ago, Lee and Kenworthy (1931) argued that the social worker's role is "first the provision of certain service opportunities or special kinds of experiences . . . and second, a direct effort to change the attitudes [italics added] of those persons most closely associated with children" (p. 111). This underlying assumption, that parents who abuse and neglect their children need to "change their attitudes," significantly hampers the establishment of meaningful family-based care. Solution-based casework and others (e.g., Adams & Nelson, 1995; Hartman & Laird, 1983; Lee, 1994) suggest an alternative view of individuals and families.

CURRENT CHALLENGES TO CASEWORK

As stated, due to an endorsement of the psychiatry and psychology traditions, social services tend to emphasize individual pathology, diagnostic categories, and client naivete. Emphasis on individuals and their deficits is fully institutionalized, i.e., within the current reimbursement system, the release of funding is often tied to diagnostic categories (e.g., DSM IV). However, the rash use of diagnostic categories is wrought with disadvantages. For instance, diagnostic labels can be misleading, inaccurate, ethnocentric (e.g., culturally insensitive), rigid in their description of healthy behavior, dismissive of context, and can create an environment wherein professionals easily assume that individuals are their symptoms. The "deficit orientation" manifests itself in service delivery in this manner: (1) services are compartmentalized and fragmented since recipients are diagnosed and referred to specialists, (2) services are reactive since they are generally available only once maladaptive behavior has escalated, and (3) the resources within the community at large are dismissed since service providers too frequently assume client improvement is dependent on providers' wisdom (Adams & Nelson, 1995; Kemp et al., 1997). Each of these issues is among the major challenges in human services and casework today.

Compartmentalized and Fragmented Services

Social service agencies and private providers (e.g., therapists) depend on individuals being "clientized"—formally processed and fit into a funding category. This creates a "compartmentalized" system of service delivery, i.e., if a client meets specific, predetermined categorical criteria, he/she is likely to be referred to a specialist, or several specialists if deemed necessary. As described by Peters (1993), one pregnant teenage girl, also on welfare and a juvenile offender, was expected to deal with "at least six different government case workers, each regulated by a different set of rules—many at odds with one another" (p. xviii). As suggested by Adams and Nelson (1995), "[W]orkers then think of their jobs in terms of lining up their clients with discrete packages of service from private providers and filling out the paperwork required to justify the expenditures they wish to incur" (p. 93). Under this arrangement, care is likely confusing to service recipients. Further, given the logistical nightmare and costs involved in coordinating care between providers (who typically are dispersed throughout the community), it is nearly impossible to create coherent and complementary service plans. Compartmentalized care is fragmented care. At best, fragmented care is inefficient. More likely, however, fragmented planning contributes to unacceptable recidivism rates. Reducing the likelihood of relapse of destructive behavior requires (1) the active engagement of clients and (2) carefully coordinated planning between all involved.

Reactive Nature of Service Provision.

Casework practice, like other human service systems, is partially shaped by financial constraints. Adams and Nelson (1995) argue that the human service system is significantly influenced by managed care and shrinking state and federal funds:

> Public social services have responded to funding constraints and policy mandates by targeting services on the most critical "cases," and are increasingly contracting with private providers to furnish discrete packages of service. They have sought to protect themselves from scandal—a child suffering further abuse despite being known to the child welfare agency—

by prescribing ever more exactly what procedures workers must follow. Attempts to substitute rules and procedures for the professional judgment of line workers have been reinforced by funding mechanisms that specify the kinds of diagnosis or other category the service user must fit before help can be provided. . . . The resulting services are fragmented, unresponsive, and stigmatizing. They require people to wait until there is a crisis . . . before they can get help. (pp. 1–2)

In this environment, social and casework services are often only provided when problems are advanced, i.e., services are reactive rather than proactive. Indeed, since funds are generally accessed only when problems have escalated, the "scope for preventive work is limited. . . . [The] process typically requires a crisis. A parent must hurt a child or the child must commit a seriously delinquent act before help is forthcoming" (Adams & Nelson, 1995, p. 93). Due to emotional impact on workers, cases are often prioritized based on the severity of injury, an assessment criterion not always related to risk. Finally, the bureaucracy demands formal processes and careful adherence to policy. This often is experienced by service recipients as rigid, dehumanizing, and overly formal.

The Community at Large Is Underutilized.

The individual-focused, deficit orientation assumes that conflict predominantly resides within individuals, that individuals are largely unaware of their needs, and that they therefore require the assistance of enlightened professionals. In this light, services target individuals, with particular emphasis on their deficits (e.g., lack of insight) and/or their excesses (e.g., anger). This places the client in a subordinate position, is insulting, and hinders the development of creative processes and partnerships that inspire individuals to recognize their own resources (McDaniel et al., 1992). Not uncommonly, clients who recoil under these conditions are labeled resistant, not amenable to services, and uncooperative.

This intrapsychic, deficit orientation centers services around individual clients and their "pathology." With this arrangement, where professionals instruct naive clients, "[T]he social service or mental health system becomes central, at least in the eyes of professionals, to the resolution of children's and family problems" (p. 62). When professionals see themselves as central, i.e., as the bearers of the solutions to clients' problems, the naturally occurring network of family, friends, and community is frequently left untapped. Current casework practice too frequently focuses interventions on individuals, families, and their deficits. Instead, professionals are seen as central change agents. Consequently, the utilization and development of naturally occurring change networks within and across the community is much too often unrealized.

RISING PRESSURE FROM THE WELFARE TO WORK
MOVEMENT

The recent changes brought about by the welfare to work legislation signed by President Clinton in 1996 have created new challenges for the social service system. As states began to adopt changes in their requirements for receiving welfare, many states experienced significant (and newsworthy) declines in their welfare rolls. These early successes in states like Wisconsin and New Jersey encouraged other states to significantly tighten their welfare eligibility requirements. Many on the welfare rolls responded to the threat of loss of benefits by finding work or entering a job-training program. The tightening of eligibility requirements occurred during a period of economic prosperity, thus allowing many recipients to make the shift to self-reliance. Record low unemployment nationally benefited areas where the job market offered varied opportunities for first-time workers. Within the first two years of the landmark legislation, welfare rolls dropped noticeably.

However, many social researchers began to notice a difference in those families still left on the welfare rolls and in jeopardy of losing their sustaining support (Wilson, 1987; Olson, Berg, & Conrad, 1980). Many in this category were significantly more entrenched in personal patterns that made daily work a challenge. The too common myth that "these people don't really want to work" was not supported by those studying employment restraints (Herr, Halpern, & Conrad, 1991). In fact those left on the welfare rolls were found to want to work, and valued work as a life accomplishment, yet held other beliefs that limited or restrained their ability to accomplish the task.

Client Restraints to Employment

Significant factors in continued unemployment for many welfare recipients appear to be restraining attitudes that form a self-defeating constellation of beliefs. These beliefs feed a destructive pattern of (1) attempts to reach the goal, followed by (2) small failures that lead to conclusions of hopelessness and result in (3) further discouragement and (4) retreat from action. Significantly recurring thoughts in this constellation are often an overwhelming belief that the system is stacked against welfare recipients, that they are personally inadequate or ill-equipped to succeed at work, or that having to work is somehow equated with a denial of their rights, in essence an act of punishment and therefore not personally beneficial. Additionally, the social support systems that would normally encourage and reinforce efforts at obtaining work are lacking or are even considered counterproductive. Some recipients had the perception that they were betraying other family members and friends by "showing them up" or "being uppity." When work was equated with cooperating with an oppressor, the restraints to economic self-reliance were significant.

System Restraints to Employment

Additionally, the social service infrastructure was not set up to address attitudinal beliefs about work in individuals, families, or their social networks. Eligibility requirements developed a social response system that was largely numbers based, largely disconnected from other family concerns about family member safety, education, or developmental needs. Welfare workers and child protection workers did not interact with each other even though they were working with the same family. This compartmentalization kept practices from one field from influencing another. For instance, this compartmentalization of personnel and tasks prevented empowerment models popular in child protection or relapse prevention strategies popular in mental health from influencing those working in welfare delivery systems. Conversely, information held by welfare workers was not available to the child protection teams. Collaborative models of service delivery that overcome these problems are being explored and implemented. These models require a common conceptual map for the partners to use to communicate common goals and strategies. Chapter 9 discusses how a solution-based casework approach serves to teach critical skills of self-reliance in an empowering partnership with families and community providers. Chapter 11 details the experiences of workers who have been involved in implementing this approach.

EMERGING RESPONSES TO THE CRISIS IN CASEWORK

A social service system that tends to emphasize client deficits, that is largely compartmentalized and reactive, and that too frequently dismisses community resources diminishes our ability to assist clients in their efforts to reduce the occurrence and recurrence of maladaptive behavior. Indeed, caseworkers routinely encounter individuals who repeatedly behave violently and / or repeatedly neglect the needs of vulnerable children and the elderly. The phenomenon of opening, closing, and reopening files—sometimes over a period of years and even across generations—is widely known. Few would disagree that recidivism rates of destructive behavior are unacceptable. Systemic change, including change in our underlying assumptions about service provision and the people we serve, is needed.

In offering a remedy to a social service system that tends to dismiss community resources and regard professionals as the central change agents, Adams and Nelson (1995) suggest "community and family-centered practice," a "de-centering of human services," and a "new paradigm for practice":

> If we take the de-centering of human services seriously, however, we see that it would be better to recognize that most of the caring and controlling in the community is normally done informally within families and neighborhoods. The task of the professionals, then, is to find ways to join the community and help it in carrying out its work of caring for its members. A related problem is the professional tendency to see the community as a resource that the worker can use to supplement his or her repertoire of interventions, putting together a bag of resources from different places—a support group here, a helpful neighbor there—and presenting them to the consumer. Instead of that, we see changing the community itself as a part of the task and the service user as a contributor to the process. Professionals do not, in this approach, use informal networks for their purposes, as a bag of resources to reach into, but seek to enable and support social networks to help them function more effectively. In this sense, the community both has resources for addressing its concerns and is the locus of problem- perpetuating patterns of interaction. (pp. 7–8)

Neighborhood Place, a community partnership model based in Kentucky, and Patch are two applications of community-based social work. Patch, developed in the United Kingdom in the 1970s, has been adapted and implemented in the United States, primarily in Iowa and Pennsylvania. Neighborhood Place and Patch share similar assumptions and objectives and are responses to the challenges previously described. The solution-based casework model was developed to provide professionals with a conceptual map that would complement programs like Patch, Neighborhood Place, and other efforts at collaborative community and family-centered social services.

Echoing early social work traditions, Patch and Neighborhood Place proponents argue that social service delivery ought to be proactive rather than reactive, flexible instead of bureaucratic, and focused on strengths rather than deficits (Todahl & Christensen, 1999; Adams & Nelson, 1999). Patch and Neighborhood Place both advocate:

Localization of Services.   Services are located strategically in regions within neighborhoods. This allows for social work practice that depends on familiarity with the community and active community involvement.

Integration of Services.   Historically fragmented, multidisciplines, e.g., health care, employment services, protective services, education, and psychotherapy, actively collaborate with one another. This is promoted by central location of disciplines, i.e., instead of being housed in separate buildings across town, disciplines are located in the same building within regions that are mutually served.

Active Community Involvement. Soliciting active participation of community members and fostering helpful networks assumes that most of the "caring and monitoring is done informally in the family and neighborhood." The role of professionals is to "build the caring and capacity of the people and the networks involved" (Adams & Krauth, 1994, p. 103). In this light, "workers see their tasks in terms of building partnerships, not only with other agencies, but with consumers, family members, and other local people, as well as with neighborhood organizations, churches, and groups" (ibid., p. 97).

Community Work Is Central, Not an "Add On" to Overly Taxed Job Descriptions. Knowing the community, its members, its services, and its sentiment is not a nicety of Patch or Neighborhood Place—it is central. This knowledge promotes proactive and preventive care. "Working 'within the community' means that workers do not just focus on clients and their networks, but also on particular groups or streets within the area. They now call upon a range of community-based resources, from workers in other agencies (who they know in a way as never before since many are centrally located in multi-disciplinary teams), to self-help groups, individual volunteers and voluntary groups" (Bayley, Seyd, & Tennant, 1989, p. 54).

Emphasize Strengths and Diversity. Emphasis is placed on client competencies and diversity is valued. When individuals engage in destructive behavior (e.g., child abuse and neglect, partner battering), both problem behavior and exceptions to problem behavior are addressed. Patch workers have found that "as they looked at people's strengths they started to see themselves less in the role of saviors who told families what to do and more in the role of partners developing plans with families" (Adams & Krauth, 1994, p. 97). Neighborhood Place workers have experienced a very similar phenomenon.

Teamwork. Teamwork between workers is invaluable for Patch and Neighborhood Place. Teamwork allows workers to "(1) develop a detailed and comprehensive knowledge of the locality they serve; (2) to bring a wide range of skills to bear on the tasks they need to undertake at family, neighborhood, and service system levels; and (3) to develop a common vision and strategy" (ibid., p. 98).

Partnership with Individuals and Families. Patch and Neighborhood Place both believe that fostering partnerships at several levels is essential to community-oriented care. Partnerships must be struck between professionals, between professionals and community network systems, and between professionals and their immediate clients. Forming meaningful partnerships with consumers requires that professionals recognize consumers' strengths, aptitudes, and resources.

Change at the Neighborhood/Community Level. The site of change includes individuals, families, and the neighborhood. Patch and Neighborhood Place both assume that individual and family problems are in part correlated with problems within neighborhoods and communities. Therefore, efforts are made to promote change at each level of the "system," including individual, family, worker, agency, neighborhood, and community. One patch worker stated, "I'm seeing more and more that we as patch team members can help facilitate change in the neighborhood" (ibid., p. 98).

Although services of this nature do currently exist beyond Patch and Neighborhood Place, they are typically marginalized, and/or are transient pilot projects (Schorr, 1993). A crucial difference between status quo social work and community social work is the "degree to which different levels of work [are] seen as legitimate professional practice" (Adams & Nelson, 1995, p. 67). Community social work argues that "indirect intervention," including efforts to truly get to know one's community, are completely legitimate and indispensable. Typically, these activities are not legitimized and, therefore, do not receive "appropriate thought, planning, and workload weighting by management" (p. 67).

Solution-based casework complements efforts such as Patch and Neighborhood Place by providing a model that emphasizes collaboration between professionals, client competency, working partnerships, service integration, community organizing, teamwork, and family involvement. Further, solution-based casework adds to macro-oriented community-based social work by its emphasis on specific casework skills that are common to the service network and in language that is familiar to families. Moreover, by unifying concepts for case assessment and case planning, solution-based casework offers a conceptual and skill-based road map for intervening with individuals and families. Finally, solution-based casework dismisses the predominant deficit orientation and replaces it with an emphasis on client and community resources. Indeed, solution-based casework argues that professionals ought to facilitate a process whereby clients identify those moments when they have managed stressors safely (rather than simply instructing clients how to behave differently). That is, instead of conversations that repeatedly recount failed efforts to cope with life, social service professionals and their clients identify and detail situations when stressors were effectively handled. It is assumed that exceptions to maladaptive behavior actually occur frequently. The task, then, is to understand those moments and to build on them. In this process clients construct their own solutions. Rather than spinning solutions for clients, professionals help clients identify and implement their own underutilized successes. This creates a notable shift in the educator-student relationship that has historically existed between social service professionals and their clients. Historically, many professionals have readily assumed that adults who behave abusively or who neglect their children need to be educated about how to behave and emote. This suggests that clients are naive and places them in a passive role in relation to professionals. A solution-oriented conversation instead elicits exceptions to abusive behavior, e.g., "When have you been close to hitting your son, but didn't?" or "What is different about those times vs. the times when you've behaved violently?" This shift in the conversation seems to embolden discouraged clients, is instrumental in establishing working partnerships, and can loosen the grip of maladaptive processes. Instead of being bound by their maladaptive behavior, clients are instructed by its exceptions.

Part II

Assessment

Chapter 3

Anchoring Casework in Everyday Life Events

"SORTING THINGS OUT" TOGETHER

As we have said previously, solution-based casework anchors itself around three basic tenets: (1) the commonality of challenges in family life, (2) the importance of focusing casework on those everyday challenges, and (3) the necessity of locating individual skill development in the context of those specific family life challenges. While these three concepts are interlocking and dependent on one another, the model rests on the theoretical and conceptual foundation that all families face similar challenges and tasks in order to meet the needs of everyday life. Whether one is a third-generation welfare client or a supervisor of social services, a student or a college professor, one can appreciate the mundane and all too real struggles of how to be patient when teaching a child something new, or who should speak to the in-laws about a disagreement, or how to keep a family member from abusing alcohol or drugs, or how to help a family member face discouragement over a dream that seems unachievable. This acknowledgment of the universality of family life does not diminish the significant differences that exist economically between families; it simply reminds client and provider alike that it is within these daily life dramas that we all live and work out our individual needs and idiosyncrasies. Our challenge in casework begins with the desire to form a partnership with families based upon the recognized commonality of family life. This challenge requires us to help the family make sense of what is happening and to come to a common understanding of what everyone needs to do to make things go better. This "sorting things out" function of casework is what we call in the profession *assessment and case planning*.

PARTNERSHIP CHANGES THE MEANING OF ASSESSMENT

In a postmodern world flooded with viewpoints, the challenge to "sorting things out" becomes one of discernment of what information is truly important. Gregory Bateson (1951) argued effectively that the acquisition of information was based on one's ability to notice difference. The more data that comes in, the higher the allowance must be for filtering out data as "nonimportant," i.e., information that doesn't register as making a difference to our conclusions. Otherwise, our experience in this information age would quickly become one of information overload. Our conceptual grid or map of how we process data about the families we work with becomes very important in determining what data we end up considering as informative.

How does this phenomenon affect our assessment of the families with whom we work? From a solution-based perspective, we believe the way we organize our thinking about families will determine what data we recognize as important. If our conceptual map is honed on recognizing and identifying evidence of pathology, we will filter out all other data as unimportant or irrelevant. If we see the family as sick or dysfunctional, and view our own family as healthy and functional, we will see little in common with the client other than the client's need to be more like us. By continually studying deficit populations and their problem characteristics,[1] we further confirm an entrenched and collective view that these families are "dysfunctional." This attitude can lead, in the extreme, to caseworkers adopting the view, "These people don't care about their kids, so why bother?" Rather than taxonomies of pathology guiding our work with families, we suggest focusing on the very real and practical aspects of everyday life in the family.

KEEPING OURSELVES FOCUSED ON EVERYDAY LIFE

In spite of all the best efforts of a good caseworker, and sometimes because of those efforts, casework can get too fancy. The process of working in a social service or mental health system has a subtle effect on the way we do our business, often creating unintended results. An effort to truly understand what is happening in a family can too easily become a diagnostic exercise, where every possible issue in the family is documented.[2] A process to help the family improve their own attempts to solve their problems becomes a process of trying to get the family to cooperate with our proposed solutions. A desire to provide the family with creative alternative ways of viewing their problems becomes an insistence that they face up to seeing their problems "as they really are" (i.e., the way we have come to see them). Solution-based casework attempts to help the caseworker and supervisor resist the subtle pressures of our system to organize the family's reality on our terms. The best way to resist this pressure is to continually focus on the life events that happen on a day-to-day basis in the family.

ROUTINES ARE AT THE HEART OF FAMILY LIFE

Events or routines such as the one for everyone getting up in the morning, or getting dinner on the table, or keeping track of people on Friday nights are the events that constitute family life. It is in these patterned everyday life events that families live and sort out their needs. It is in these events that solutions to the "sorting" must also take place. Different routines are attempted, sometimes in a trial and error fashion, until something more or less works well enough that it no longer is noticed as an event that needs attention (Terkelson, 1980). Of course, it may come back to family attention if the attempted solution isn't up to satisfying the competing needs once circumstances change.

Example

For instance, the Friday night routine in the Smith family (adolescent stage) has consisted in the past of the kids (ages sixteen and fourteen) grabbing dinner at the kitchen counter, while discussing with their mother their proposed activities for the evening. In the past, this process usually didn't include Dad (still at work), but did involve considerable negotiation with Mom over where, when, how (transportation), and with whom these proposed activities were supposed to take place. Dad would usually arrive after most of this was settled, only getting involved if Mom needed him to confirm her "no." This routine worked well for them until a couple of weekends went by in which the oldest son, who was now driving, called home from a friend's house to inform his mother of his plans, rather than coming home directly after school. While the son was exercising new freedoms, he was also afraid that his father might say no to his requests and by calling in early he neatly avoided his father. The first time the son called, the mother was upset that he had not instead come directly home first, but she didn't want to overreact and ended up asking him what he was going to do about dinner. He informed her that he had already eaten. Since she had always been concerned about his eating, a brief argument about nutrition took place, ending with the son telling her not to worry so much and that he would call in later. Hanging up, she felt uneasy but "shook it off" as there were other tasks to be done. When Mr. Smith came home, he asked where everyone was, and Mom's unease came back as she tried to explain the call to him. Mr. Smith was more suspicious of his son (a boy a lot like himself) and "gave her a dig" for not even finding out where he was, an issue that had slipped her mind when the conversation became heated over what the boy was going to do for dinner. The Smiths dropped the subject when it looked like it might threaten their evening, and they made no plans to alter their routines to adapt to the increased independence of their son. It wasn't until the police called a couple of Fridays later that they realized they had a problem that required some kind of attention: Their son had been one of many picked up at a loud open-house party. He was not charged—he was simply in the wrong place at the wrong time. Prior to the call, the Smiths had not recognized any significant (attention-requiring) change in the everyday life of their family—it all just seemed to happen. They hadn't noticed that they didn't have a rule about "going places" because up until now (son starting to drive) they didn't really need one.

THE PROBLEM WITH SOLUTIONS

This time, the Smith family was able to quickly readjust to the developmental challenges they were facing: their solutions were practical changes in the routines of their everyday family life (particularly the Friday night routine). The Smiths met with their son and established rules appropriate to a driving teenager and the consequences for not following them. Some families' solutions, however, are not only inadequate to the problem at hand, but may even complicate the resolution of their developmental difficulties. Inadequate solutions tend to be "more of the same" (e.g., lack of notice, retreat, overreaction) thus reinforcing the routine (pattern) that is not working. The "solutions" serve to discourage the family members and erode their ability to recognize the original developmental problem the further the solution gets from the everyday life problem that originally spawned it.

For instance, imagine that the Smith family in the example above had framed the problem as totally residing within their son (i.e., "I don't know what's wrong with him, Doc"). Their embarrassment and anger with their son would increase the pressure on him without providing him a process to responsibly exercise his growing autonomy. Or let's further complicate the situation by imagining that Mr. Smith has a temper that can be triggered when he thinks his control is being threatened (e.g., Mr. Smith strikes his son in an argument-turned-shoving-match about curfew). While few caseworkers would see this action as a solution, it is in fact an attempted solution (reestablish authority) by the father that could complicate and engrain a problem that started as a temporary developmental problem. Such "attempted solutions" to the everyday life problems in a family make it harder for the family to recognize, or locate, the problem in everyday life (e.g., What rules are we going to establish regarding asking for permission to do something?). Instead, the problem is located within some individual, not unlike how casework might define it if not focused on the everyday life events of the family. Casework almost always involves family situations in which the original developmental challenge (problem) has become "fuzzy" in definition and the attempted solution (individual loss of control) is creating a risk for family members.

However, as we can see in the Smith case, even if the father regained control of his temper, the family would still need to resolve the developmental issue regarding their teenager. Without a family developmental focus to the Smith's family work, it would also make it more difficult to engage Dad in working on his temper. If the sole focus is on his temper, he can feel singled out and even undermined (e.g., "You are siding with my son!"). In some instances, other family members may also feel like Dad is being attacked and move to defend his actions, placing this whole issue in the lap of the caseworker. When all of the attention is placed on individual self-control objectives, the Smith family may still be at risk because they have not been helped to develop a reasonable plan to manage the increased autonomy of their son. It should be noted that the reverse is also true. If casework merely focused on "the Friday night routine" and did not help Dad address his anger, the family would remain at risk. Focusing on the everyday life of families and helping them recognize their patterns at the family developmental level as well as the individual level keeps casework from being merely reactive and moves it toward solution-based prevention.

OVERVIEW OF FAMILY DEVELOPMENT

Although the field has seen several different ways to organize and discuss family developmental issues (Haley, 1987; Duvall, 1957, Carter & McGoldrick, 1988), there appears to be general agreement that family tasks develop in close coordination with the needs of individual development and environmental stressors. Carter and McGoldrick propose that problems result when too many needs go unmet, resulting in an interruption in the family life cycle, and that the goal of casework is to assist the family in restoring its developmental progress. Their work focuses on assessing the developmental stage of family life, and the interactional patterns that vary with each stage of the life cycle, from early marriage through the birth of children to the postparenting years. Although many families do not proceed in a linear fashion through these stages,[3] or do so with unique cultural characteristics, the commonality of family experience is still a very useful model for the caseworker to fashion a view of the family. Our discussion of these stages will center on how the tasks of each stage are realized in the everyday life of the family. Understanding how everyday life events are related to good casework will be critical to the discussions on case planning and case management. Because we believe that an understanding of family development provides an important conceptual umbrella for organizing and locating our work with families, we begin with a brief overview of the family life cycle and the everyday family life challenges that are typical of each stage.

BEGINNING COUPLE

The beginning couple stage historically commenced with marriage and continued until the first child was born. While this certainly is still the case for the majority of couples, in our rapidly changing society many couples are beginning some of the tasks of marriage before a commitment to marriage is ever made. This phenomenon is usually thought of as something only practiced by the poor, but an increasing number of young middle-class couples, previously divorced couples, and the elderly are choosing to live in a relationship with some similarities to marriage, but not to marry. Couples who live together but do not marry have different challenges in this developmental stage, as will be discussed.[4]

Regardless of the challenges created when coupling precedes commitment, the first tasks of a new young couple are to (1) differentiate from their family of origin, (2) negotiate new boundaries with friends and relatives, and (3) resolve conflict between their individual needs and each other's needs (Carter & McGoldrick, 1988). Everyday family life in this stage of the life cycle will typically revolve around questions similar to the following:

- Who deals with whose in-laws?
- How often do you visit each family, and how long do you stay when you visit?
- What can you tell your relatives about your spouse?
- What friends is it still OK to see occasionally?
- What are the rules about seeing them (i.e., when, where, how late, etc.)?
- When can people come over to visit and how long can they stay?
- How much attention do you give your spouse when around friends?
- When can you use the bathroom?

- What should be done with the toilet seat (i.e., up or down)?
- How will you spend time together and time apart, share intimacy?

The number of small increments of adjustment in everyday life is staggering for the young couple and goes far beyond those mentioned above. Most of these issues get resolved without much discussion or conflict, but any one of the issues can trip a given couple up and lead to developmental conflict. In fact, most of the conflict couples experience in early marriage is around the details of life together (e.g., when to get up, when to got to bed, what to eat, where to eat, hair in the sink, caps off toothpaste). Life events may or may not wait for the resolution of developmental tasks, for instance the birth of a child. The young couple best handles the addition of a child if they have accomplished enough of the earlier tasks so they feel ready to focus their attention on the enormous needs of a newborn child. When conditions are less than ideal (unwed parent, absent parent, lack of established independence), the tasks don't change but do become more difficult and complicated. However this shift in organization occurs, the common characteristics are something all new parents can identify with, regardless of the their socioeconomic level, cultural characteristics, or prior success in preparation.

INFANT PRESCHOOL FAMILY

The developmental tasks for the family of young children often begin with the decision to start a family and continue until the children enter school. Whatever their level of preparation, the couple (or single parent) is quickly faced with the strong attachment needs of the newborn baby. In the first two years of life, the child's primary developmental need is to form an attachment to one or more family members. When infants have a secure attachment to the caregiver, they are more likely to develop problem-solving and social skills from two to five years of age (Sroufe, 1978).

As the child grows, parents must establish rules that maintain safety and parental authority and still encourage growth. During toddlerhood, children begin to develop their sense of autonomy or separateness. Toddlers develop autonomy by climbing and pulling to get things without asking. To achieve autonomy, the toddler needs the parents' support. Children need to be encouraged to make choices and take responsibility for feeding and dressing themselves. The parents' developmental tasks expand to include learning to cooperate so they can balance limits with freedoms, as well as create an environment that is supervised and safe from hazards.

Whatever the level of parental cooperation (or availability), families must organize themselves as best they can to feed, clothe, clean, supervise, teach, discipline, and nurture their small children. In each family, there are days when this goes better than others.[5] If it goes "good enough, often enough" (Terkelson, 1980), the child will have enough needs met to begin school with a chance of meeting the challenges of the next stage.

Some of the typical challenges facing the family with infants and preschool children are illustrated by the following examples:

- Who gets up in the middle of the night to feed the baby?
- What do you do when the baby cries and can't be soothed?
- Who will stay and watch the baby if one or both parents have to leave?
- How do you keep things you have never worried about away from the baby?
- When do you have sexual intimacy?
- Who watches the baby when meals or other chores are being done?
- When can you relax with friends and still look after the baby?
- How, when do you toilet-train a child? And who should do it?
- How do you prepare a child for day care?
- How do you teach a child right from wrong?
- What is right and wrong in this family?
- How should you discipline the child? Who should do it?

The list of possible questions can go on and on. The resolution of each task results in new behavior and gives the family clues as to how the other tasks of this stage can get resolved.

SCHOOL-AGE FAMILY

A couple may have difficulties resolving some of the tasks associated with having a small child, but other tasks will go just fine. Social scientists view this next stage as beginning when the first child enters school. The family system often becomes vulnerable to influences and forces from outside systems, such as neighborhood and school. The family must learn to relate to these new and competing systems. Rules (ways of operating) must permit contact with people outside the family in order for the child to experience relationships for himself or herself. Some of the new ways of operating (rules) that must be established are as follows:

- How will you help with school work?
- Who should help with school homework?

- How will you deal with school evaluation?
- How much should you expect at school? At home?
- How do you get him/her up and off to school in the morning?
- What time do you decide bedtime is? Who enforces it?
- Do you have consequences? Are they consistent?
- What friends are OK at that age? Can they go to someone else's house?
- Do you talk to the teachers? Who talks to the teachers?
- Who transports the child and when? What events are OK?

The extent to which these and countless other questions can be negotiated will often determine how a family manages this stage of the life cycle. Parents may also be undergoing physical and emotional changes as they leave their youth and approach middle age. They may experience stresses and pulls of their own from their rising (or falling) work responsibilities as well.

ADOLESCENT FAMILY

The adolescent family is the next major shift in family life cycle development, occurring between the time the first child reaches puberty and the time the last child starts to leave home (launching stage). When adolescence occurs, the everyday life events of the family must again change. Parents try to allow the adolescent more autonomy, and boundaries (hopefully) can become more flexible. Parents can no longer maintain complete authority and must accommodate themselves to the adolescent's increasing competence. They must also retain some supervision and control in some critical areas, even as they loosen the reins. The way in which critical tasks of communication and negotiation have been resolved in previous stages will again affect resolution of challenges in this stage.

As everyone knows or remembers, adolescents often challenge and test family rules and regulations concerning privacy, control, and responsibility. Adolescents often challenge the family system with new values and behaviors. They may act like children one minute and like adults the next. Parents often do not know how to respond to the adolescent:

- Should parents set limits?
- What behaviors should be taken seriously?
- Should you let him/her try and fail?
- Can you risk letting him or her fail?
- Should you ask about his/her friends?

These questions, and the examples that follow, become all the more difficult for parents who are themselves feeling rebellious in their work or relationships:

- Should they have a curfew? What should it be? What if they are late?
- Do they need to report their whereabouts? What if they don't?
- What can they wear? Where can they wear it?
- Who can they be friends with? Can they be alone with their friends?
- How much telephone time is enough? What if they want it secret?
- What chores are reasonable, how often, and do they have to do them well?
- What are the consequences for not following the rules?
- Who needs to agree about the rules? How are they known?
- How are rules changed or adapted?

LAUNCHING FAMILY

As the adolescent children grow and mature, the family prepares to launch them into independence. The young adult may leave home or in other ways assume major responsibility for him- or herself. In this stage, the young adult and the family attempt to decrease the dependence of the youth on the family. The ability of the young adult to differentiate from his or her family of origin will lead to increased autonomy with future family members and friends.

The launching stage is also marked by the greatest change in membership in the family. Young adults marry and bring new spouses and children into the family, parents become grandparents, and new roles are established within the system. The family may also lose members through the death of parents and grandparents. Because family membership (or availability) changes so much during this stage, everyday life events that have been routinely handled by certain family members must now be realigned and handled by someone else.

How do these developmental forces resolve themselves in the everyday life of the family? They resolve themselves through small tasks and challenges that occur on a frequent basis each and every day. For instance:

- What rules still apply to a young adult living at home?
- What about consequences, can you still make them stick?
- How much of their individual support should they be responsible for?

- What is OK and not OK about the friends that they keep?
- Do you "bail them out" if they get in over their heads on something?
- What do you do about our lives as they begin to move out of the family?
- How do you start preparing for later life ourselves?
- How do you parent and grandparent at the same time?
- Do you make their significant others a part of the family? How do you do this?

POSTPARENTAL FAMILY

The postparental family, often referred to as the "empty nest," is typically thought of as beginning when the last child leaves home. However, this stage usually begins with a gradual realization and adaptation of new arrangements around developmental tasks.

A critical role for the postparental family is often grandparenthood. The grandchild establishes a common bond between the grandparents and their adult children. Grandparenting helps the postparental family adjust to retirement and the loss of a loved one. Newgartin and Weinstein (1968) studied seventy sets of middle-class grandparents and found that most expressed satisfaction with this role. Poor families may not experience the same rewards as middle-class counterparts because the role of grandparent often comes too early (Hines, 1988), at a time when other life stressors are still very high.

Everyday issues present during the postparental stage of family life revolve around the encounters that the older generation has with the younger:

- What involvement can or should the older generation have in discipline?
- What amount of help will they provide in child care?
- What should be the financial relationship between the generations?
- How much help should the younger generation give the older generation?
- What role can the older generation play in day-to-day family life?
- How long should the older generation visit, how often, what time of day, etc.?

DIVORCE AND REMARRIAGE

The divorced, remarried, or blended family is yet another lens by which to view the challenges of everyday family life. Like the stages of the family life cycle, the stages of remarriage include common developmental tasks and transitional periods. It is noteworthy, however, that remarried families must go through two sets of developmental processes simultaneously: those appropriate to the age and stage of family members and those related to the stage of the remarriage process (Whiteside, 1982). The challenges are shared by anyone who goes through divorce and remarriage, and are only partially affected by the distinctions of race, age, or economic condition. The remarried family goes through the following developmental stages: separation and divorce, single parenthood, courtship, and remarriage. For the purpose of this discussion meant only to illustrate how these events affect everyday life, we will include all of these stages in the example of developmental questions that follow:

- Who makes the rules now? Who enforces them now?
- What do you do when everyone is very upset and sad?
- What do you do to avoid saying or doing something hurtful when upset?
- Do you talk about your problems or try to ignore them and stay strong?
- Who do you tell what (who said what, who is dating whom, etc.)?
- Who belongs to the family?
- What property belongs to you? What room is yours?
- Who is in charge of the children? When are they in charge?
- What is the role of steprelatives?
- Which rituals (holidays, food, church, etc.) are maintained, which are not?
- Which set of rules are you following?

KEEPING YOUR FINGER ON THE PULSE OF FAMILY LIFE

As stated earlier in this chapter, family life revolves around the everyday challenges that occur on a daily basis. These patterned interactions are where the family evolves its arrangements for satisfying diverse and competing needs. By focusing on the everyday life events as an organizing principle of casework, the assessment and case planning process stays close to the family, where it can be practical and useful. It is within the family's domain that problem patterns should be located, not within the domain of the professional helper. Conversely, definitions of problems that do not place everyday family life events at the heart of the work do so at the risk of losing the family partnership.

EVERYDAY LIFE AND PATTERNS OF DISCOURAGEMENT

It is understandable why developmental challenges lead to moments of discouragement for all families. Developmental challenges that go unmet for any length of time can lead to a lack of hope. A lack of hope can lead to a deepening of discouragement in which efforts to face new tasks are met with diminished expectations before they are even attempted (Carter & McGoldrick, 1988). Families who experience extreme difficulty in adapting to life events often become discouraged to the point that they no longer attempt solutions. Michael White (1986) has characterized such families as problem saturated. Their attempted solutions to everyday family life problems are simply not "good enough" to meet the current developmental needs of the family members, and so tension and conflict increase (Terkelson, 1980). With increased conflict over needs comes an increased effort to compensate for unmet needs. The efforts to compensate for unmet needs often lead family members into behaviors that allow momentary self-gratification at the expense of other family members. These behaviors (e.g., retreat, use of substances, physical expression of anger) in turn create more stress, more conflict, and further unmet needs. What begins as an everyday developmental issue can grow into escalating cycles of patterned behavior that can lead to pervasive discouragement. It is not unusual for such families to feel that their problems actually dominate family life and, over time, their experience convinces them they lack the resources to overcome the problem (White & Epston, 1990). This entrenched and discouraging view of themselves tends to obscure their awareness of how they enter destructive patterns around everyday life events, and blinds them to existing and potential solutions that are within their power to implement (de Shazer, 1988). Because family members often personalize these struggles, they typically are only vaguely aware of the interactive nature of their family and individual response patterns to the daily developmental stressors. As reflected in comments such as "and then we start all over again," and "I knew we were going down the same old road," members are cognizant that a pattern exists, but are not confident in their ability to avoid the pattern, interrupt it once it starts, or escape it before harm occurs if avoiding and interruption fails.

This cycle of discouragement goes beyond the family and includes those social systems charged with assisting the family (e.g., social services, mental health, schools, and the courts). As we begin to look at assessment in the next chapter, we will discuss how to resist this pull toward discouragement and to assist the family in recognizing its problem patterns. The ability for staff and families to recognize helpful and unhelpful patterns in their lives is closely linked. As staff learn to "hear" a family discuss their pattern, staff can help the family focus on how the pattern is realized in their everyday life.

NOTES

1.   Graduate school and job-related training programs are not immune from contributing to a perspective that views families as if looking through a lab microscope. For instance, classes in abnormal psychology routinely identify the pathology of the week to "look at." Social work courses can also unintentionally contribute to this distancing perspective by covering family problems in "family dysfunction of the week" format (e.g, alcoholism in the family, child abuse in the family, family violence). Information separated from its everyday life context does not distill a sense of commonality in the challenges of family life.

2.   Much of the subtle pressure to view families this way comes from our colleagues in the typical case staffing meeting. Too often we challenge our colleagues over possible areas of pathology they may have overlooked (e.g., "I suspect she was sexually abused as a child, sounds like a dysfunctional family background. . . . Did you ask about that?").

3.   Poor families have generally less calendar time for the meeting of developmental needs (Hines, 1988). Family members have children and become grandparents at far earlier ages than middle-class families. This means there is much less time for getting organized to meet the needs of emerging members.

4.   Although gay and lesbian couples would fit this general category, we will not be discussing their additional and somewhat unique developmental challenges in this text. The importance of understanding the similarities and differences in everyday family life events does not change, however.

5.   This idea that ability is often situation specific will be discussed in greater depth in Chapters 4 and 5. The solution-based casework model places considerable importance on collecting information on the "exceptions" to problem pattern situations because these exceptions can hold the key to future solutions.

Chapter 4

Recognizing Patterns

ASSESSING PATTERNS IN EVERYDAY LIFE

Briefly and generally stated, the caseworker needs to answer three assessment questions to keep the problem definition located in the everyday life of the family:

1. What everyday life task(s) is the family having difficulty with?
2. What are the details of the family interaction when they try to accomplish these tasks?
3. How do key individuals in the family fail to do their part in meeting the current tasks?

Posed in common terms the questions are:

1. What is the family trying get done?
2. What actually happens when they try to get it done?
3. How does someone "lose it"?

These assessment questions sound easy and logical to frontline workers, yet the investigative responsibility of protective service agencies often predisposes assessment to focus primarily on whether or not the neglect, abuse, or out-of- control behavior has occurred, rather than the more inclusive question of how it occurred. Concurrently, investigative workers often feel pressure to collect indications of pathology or dysfunction that can be readily identified by the caseworker, whether or not they are directly related to the conflict in question. The presence of pathology is then used to "explain" why the neglect or abuse occurred. Such an emphasis puts all of the expertise within the social worker (presumed healthy) and the deficits within the family (presumed unhealthy / sick). Although collecting this information is potentially useful, if the assessment lens is primarily focused on whether or not there is evidence of pathology, it will be difficult for the caseworker to maintain a perspective that locates the problem within the developmental challenges the family and its members are facing. When pathology is the primary lens of assessment, case plans are at risk of simply listing the pathologies identified and assigning a treatment package or experience to each (e.g., child abuse = parenting classes, presence of alcohol = alcohol counseling, past sexual abuse = victim counseling, domestic violence = perpetrator group).

While all of these experiences may be useful to many families, without situation-specific information, measuring treatment outcome is at risk of becoming little more than deciding safety issues based on compliance with treatment attendance. This is particularly the situation the longer a case stays open and the further the presenting developmental problem recedes into the background. If a father strikes a child with a belt and leaves bruises, caseworkers need to know more than whether or not the abuse occurred, or how many anger management classes the father attended, in order to be reasonably confident that the child is safe. A focused understanding of the developmental tasks the family was facing (e.g., getting the kids bathed and off to bed), how the family was responding to the tasks, and the specifics of how father lost self-control, will lead the caseworker toward a case plan that targets both the developmental task of the family and the father's ability to control his emotions and behavior during that task. When problems are defined within the everyday life of the family, the family, the caseworker, and the service providers are able to agree on the outcome goals (specific prevention skills) and can organize their collective resources accordingly. Conceptually locating the problem firmly in the everyday life events of the family keeps the caseworker focused on assessing the family's patterns of response to the challenges presented by their stage of family life. Assessing the specifics of that pattern helps individual family members define the struggle they are having in doing their part to accomplish the task. Assessment begins with the worker and family collectively recognizing these patterns and bringing them into sharpened awareness. This type of assessment requires a partnership, a partnership to define the problem in terms familiar to the family's life, a problem definition that keeps the resolution of the problem within the competence of the family. Assessment is as much about reestablishing hope as it is about assessing the challenges to that hope.

CREATING A PARTNERSHIP TO FIND SOLUTIONS

Historically, social service and mental health providers have too often assumed a posture of objective expertise, perceiving themselves as disseminating professional truths to a relatively naive client population. In this environment, clients who did not accept the professional's recommendations were apt to be labeled resistant and their contribution to the change process was largely minimized (Patterson & Chamberlain, 1992). Recently, however, there has been an increased interest within the social services in placing a premium on establishing partnerships with clients that attempt to reinforce client growth. This partnership reflects the caseworker's awareness that the challenges the client faces are in many ways universal.

As we have discussed, family caseworkers should conceptualize symptoms or complaints as "problems in living" arising out of the family's current inability to accomplish current everyday developmental tasks. Instead of diagnosing disease or deficits, caseworkers should join with the family around their frustration with resolving certain family issues and should reinstill hope that the problem will get solved. Assessment is based on the shared belief[1] that the family can meet any challenge if they can just figure out what goes wrong and can develop a plan of action to change their old way of doing it (old pattern). Based on this hope, it is necessary for the caseworker to focus everyone's attention on a detailed description of the problematic family events.

It is assumed that the family has frequently attempted to solve the problem(s) on their own, but have too often been unsuccessful. The caseworker, therefore, is quite interested in their attempted solutions as well as the members' beliefs regarding why those solutions have not been successful. The caseworker is interested in how individual members have struggled with attempted solutions. Deficits in family functioning are not ignored, but rather are seen as part of a larger question: How is this family going to meet the needs of its members at this particular moment in their life cycle? The relationship between the caseworker and the family member becomes a partnership that focuses on problem-solving. When workers fully adopt this approach to casework assessment, it is possible to extend this partnership to contentious situations, for example, when it becomes necessary for a family to separate in order to ensure safety.

TECHNIQUES FOR BUILDING PARTNERSHIPS

Partnership goes beyond interviewing technique; it begins with how the caseworker thinks about the family with whom he/she is working. It is not merely abstract theory that families go through predictable life stages and are faced with common developmental challenges: it is a way to think about each and every family situation that needs our help. Thinking developmentally is therefore the first "technique" that a caseworker must master. Although there are several techniques that could be additionally discussed, we want to focus on three that are specifically useful within a solution- based approach to casework: (1) separating intention from action, (2) normalizing family struggles, and (3) externalizing the problem. After discussing these techniques, we will discuss how to help a family describe their problem in everyday life terms.

Separating Intention from Action

"I didn't mean to do it!" Such a statement usually draws the ire of those in a position of protection. Our response, whether spoken or not, is too often something like, "Then why did you do it if you didn't mean to do it?" or "You wouldn't have done it if you really didn't mean to do it!" Both responses are logical extensions of a belief that people only do what they want to do. And while the justice system must hold us all account-able for our actions and not our intentions, we also know that the human personality is not simply of one mind. Most of the time we are of at least two minds on any given subject or situation, let alone one in which our emotions are running high. It is not difficult to recognize the familiar, even universal thought process that says "Part of me wants to . . . , but another part of me is afraid to." Rather than treat these separate parts of the client as resistance to responsibility, we can instead give voice to both parts of the person's personality, the part that didn't want to hurt his/her child for instance, and the part that can't believe the person did what he/she did. There may also be a part that feels blamed and misun-derstood, as well as a part that feels self-hate and disgust. Human beings are complex creatures with multiple intentions in any given situation. A solution-based caseworker recognizes this phenomenon and seeks to take advantage of it, choosing to form an alliance with those parts of the person's intentions that do not want to repeat what has occurred. Separat-ing intention from action allows the worker to partner the client in a common desire to avoid any similar action in the future. This desire does not reside in only the heart of the caseworker (as in a traditional practice model), who must then teach or require the family member to "start to care." Two techniques that help separate intentions from actions are (1) statements that help normalize the pressures and challenges clients currently face and (2) statements that help clients create a little breathing space between themselves and the problem (i.e., statements that external-ize the problem).

Normalizing Family Struggles

Depathologizing the family, and the intentions of its members, will greatly increase a client's receptivity to joining the caseworker in partner-ship to assess new ways of behaving. Much unnecessary time is wasted and casework relationships weakened by assessments of problems that elicit family members' defenses. Indeed, families often start out defensively in their relationship with caseworkers. This is particularly true for families who have had previous involvement with the social service system. Consequently, it generally doesn't take much stimulus from the worker to trigger more defensive posturing in families during the first visit. Caseworkers can minimize this risk by depicting the family's problems as part of the struggle of negotiating difficult life cycle stages. The destructive behavior should not be condoned or endorsed, but the worker can and should demonstrate an understanding of the pressures of modern life and awareness of common developmental tasks facing the family. When first experimenting with this approach, caseworkers may experience a desire to first ask numerous questions about the suspected abusive or neglectful behavior that elicited the referral, rather than thoroughly attempting to understand the context (what the family was trying to accomplish prior to the alleged destructive behavior). If the initial line of questioning completely revolves around the possible offense, the family and/or certain members will undoubtedly recoil. The solution-based caseworker anticipates a degree of defensiveness and reduces it by readily normalizing contextual family events. Caseworkers who successfully accomplish this task gather better information, better understand risk, and create cooperative working partnerships with families. Figure 4-1 illustrates possible normalizing language.

Figure 4.1.   Possible normalizing language.

Presenting Problem	Possible Normalizing Language
Mother who beat her child (prior abuse victim)	*"I understand you were trying to get her to sleep the night without crying and waking everyone up? I found that so difficult when my first child did that, particularly if I had to go to work the next day. You must feel terrible. How did the evening start?"*
Stepfather who slapped his teenage stepdaughter	*"You know, so many dads are telling me that raising a daughter in the 90s is really difficult, with all the influences out there, whether or not they are in a blended family like you are! What was the argument about?"*
Mother who neglects her children due to depression	*"I've met a lot of young mothers lately that are struggling with the same problems you are, it's odd, they all thought they were the only ones! Tell me about your child."*

Externalizing the Problem Pattern

In addition to normalizing the family's experience, another way case-workers have found it useful to create a working partnership with fami-lies is to use language that "externalizes" the problem. For example, asking clients, "How long have you had to struggle with this problem pattern?" "Has the yelling problem been around for awhile?" "What would you be doing more of in your family if this problem wasn't trying to run your lives?" Such questions move the family slightly outside the actual problem, disarming their personalization of the problem (blaming), and helping them to consider more independent action (White & Epston, 1990; White, 1988). If the family can discuss the problem in external terms, then they and the caseworker can work together as a team to overcome it. If certain family members have become identified as embodying the prob-lem, then finding ways to externalize the problem is helpful in freeing all family members to work against the problem rather than spending their energy defending themselves.

Externalizing the problem does not mean minimizing personal respon-sibility. For instance, even in work with sexual offenders, who often cover their destructive patterns with extreme minimization, distortions, and denial, there are helpful ways to give them the room to face their moral responsibility. For instance, a caseworker might externalize the problem by saying "I understand you want to fight this cycle of abuse that you have been caught up in. I wonder what it would take for you to feel honor again and not pass this cycle on to future generations?" The "cycle of abuse" then becomes the enemy, and rather than defending him- or her-self, the offender can "undermine" the cycle by giving the caseworker as much detail as possible about what the cycle's pattern looks like. Figure 4-2 provides additional examples.

Externalizing is not limited to a single rephrasing of problems the family members face, but is the natural outcome of the caseworker posi-tioning him- or herself as the family consultant (partner) in attempting to find solutions to their problem patterns. Working together against a com-mon foe provides the family members respect: respect for their desire to change, and the room to negotiate without unnecessary loss of personal integrity.

RECOGNIZING DOMINANT PATTERNS IN
EVERYDAY LIFE

Preventing the relapse of dangerous behavior begins with assisting individuals and families to recognize patterns (interactional sequences) that culminate in destructive behavior. Many families, when discussing

Figure 4.2. Possible externalizing language.

Presenting Problems	Possible Externalizing Language
Mother who beat her child (prior abuse victim)	*"Maybe you would like to put an end to this cycle of violence that has been passed on to you; would you like to be one to defeat this monster and keep it from hurting future generations?"*
Stepfather who slapped his teenage stepdaughter	*"When you described on of those episodes when everybody gets into it and you end up losing it, you seemed to be saying that you hate these episodes because they keep you from being the father you really want to be to your stepdaughter."*
Mother who neglects her children due to depression	*"This dark curtain that you mentioned, tell me about a time when you fought back, or slipped by, or fooled this dark curtain that descends on you."*

their conflicts, will say, "It just happens," or "All of a sudden (s)he just went off." They typically do not place the incident in a recognizable sequence of events or locate it in a family routine. These events flow like an uninterrupted experience just beyond their conscious awareness. However, everyday life patterns that end in destructive emotional or physical trauma must remain the focal point of assessment, case planning, case management, and case closure.

There are several benefits of organizing case planning around the everyday life events within which destructive behaviors occur. For instance, the individual who behaves dangerously can more readily recognize how his/her behavior influences and is influenced by the family context, and this knowledge informs individual skill development. Further, the family is more apt to receive usable assistance interventions that emphasize pertinent and particularly challenging pragmatics of family life. And, finally, since the dangerous behaviors are highlighted as familiar to all involved, service providers are able to more readily measure success in the specific life events that have been a problem in the past.

HELPING THE FAMILY DESCRIBE THE PROBLEM IN EVERYDAY LIFE TERMS

As we have discussed, it is typical for all of us to see stress and discomfort as the result of someone else's behavior. Assigning blame, arguing over who started the problem, comparing the current "injustice" to every other possible example of perceived slight that has occurred in the past is all so familiar to family life, "This is just like you." "You are doing it all over again," or "It all started when we married, you never . . ." are all familiar echoes to arguments most of us have had at some point in family life. If we are to help the family relocate their problem in the developmental issues they face, then casework assessment has to have ways of interviewing that draw the family's attention to the patterned and sequential events that have given rise to their hurt feelings. A context for their feelings must be co-constructed with the family if they are to be engaged in working on contextual issues.

A beginning step to organizing the family's attention toward everyday life tasks is for the caseworker to consider what some possible or likely contexts for conflict in the family might be. This is why we have stressed that understanding family development is so important. For caseworkers who have lived through all the stages, personal experience of the challenges can be a great benefit. For the younger caseworker, or for caseworkers who do not marry or have children, being informed through reading either professional texts or great literature will be necessary. Older workers can often reassure younger workers that experience is not always an advantage. As they point out, sometimes it makes objectivity that much more difficult.

A second step in caseworker preparation is to have a structure for organizing everyday family life tasks. Such a structure for organizing possible family level objectives appears in Figure 4-3. When the worker develops (or is provided) a grid for organizing casework around everyday family life, it increases the likelihood that discussions about what to work on with the family will be directed toward family developmental tasks.[2]

Tracking an Interactional Sequence

A critically important technique in helping the family define their problems in developmental terms is to discuss the sequence of events that led up to and followed the family event that everyone is concerned about. This is sometimes referred to in relapse prevention terms (Lane, 1991) as mapping a pattern or cycle work.[3] Casework assessment has always had an element of this sort of inquiry, an aspect of casework usually conducted to ascertain who did what to whom. Too often in the past, this inquiry has been conducted as part of an investigation to substantiate abuse or neglect (i.e., did it or did it not happen?). Rather than a simple binomial question, a solution-based caseworker asks a more complex question: "How did a family, who did not set out to hurt or harm each other, get into a position where things (everyday life event) got out of hand (or never got done in the case of neglect)?"

Figure 4.3. Sample menu of family level objectives. *Note:* List is not complete, only presented as a sample.

Adaptation to Crisis

Will use their "_____" plan to adapt to changing circumstances in the family.

Will provide family members opportunities to discuss to changing conditions in the family.

Behavior Management of Young Children

Will use their "_____" plan to teach their children limits of behavior as described in tasks.

Will use their "_____" plan to learn to use the toilet as described in tasks.

Will use nonaggressive forms of discipline, without corporal punishment, as described in tasks.

Behavior Management of Adolescents

Will use their "_____" plan to set family rules and consequences as described in tasks.

Will use their "_____" plan to resolve disagreements with teens as described in tasks.

Will use nonaggressive forms of discipline, without corporal punishment, as described in tasks.

Blended Family Issues

Will use their "_____" plan to work cooperatively together as described in the tasks.

Will negotiate reasonable arrangements to prevent escalation of conflict and disruption.

Chores and Routines

Will use their "_____" plan for (insert time of day) chores and routines as described.

Will structure (insert time of day) chores and routines to prevent conflict as described in tasks.

Home Cleanliness/Sanitation/Safety

Will use their "_____" plan to keep their home hazard free as described in the tasks.

Will maintain home in a clean, sanitary, and safe condition as described in the tasks.

Hygiene (Family)

Will use their "_____" plan to teach children about personal hygiene as described in tasks.

Will ensure healthy and clean family members as described in tasks.

Medical Care/Mental Health Care

Will use their "_____" plan to follow medical advice as described in tasks.

Will maintain proper medical and mental health care for the family as described in the tasks.

Nutrition

Will use their "_____" plan to maintain quality nutrition as described in tasks.

Will manage purchasing, and cooking of meals to ensure nutrition as described in the tasks.

Physical Safety

Will use their "_____" plan to keep children safe from physical harm or its effects as described in tasks.

Will arrange for personal safety for self and/or children as described in the tasks.

School Attendance

Will use their "_____" plan to get kids to school on time as described in tasks.

Will manage mornings and work with school personnel to ensure attendance as described.

Sexual Abuse

Will use their "_____" plan to help their child cope with abuse and ensure safety.

Will ensure the removal of person causing harm to child as described in the tasks.

Sexually Reactive Behaviors

Will use their "_____" plan to help children become less reactive and safe from abuse.

Will support child in coping with sexual reactivity as described in tasks.

Will provide supervision of child to ensure safety from sexual activity as described in the tasks.

Shelter

Will use their "_____" plan to secure a safe and adequate home as described in the tasks.

Will ensure that safe and secure shelter is provided to family members as described in the tasks.

Supervision

Will use their "_____" plan to ensure supervision of children as described in tasks.

Will negotiate roles and responsibilities for secure child care at all times as described in the tasks.

For instance, recall the Smith family discussed earlier in this chapter. The Smiths were having problems over the rules for their son when he wanted to go someplace. The son had gotten into some trouble for going places without permission. Assessment questions like the following might help the assessment caseworker and family understands the "how" of their problem pattern sequence.

- When did you first notice there was an issue with your son's "whereabouts"?
- How have you established rules and consequences for him in the past?
- Has his "whereabouts" been an issue on other nights, or mostly Friday?

- What has been your way of handling Friday nights in the past, your routine?
- How did Friday begin, has this thing been building up for a while?
- Walk me through the events of Friday night, will you?
- What happened then? Then what did you think? So what did you do?
- Is that what you wanted to say? Then what happened?

Through such sequential questions, the caseworker has the opportunity to summarize the developmental issues the family faces. For instance, with the Smith family the caseworker might say, "So you were trying to give your son some freedoms and your son was not keeping his end of the bargain. It sounds like you want to clarify or revamp your family rules about getting permission to do something [family level objective] as well Dad wants to be able to keep his temper no matter what [individual level objective]. Have I got it right?" Such a shaped summary allows the family to define their problems on both a family level (rules about going places) and an individual level (controlling temper).[4] Without tracking the sequential interaction of the precipitating event, the caseworker has difficulty locating and defining a family context for the behavior in question. It must be continually stressed that conflict over a developmental family issue does not explain or offer causal explanation for someone losing self-control during such conflict. This would be tantamount to blaming the victim for someone else's lack of self-control. There obviously is no justifiable explanation for harming oneself or someone else. However, by tracking the self-control problem back to the developmental conflict arena in which it occurred, caseworkers (1) provide the family a way to engage their member who has lost control, (2) maintain casework's focus on high- risk events in everyday family life where change can be measured, and (3) ensure that longer-term prevention steps are taken to reduce overall stress where the family has been experiencing it.

Searching for Exceptions to Everyday Life Patterns

Another technique for helping families focus productively on the routines of everyday life is to help them recognize situations in which the problem doesn't exist (Berg, 1994). Families who have repeatedly experienced a sense of failure typically find it difficult to recognize moments when they successfully manage conflict. As such, they may say, "He never tells the truth," or "We always have trouble with her." Such expressions clearly do not reflect the specific situations in family life in which the behavior is located. Professionals can help families[5] toward solutions by accepting their narrower view of the problem, while at the same time helping them search for and identify any exceptions to the pattern. Identifying moments when someone didn't lie, or conflict was avoided, or the family handled anger safely gives everyone an opportunity to explore the differences (i.e., how the exception became possible). What unique characteristics of that moment allowed the maladaptive pattern to be averted? The premise is simple: since an exception to maladaptive behavior occurred at least once, it may occur again if and when similar conditions are recreated.

For instance, imagine the Jones family, who, as they perceive it, always argue over finances (an everyday life event that, for these individuals, escalates to violence). Their latest disagreement culminated in a shoving match. Mrs. Jones was successful in pushing her husband out of the house. She then threw their bills, paperwork, and eventually several of his belongings out the windows of their home. He retaliated by throwing rocks and breaking several windows. Meanwhile, their young child stood screaming at the front door. Neighbors became rightly concerned and called police. Working with the caseworker, the couple expressed little hope that anything could be different because they always argued over money. When searching for exceptions to a clearly evolved pattern, the caseworker asked them to describe an incident in which they found themselves in one of those high-risk situations (in conflict over finances), but averted dangerous behavior. The couple agreed that must have occurred and they eventually identified several situations. The conversation then detailed how they avoided danger, which included (1) what the other could do to lesson the tension in those moments, (2) actions identified that fostered escalation, and (3) actions identified that avoided or interrupted their cycle. Bolstered by this knowledge about their individual and collective patterns, they agreed to more routinely exercise these skills and experiment with other adaptive behaviors. These changes began with a search for exceptions.

DECISION-MAKING IN ASSESSMENT

Casework assessment in child protection situations always requires (1) decisions to be made regarding whether or not to open a case and (2) whether or not to establish alternative care arrangements. As has been previously discussed, these decisions often drive the assessment/investigation away from a partnership model rather than allowing the assessment partnership to arrive at the decisions that need to be made. This text will not go into the specific criteria that are used to make risk decisions because of the wide variety of state and local jurisdictions that influence the criteria and because of other excellent texts available on the subject. Common risk factors such as the age and vulnerability of the victim, prior offense record, presence of substance abuse, presence of domestic violence, and severity of the abuse/neglect enter into such decisions. Solution-based casework does provide a framework for the caseworker to make these difficult decisions in partnership with the client.

For instance, take the difficult situation of having to place a child out of the home due to risk factors. Many times the experienced assessment caseworker has a "gut feeling" on the first home visit as to whether or not this is a family situation that will require out-of-home placement. If the caseworker jumps ahead in his/her thinking to issues related to the child's placement, he/she will soon be letting the decision about placement drive case assessment and planning. Developing a partnership will be given only lip service as the caseworker proceeds with casework issues such as documenting risk and getting the proper paperwork filled out. This process will accelerate as the family members pick up signals that the worker has moved on without them. As the family senses this movement, they will become reluctant to cooperate. The worker, now headed in a direction of documenting risk, will tend to see their resistance as further signs of pathology or dysfunction. The relationship will become contentious and will tend to convince the caseworker that the situation needs dramatic external action.[6]

This discussion is not to imply that an effort to remove a child is not solution-based, only to stress to the reader that a solution-based caseworker doesn't wait to practice a partnership model until getting all the information he/she needs to take protective action. On the contrary, experienced workers with solution-based casework are able to take strong actions, even termination of parental rights, within a model of partnership with the family. While this type of action is often a difficult one for parents, a partnership can still be formed around doing whatever is best for the child.

In Chapter 5, we will discuss the next step in assessment. After helping the family come to an initial recognition that their problems might be related to the pattern of problem resolution, and helping them consider that a better plan might help them achieve the outcomes they are seeking, assessment can move on to a more detailed and useful understanding of patterns that have placed them at risk both at the family level and at the individual level.

In words, it might go something like, "Let me see if I understand what you are saying. You're saying that you are all unhappy with the way your family has been arguing over chores,[7] and that you need a better plan for doing chores [family level objective], and you also think everyone needs to change themselves somewhat. For instance, Dad, I have heard you say that you really want to get better control of your temper [individual level objective]." Chapter 5 will focus on the specifics of how the caseworker can help the family learn enough about the details of the family and individual patterns to develop an effective plan of action at both levels.

NOTES

1. This "shared belief" is often one that must be first held by the worker on faith and experience. It is not the result of assessment, but a foundation of assessment. The caseworker chooses to believe in the family's restorative ability, and then goes about discovering with the family a reasonable plan of action to realize that outcome.

2. The menu of objectives in Figure 4-3 provides objectives in each category that can be named by the family. An example might be "Our Getting Organized Plan." More will be said about *family-level objectives* in Chapter 7 when specific suggestions are given for their use in case planning.

3. Cycle work will be explored in further depth in Chapter 5, when we discuss organizing assessment and case planning around specific prevention skills for individuals who have self-control problems.

4. Organizing a case plan around family-level objectives and individual-level objectives will be discussed in Chapter 7.

5. This same technique is useful when assisting individuals to identify the differences between the times they are vulnerable to being a certain way as compared to times when they can resist or avoid being that way. Use of this technique with individuals will be further discussed in Chapter 10.

6. For an excellent depiction of these accelerating events where two cultures of intent collide, see Salvador Minuchin's portrait of a social service case from the client perspective (Minuchin, 1984).

7. Chores are used as an example only—it could be any family life event.

Chapter 5

Assessing Problem Detail

RELAPSE PREVENTION REQUIRES SPECIFIC SKILLS

We have discussed how good casework requires a close working partnership with families, and we have seen how this partnership allows the
caseworker to help the family recognize patterns in everyday life that are
difficult for family members. But what do you do about those patterns?
How do you ensure that knowing what are high-risk situations for a
family will make any difference in lowering the risk to vulnerable members? How do you measure prevention?

The third basic tenet of a solution-based approach to casework is the
importance of identifying and targeting prevention skills as measurable
outcome. In situations of potential risk to family members such as abuse
or neglect cases, it is not enough to send the family to counseling and then
wait for the mental health provider to say that everything is better and the
kids can go home or the case can be closed. Measuring risk reduction
must be more than reporting on the number of therapy sessions attended.
Risk reduction is best measured by documenting the acquisition and use
of specific skills at specific high-risk times. Questions such as, "What
skills should be targeted?" "How does the caseworker go about assessing
them?" and "How are objectives to be determined?" are essential concerns of the caseworker. This chapter will address these questions to
provide the worker with the action steps necessary to help family members acquire relapse prevention skills.

WHAT SKILLS SHOULD BE TARGETED FOR OUTCOME?

Casework in today's world cannot and should not rely on vague un-
measurable goals for decision-making. Because the mental health and
social services fields have been fertile ground for theory development,

a professional tolerance has been established for "personalized approaches" to casework. Although this tolerance continues, there is increasing evidence that the field does agree that some minimum outcome skills[1] are considered essential to preventing relapse. Although this consensus has a fair amount of variance in it, most practitioners agree that the following list of skills should be considered necessary as a minimum and therefore targeted in all cases where prevention of a given problem pattern is important:

skill in identifying high-risk situations,
skill in recognizing early warning signals and triggers,
skill in avoiding high-risk situations,
skill in interrupting the problem cycle if the situation was not avoided,
skill in escaping the problem cycle if the situation was not interrupted

High-Risk Situations

As human beings we like to summarize our experience into descriptions that explain our feelings about them. In short, we exaggerate (ignore contrary information) for emphasis. This universal tendency results in statements about politicians (they are all liars), gender (men have no feelings), or family members (she has no patience). While all of these statements may contain elements of truth, it is clear that they are summative and do not account for variance demonstrated in different situations. For instance, the reader can identify certain situations in which politicians don't lie, men have feelings, and family members manage some patience. If you accept the premise that behavior is not unidimensional, then it is reasonable to assume that there are certain situations in which people are more at risk to behave in an "unwanted" way. If clients can identify these high-risk situations (e.g., when I'm tired, broke, and told I'm not needed), then they have the beginning information necessary to alter these situations. Without such skill in identifying high-risk situations, they are unable to make plans to avoid, interrupt, or escape those situations that could lead them to trouble.

Early Warning Signals

We all try to improve our ability to sense trouble coming ahead. Sayings such as "I'll see it coming next time" or "I know my limits now" are statements about our skills in detecting early warning signals of trouble. Although we will discuss this skill in more detail later in this chapter, it is important to stress here that if clients do not improve their skill in recognizing their own warning signals, they will have difficulty implementing new behavior because they will continually enter high-risk situations without "alarms going off." In this case, even though clients may have a plan of action, their early warning signals (identifiable thoughts and feelings) and late warning signals (physical sensations and planning) do not trigger their alternative plans to interrupt or escape the high-risk situation.

Skills in Avoiding (Preventing) High-Risk Situations

When parents tell their children not to cross the street, not to play with older children, or to get plenty of rest, they are teaching their children how to reduce their risk of getting into trouble. These parents and children construct their lives in such a way as to reduce the total number of times they get into awkward, uncomfortable, or even dangerous situations. When parents of adolescents develop rules for curfew they are having their children practice skills in avoiding certain high-risk situations.

Once our client families recognize when they are specifically at risk, they are in a position to develop specific plans to avoid those situations. Skills are developed through testing these plans in the everyday life of the family.

Skills in Interrupting High-Risk Patterns

This is probably the hardest skill for all of us, regardless of the problem arena. Interruption skills are used in difficult (high-risk) situations that were not avoided for some reason. By definition then, we are already "at risk" and are now in a position where we have to extricate ourselves from the problem. For families struggling over adolescent freedoms, it might mean interrupting a tense and potentially volatile conversation about curfew until the teen's friends go home and cooler heads can prevail. The same skills apply on the individual level as well.

For instance, a problem drinker decides he needs to avoid alcohol to preserve his family life. He is successful in avoiding situations with alcohol until one Friday he decides to go to lunch with some friends from work. The group ends up at a restaurant bar that is having drink specials. If he stays, he knows his risk will go up and he will feel himself wanting to participate. He doesn't want to make a scene; he even sees the thought "Maybe just one" race across his mind. At this point he needs to interrupt this pattern—he has "been here before" and knows where it (the pattern) is headed. If he has rehearsed this moment and has come up with a plan, he has a better chance of graciously excusing himself "for work reasons he just remembered" and getting out of there. Interruption skills are plans to be used when high-risk situations were not or could not be avoided but full relapse is not imminent. In this example, he came very close. If these interruption skills had failed and he had kept thinking about ordering just one drink, he would have needed an effective safety plan to escape the situation before relapse.

Skills in Escaping High-Risk Patterns

Counting to ten, going for a walk, or locking oneself in the bathroom are all skills in escaping an imminent relapse to unwanted or hurtful behavior. The high-risk situation obviously was not avoided, which means that the warning signals were not heard or they were ignored. Any efforts at interrupting the escalating pattern were ineffective, either because they were not practiced before and were therefore unavailable or they came too late in the pattern buildup to be effective. At such moments all one can do is to leave the situation immediately: not always an action without some costs, but better than relapsing to more negative behavior. Although these skills are clearly not a solution by themselves, they are an important component of relapse prevention plan. By the time a pattern problem escalates to escape skills, family members have few options and are at increased risk. They certainly need these skills, but as backup only.

STEPS TO PROMOTING PREVENTION SKILLS

How does the caseworker go about assessing these skills? Relapse prevention includes four basic steps: (1) recognition of patterns, (2) learning the details of high-risk patterns, (3) practicing small steps toward change, and (4) creating a relapse prevention plan. Each of these steps is important in constructing a case plan that is tailored to the unique characteristics of individuals and families (and therefore particularly relevant), is measurable (and therefore creates accountability), and pinpoints risky behavior (thereby reducing the likelihood of relapse). Further, each of these steps moves clients along in their efforts to master skills that will ensure safety.

STEP 1:   RECOGNIZING PATTERNS IN HIGH-RISK SITUATIONS

As previously described, individuals and families who are engrossed in maladaptive behavior generally have little knowledge of their individual and collective actions, how they contribute to escalating conflict, and when they are prone to destructive behavior. One may become angry, strike, and then cover his/her transgression without ever recognizing triggering events. Without assistance, some may be unable to recognize gradations in their emotions, or to identify the conditions in which they are prone to violence. A similar cycle can be identified with neglect: the guardian(s) may report constant fatigue and be unable to identify any events, thoughts, or feelings that led to his/her depressed state, let alone identify exceptions to his/her motivation. Therefore, developing the ability to recognize and understand that behaviors are embedded in interactional patterns is the first step in reducing the recurrence of maladaptive conduct. For instance, it is very useful for a parent who has previously said, "It just happens, I have no control over it [abusive behavior]," to begin to consider the who, what, when, and where surrounding his/her destructive actions. When clients engage in a conversation that helps them to recognize key sequences, previously unnoticed adaptive and maladaptive behavior becomes obvious. Steps 2 and 3 provide a framework for building prevention skills.

STEP 2:   LEARNING THE DETAILS OF HIGH-RISK PATTERNS

Since destructive cycles have evolved from nonproductive efforts to resolve conflict in daily living, it is essential to assist clients in delineating the everyday events that led to protective service involvement. Illuminating triggering events has the advantage of obvious relevance to the family, and also begins the process of building accountability. The aim is to thoroughly diagram the vulnerable and explosive moments within the life of the family.

The process of identifying and exploring specific destructive interactions in a family often creates a defensive and protective response by the family. The family and sometimes the caseworker may have a desire to place blame as a way to deal with this stress. The process can also be complicated by a caseworker's expectation that the transgressor should admit wrongdoing. Indeed, professionals often assume that services can not be productive until perpetrators overtly admit guilt and accept responsibility. It is not without reason that this is assumed; admission of guilt is positively correlated in our experience with a desire for change. However, an admission of wrongful behavior is difficult for anyone, particularly heavily defended (e.g., traumatized) individuals and families. Confessing to a shameful act is a significantly large step. Therefore, intervention need not be dependent on such a difficult first step. In other words, admission of guilt does not have to be the first line drawn in the sand. When the professional relationship is defined in an either/or context, someone will lose. Instead, when professionals and families engage in a disarming, solution-oriented conversation about (1) the challenges in everyday life, (2) specific high-risk behavior, and (3) how they can draw on their resources to prevent further conflict, transgressors are more apt to begin activities that lead to accepting responsibility, and fully engage in the change process.

Mapping the Pattern (Cycle Work)

Entrenched, nonproductive patterns can be thought of as cyclical in nature (Lane, 1997) and self-perpetuating (Figure 5-1). Assisting clients in mapping their patterned behavior (cycle work) is a powerful assessment and case-planning tool. Because cycle work is considered intrinsic to a solution-based approach to casework, we will discuss its use in a fair amount of detail. The first step in learning how to use this tool is to understand how conceptualizing problem patterns as cycles helps the caseworker and client make sense of what is happening in the individual and family.

Patterned Behavior in High-Risk Situations

A *triggering event* (e.g., comment, thought, act of omission) initiates an escalation of tension. For some people this might be as simple as being spoken to with a raised voice, for others it might be a critical comment, or for others it might be simply being ignored. The thoughts and emotions that follow triggering events often include a sense of injustice and are frequently self-punitive (e.g., "I'll never be loved," "Why does this happen to me?" "It's not fair"). This *early buildup* phase typically involves blaming others. In high-risk situations, tension often mounts within the individual, as manifested in physical signs (e.g., muscle tension, rapid heart rate), fantasy, and the construction of excuses (*late buildup*). In problem-saturated individuals and families, the release of tension is often manifested in some sort of *harmful incident* such as self-abuse, aggressive retribution, or as a symbolic act meant to punish both self and others (e.g., sexual promiscuity). Typically, the process includes a *justification phase* wherein the individual attempts to exonerate his/her action and avoid responsibility and/or wherein apologies attempt to pacify those involved.

Case Example

The young mother (Ms. Smith) whose situation we discussed in Chapter 1 had admitted to the caseworker that she had a significant temper problem, particularly when her son was being verbally or physically aggressive toward her. She would get angry at other times but reported being able to manage her anger then. When the caseworker asked her about the sequence of events that led up to the incident in question, they

Figure 5.1. Cyclical nature of entrenched, nonproductive patterns.

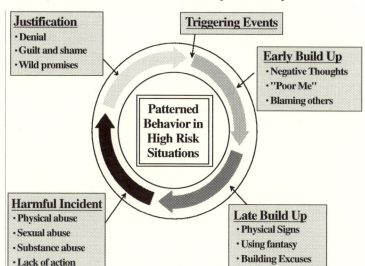

Justification
- Denial
- Guilt and shame
- Wild promises

Triggering Events

Early Build Up
- Negative Thoughts
- "Poor Me"
- Blaming others

Patterned Behavior in High Risk Situations

Harmful Incident
- Physical abuse
- Sexual abuse
- Substance abuse
- Lack of action

Late Build Up
- Physical Signs
- Using fantasy
- Building Excuses

learned that the mother was more at risk when she was exhausted due to lack of sleep (she has an infant daughter), or has been discouraged about finances (near the end of the month) such as when the father of her four-year-old son has not sent his child support payment. As Ms. Smith recalled the events that led to her assaultive behavior, she reported that the evening before the violent event, she waited for the child's father to deliver a child support payment. He never came. She said this event triggered in her considerable negative thoughts about the father, herself, and all the things about their four-year-old son that reminded her of his unreliable father. This early buildup continued until she cried herself to sleep, after drinking wine (something she usually doesn't do unless she's depressed). Her mood continued in the morning, with flashes of anger at her child and even angry thoughts about her infant (e.g., "Why did I have you?"). She slapped her infant's bottom for crying when she changed her diaper, and then stomped out of the room angry at herself, leaving the child unattended on the bed. She reports feeling flushed, dizzy, her fists were clenched, she mock pulled at her hair, and she fantasized just running out the door (late buildup).

Moments later, she heard her baby scream and ran into the room to find her four-year-old son (Sam) trying to diaper the baby, holding a pin in his hand. She flew into him, jerking his arm harshly. In this melee, the son accidentally stuck his mother with the diaper pin and she became enraged. She lashed out at him and struck him several times with her fists. She remembers screaming at him, being shocked at hitting him so hard, and experiencing a feeling of panic. She grabbed the baby and ran crying to her mother's home nearby. The incident was reported and the offending mother initially minimized what had occurred. She minimized to the assessment worker her loss of control and justified the bruises (it was accidental, he stuck me, he bruises easily), yet privately promised herself she would never behave in that manner again. She agreed with the worker that mornings are her most difficult time, particularly when she is tired, is financially stressed, and/or has been drinking the night before (high-risk situations).

While the caseworker has assessed significant environmental stressors for this mother (e.g., unreliable child support) and will work with her on these concerns, the worker recognizes that these stressors may not be within the mother's control and ultimately the mother will need to master her temper under such high-risk situations. In assisting individuals and families who struggle to safely negotiate tasks, it is essential that triggering events, early buildup, late buildup, and justification are identified. Detailing these processes helps reduce recidivism since clients are better positioned to (1) recognize when they are at risk, (2) recognize their early warning signals, and (3) intervene before emotional intensity decreases their ability to choose safe alternatives.

In this case example, the caseworker used the morning routine to map the mother's pattern when under stress. She did this by drawing a large circle on a flip chart and labeling the middle of it MORNING ROUTINE. Starting at the top of the circle and using a magic marker, the caseworker then asked the mother to walk her through how the day usually gets started, and how she remembers herself feeling immediately upon waking. The caseworker then summarized each piece of information about the morning on the circle. Questions about thoughts, feelings, and actions would help flesh out the time line of events. The caseworker used that morning routine to explore (1) how that everyday life event was structured and (2) how the mother's ability to control herself was challenged during that event. Questions similar to the following helped the caseworker and client to map the problem pattern:

- Were you feeling upset upon waking? When did you start to notice your temperature rising?
- What happened next? What were you thinking when that happened?
- So what did you do when that happened? Is that what you wanted to do?
- How do you think he felt? Is that what you wanted?
- Then what happened next? Is that because you were thinking [what]?

- How upset were you then? What did it feel like in your body?
- Could you have stopped the situation then or were you too far gone?
- Have you ever gotten that angry and not gone on to hit? What did you do to pull yourself back that time? What was different?

These questions continue until the cycle is completely explained to the client's and caseworker's satisfaction and they have learned what it was about the situation that triggered the client, what their early warning signals of impending trouble were, and what exceptions to the problem pattern have occurred in the past that have helped the client avoid, interrupt, or escape volatile situations.

Assessment questions that assume change will occur are empowering and generally create a willingness to discuss the sequential details of maladaptive patterns. For instance, individuals are more apt to participate in a conversation about productive solutions when the question posed to them is, "When you have dealt with similar conflict in a manner that you feel good about, what exactly did you do?" Or "If this problem you have with temper disappeared one day, how would you handle similar situations? What exactly would you do?" There are countless versions of questions that assume competence, anticipate change, and forecast positive outcomes.

STEP 3: PRACTICING SMALL STEPS TOWARD CHANGE

Although we are still discussing assessment issues that enable a caseworker and family to develop a case plan, we think it is important for the worker to understand where the process is headed. When casework assessment is informed by the likely steps that will be taken in the course of work with the family, better case plans result. The caseworker should know what the likely small steps of change will be in order for the family to prevent relapse.

As mentioned, one of the small steps will be a family member's early recognition of contextual and internal signals of impending danger. One must recognize when he/she is nearing a dangerous moment in order to hamper its occurrence. Individuals who have frequently not recognized those signals benefit significantly when professionals assist them in developing that skill. For instance, a father who has been physically violent toward his teenage son needs to recognize his high-risk situation(s) and determine how he will prevent his out-of-control behavior. At the same time, the son, although not responsible for his father's violent act, needs to recognize how his noncooperative behavior (e.g., missing curfew, forgetting chores, skipping school) is not helpful to him or his family.

A particular key to the safe management of stressful, high-risk life events is the ability of members to intervene early in their cycle. Casework offers the natural practice field for such efforts. This may take different forms. Early on, it may take the form of a debriefing after a cycle gets out of hand. For instance, assume a father received a notice that his electricity was being shut off. Discouraged by this, that evening he drank heavily, something he usually only did when away from home with his friends. He fell asleep on the couch while he was supposed to be watching his child. His five-year-old son was reported by a neighbor to be "across the road in an empty lot playing alone for over an hour after dark." The worker and the father identified the following early warning signals: (1) negative thoughts: "I've had enough of this. There's no way I'll ever get caught up. I need a beer." (2) emotions: "I guess I was pretty down. I've been trying, but I can't ever seem to get the bills paid." This father felt terrible about putting his son at risk, but he did not see himself as a neglectful parent. He did not view his drinking as a "typical" problem and was a poor candidate for abstention goals. He could join with the caseworker around a plan to identify when he was at risk for misusing alcohol, and to identify his early warning signals that he was at risk of slipping into a high-risk situation for his children.

Individuals who can routinely recognize early warning signals in a safe manner are better able to develop strategies that avoid high risk or, failing that, are able to interrupt their pattern effectively. Since all problems cannot be avoided and some are too difficult to interrupt, successful individuals also need plans to escape (leave safely) when all other options have failed.

Avoiding High-Risk Situations

By avoiding high-risk situations, individuals and families enter fewer dangerous sequences and are therefore less frequently at risk. This requires practicing a series of alternative actions to entrenched routines based on detailed knowledge about high-risk situations. For instance, a mother recognized that she frequently loses her temper and argues with her daughter. She moved a step closer to creating a well thought out plan when she further identified the conditions surrounding her loss of control. She noted that these arguments only occurred when she and her daughter were alone in the house, typically on weekends when she had custody, and usually only late at night when both were tired and edgy. Although she was unclear at first how she might alter these conditions, she was encouraged that her problem times were more narrowly defined and subject to remedy.

Interrupting High-Risk Situations

Safety also depends on a predetermined plan once in the midst of a maladaptive sequence (i.e., when plans to avoid high-risk situations have faltered). As previously stated, this skill is critical and probably the most difficult to apply since it assumes emotions have already begun to escalate. However, when families are prepared—when they discuss ahead of time how to intervene in high-risk situations—they can agree to a strategy that will interrupt the cycle. If an interruption plan is not identified proactively, behaviors can be misinterpreted and safe de-escalation of conflict is less likely. Families and individuals will need to practice implementing their plans to see if they will work at stressful times. One couple with a history of angry outbursts decided that when they found themselves in an argument over their in-laws (an old high-risk situation), either one could call attention to the escalating cycle by placing his/her eyeglasses upside down (placing glasses upside down was an inside joke for this couple and therefore had particular meaning). This small step signaled a postponement of the discussion until each felt ready to resume it safely or drop it altogether. An agreement of this nature must be practiced and obviously does not guarantee safety, yet is an important skill that interrupts destructive processes. The couple identified this solution strategy when asked, "When have you started an argument but then did something that kept it from escalating?"

Escaping High-Risk Situations

Since even the best plans can fail, it is essential that family members prepare for those moments when behaviors suggest emerging loss of control and that interruption seems unlikely. In these situations, the thrust of the plan is safety and avoidance of otherwise imminent relapse. This may involve practicing actions such as leaving the situation or calling a designated sponsor. Escape plans are usually the first plans put into place—until other strategies that interrupt the cycle earlier are created and tested through practice.

With each of these situations, the caseworker plays an important role in helping individuals and families create, practice, and refine a relapse prevention plan. Each episode informs plan revision. For instance, if the intervention plan (eyeglasses upside down) doesn't interrupt the escalating sequence, the worker can collect detailed pattern information. Typically, the conflict was allowed to brew, and consequently escalated. Or individuals may not have readily recognized warning signals, they may have allowed their emotions and thoughts to dissuade preventive actions, or external conditions may have been overwhelming. Assume, for instance, that an adult daughter of a middle-stage Alzheimer's patient had been cooking for her mother after spending a sleepless night worrying about her teenage son. Further assume that she overlooked both the high-risk situation and her early warning signals of frustration, and in a fit of anger and loss of control she threw a dish across the kitchen into the wall. At that moment, despite the risk in leaving her mother unattended briefly, she recognized her lack of control as an emergency and fled to her neighbors for help. Her neighbors, who had previously agreed to be a part of the escape plan, then immediately provided care for the elderly mother.

Although the incident was unfortunate, and potentially dangerous, the key players had effectively acted on their emergency plan and their efforts were at least a measured success (i.e., no one was hurt). Casework could now map the patterned escalation and help the daughter develop and practice "exit" points (Way & Speiker, 1997) much earlier in her cycle. Obviously, families cannot expect conflict to be completely eliminated. Rather, they must focus on reducing the intensity and duration of conflict so that destructive behavior is eliminated.

STEP 4:   CREATING A PLAN THAT STAYS FOCUSED ON SOLUTIONS

Case plans that are written in client language and that emphasize everyday life events and skill development (e.g., recognition of high-risk events; plans to intervene early; plans to avoid, interrupt, and escape risky situations) increase safety and reduce relapse. Solution-based case plans have this potential (1) because they incorporate crucial behaviors that are completely relevant to the individuals involved, and (2) because individuals are held accountable for behaviors that create harm. Case planning, therefore, should target specific skill development in everyday life. For instance, Figure 5-2 lists the knowledge clients should be able to demonstrate in dangerous behavior cases.

Knowledge Needed Prior to Termination of Services

Casework planning should not choose between focusing on individual behavior or family systems issues. Regardless of the behavior in question, the severity of the situation, or the presumed availability of participants, every case should address family development issues and the individual

Figure 5.2. What will I know about my high-risk behavior by the end of treatment?

• Typical situations and or moods that lead to my loss of control.
• Physical cues and trigger actions that are my early warning signals.
• Thoughts or beliefs that have kept me from asking for help prior to losing control.
• Everyday situations with my friends that are high risk for me to lose control.
• Everyday situations with my family that are high risk for me to lose control.
• Thoughts and feelings that I have during these high-risk situations.
• Skills in self-control and self-respect that I have always had but not always used.
• My strategies for avoiding high-risk situations that lead to loss of control.
• My strategies for intervening once I start a loss of control pattern.
• My strategies for avoiding relapse in an emergency.
• What I've done to arrange external monitoring of my relapse prevention plan.
• My plan for taking care of myself and celebrating progress as I grow.

self-control issues embedded within them. Although there are several circumstances that create or require a separation of family members, or that demand intensive preparatory work by individuals (e.g., domestic violence, sexual abuse), assessment and case planning must always seek to focus individual skill development on the specific high-risk situations that occur in family life. As such, all case plans should have goals and objectives at both the family and individual level. Family goals are based on developmental tasks associated with the dangerous situations, whereas individual goals emphasize skills necessary to successfully participate in tasks without harming anyone involved.

Case Example

Recall the young mother discussed earlier in this chapter (Ms. Smith) who repeatedly struck her four-year-old son. When asking the mother about details of the event, you recall that the worker discovered that most of the tension occurred in the morning during the workweek. This is not surprising given the number of common, everyday challenges that young families face in getting small children up and everyone started on their day. The worker also discovered that Ms. Smith was particularly vulnerable (1) at the end of the month, especially when the support check was not delivered, (2) when she was exhausted due to lack of sleep, and (3) when she felt like her son was being aggressive toward her. Given this information, the case plan targeted the morning routine (family-level ob-

Figure 5-3. Partial case plan. Attached action plans are detailed plans, tailored to each everyday family life task. These plans map out how the issue at hand (e.g., morning routine) will be safely managed. These family plans are specific and therefore measurable. See Chapter 8 for examples of action plans.

OBJECTIVES	TASKS
Family-Level Objective: Will use the "Get our family through the morning plan."	1. Ms. Smith and her therapist will develop a "Get our family through the morning plan" by [date]. [Copy of action plan to be attached.] 2. Ms. Smith will discuss the morning plan with her son and explain the rewards and consequences by [date]. 3. Ms. Smith will track their family progress by logging on a calendar daily. Ms. Smith will share this log with Ms. Jones [therapist] on a weekly basis. 4. Ms. Smith will discuss her morning plan with her mother and neighbor and arrange for emergency support when necessary. A plan will be completed by [date] and shared with Mr. Brown [worker] at that time.
Individual-Level Objective: Ms. Smith will use her "Keep my cool at all costs plan" to prevent further harm to family members.	1. Ms. Smith and Ms. Jones [therapist] will create a "Keep cool at all costs plan" to prevent loss of control by [date]. 2. The plan will be shared with Mr. Brown [worker] by [date]. [Copy of action plan to be attached.] 3. By [date], Ms. Smith will demonstrate, through use of her "keep cool plan," the following: • recognition of high risk situations • recognition of early warning signals • plan to intervene early in risky situations • plan to avoid risky situations • plan to intervene in risky situations • plan to escape risky situations

| | 4. Ms. Smith, Mr. Brown, and Ms. Jones will identify Ms. Smith's existing skills by [date]. |
| | 5. Ms. Smith, assisted by Ms. Jones, will document her progress with "keeping cool" by maintaining a log of her self-control in the mornings. This will begin [date] and continue through [date]. |

jective) and the emotional pattern that culminated in Ms. Smith's angry behavior (individual-level objective). The worker and Ms. Smith set the case plan goal as "family members will live safely together" and created family- and individual-level objectives. Although Chapter 6 will go into case planning in much more detail, Figure 5-3 provides an example of a case plan in which a family-level and an individual-level objective are used to help focus the case plan.

Exceptions to maladaptive behavior do occur, and it is important to identify those exceptions and include them in the case plan. For instance, the worker asked Ms. Smith: "Tell me about a time when you were close to losing your temper, but something happened to avoid it—what happened?" Ms. Smith said that one morning her son was refusing to get dressed and she found herself becoming more and more frustrated: "I started to force him to put his clothes on, but I realized it was only going to get worse. So, I told him that he wouldn't get a movie that night unless he put his shirt on. But I can't always cool myself down like that." This skill, interrupting the escalation by using a logical consequence to manage her son's behavior, was included in the family-level task, (i.e., "Ms. Smith will use logical consequences when Sam refuses to follow the morning routine plan"). The worker also was able to help Ms. Smith recognize one of her warning signals by going back over the incident in more detail (i.e., "What were you feeling or thinking when you realized the situation was getting worse?"). The worker then asked Ms. Smith to record this signal (flushed face) and to talk to her therapist about how to use the information as part of her individual self-control plan.

REINFORCING CLIENT PROGRESS DURING ASSESSMENT

Reinforcing change has long been a part of effective casework. Working from a solution-based approach encourages the caseworker to imme-

diately notice and reinforce small increments of change even during assessment. Whether it is acknowledging a client's fortitude in resisting the
influence of an old problem pattern, or certifying expertise in defeating a
current problem that has plagued a family for some time, the caseworker
moves quickly to claim a solution skill before old patterns emerge to
rediscourage members. Since conflict is viewed as normal in this model,
the management of conflict is acknowledged and celebrated. The existence
of a difficult family situation does not overly concern a solution-based
caseworker, but how the family members handled the situation is of
utmost concern. Was there any difference in this event that would indicate
further skill growth? Did someone recognize early warning signals and
attempt to leave or alter the situation? Did the argument stop short of the
intensity of the last argument? Did anyone attempt to intervene in ways
that had been discussed? These and countless other questions regarding
how the family members managed their high-risk situation help to identify, acknowledge, and reinforce incremental changes.

SUMMARY

If relapse prevention is to be successful, family casework assessment
must focus on specific events and family members' ability to control their
behavior in response to those events. Because families are constantly
developing, and therefore changing their organization to meet their
needs, the caseworker assumes a proactive role in assisting this adaptation process. It is not unusual for social service clients to become problem
saturated to the extent that they not only have the original problems in
everyday living to solve, but have the further burden of the effects of their
unsuccessful problem resolution. Their sense of helplessness is compounded by their involvement in the judicial system and governmental
institutions. Approaching such clients from a solution-based model in-
stills a sense of hope within the context of a collaborative, pragmatic
professional relationship.

The effectiveness of this relationship is best measured by the cognitive
and behavioral skills learned to prevent recurrence of the presenting
problem. At the family environmental level, these skills focus on reorganizing everyday family routines to better meet the developmental
needs of the family. At the individual level, the skills targeted include
identifying high-risk situations, learning the details of personal patterns
when in high-risk situations, and then developing strategies to avoid,
interrupt, or escape those problem patterns before they result in harm to a
family member. The solution-based approach to casework assessment
provides a coherent map for caseworker and therapist to work collab-

oratively on the mutual task of helping a family prevent further acts of abuse or neglect.

Solution-based casework does not choose between focusing on individual behavior or family systems issues, regardless of the behavior in question, the severity of the case, or the presumed availability of participants. The challenge for the caseworker is to engage significant family members in building a consensus for change without diminishing individual culpability for personal behavior. This challenge is most acute in cases of spouse or sexual abuse, where the discussion of family interaction is at risk to infer a type of "shared responsibility " for the abuse, if the assessment and case plan does not competently make the necessary distinctions.[2]

The next chapter will take the basic concepts discussed in the text so far, i.e., building partnerships, focusing on everyday life events, and targeting relapse prevention skills, and show how the case assessment planning process makes use of these elements in the case plan.

NOTES

1. In a recent survey of mental health and social service personnel (Christensen, 1997), the author found almost universal acceptance that the five skills listed were critical outcome skills. For example, when asked if they would be satisfied if one of their clients completed casework and could not identify his / her high-risk situations and had no clear plan to avoid those situations, the overwhelming response was "absolutely not."

2. See the section in Chapter 7 for more information on this distinction.

Chapter 6

Building a Consensus for a Prevention Plan

CO-CONSTRUCTING MEASURABLE GOALS
WITH YOUR CLIENTS

To illustrate the importance of partnership in case planning, imagine the frustration and even anger you might feel if you were represented in an important legal case by an attorney who didn't listen to your ideas, but merely told you what to do and when to do it. Or imagine going to a physician who didn't solicit your input into the treatment plan, but just announced what he or she was going to do, and then expected you to go along with the plan. No one likes to be treated as a sheep, and everyone is sensitive to being ordered about. Families who are involved with social service and child welfare agencies are particularly vulnerable to these feelings because many have experienced such attitudes in public agencies or have had family members who have had negative experience with public agencies. Already guarded, casework clients often arrive at the casework relationship with a defensive and protective attitude. If they are not convinced that their input and partnership are important to the work-er, they will assume that the case plan is the caseworker's plan, not theirs, and will either resist as a way to have some control or just decide to "go along to get along." Either way, once this process gets started it can be very difficult to turn around.

SEARCHING FOR SOLUTIONS

Input from the family in searching for solutions is critical to the plan-ning process. The change that occurs "by order" is often only temporary because the family once again feels powerless and subjugated. Families are experts on themselves, even when they have become saturated with their problem. In fact, it is often the discouraging nature of repetitive problems that leads family members to conclude that their problems are insurmountable and supports their default position of just "letting the social worker work on the problem for a while." If solutions are not developed conjointly with the family, the systemic change necessary for the family will be at risk.

Start with Noticing Strengths

Since there is an inherent inequality of power in the casework relationship, caseworkers have found it helpful to use their status effectively in the validation of strengths that they have detected. When someone perceived as an authority recognizes the strengths a family has available, the receptiveness of the family to also recognize and accept those strengths is enhanced. Recognition lends validation to those strengths. Since so many families have given up hope and are understandably coming to the agency with a sense of discouragement, they find it enlightening to be treated respectfully, the intention being for the family to resolve their own issues based on their own strengths.

Notice Competence in Everyday Life Events

While most of us are trained in the skill of noticing problems, the skill does not typically foster positive assessment and case planning results. Seeing the family developmentally allows the caseworker to draw the family into conversations about competence in achieving family life events. For example, if a family with young children appears to manage getting their children up and off to school each morning without major problems, this is an accomplishment! It is not a throwaway compliment, but real data about how the family functions. How are they able to do this when other families have such difficulty with this task? Or how are they able to function so well in one area when they have such difficulty in another? Expressing curiosity about competence is a powerful tool for the caseworker to understand how the family is able to accomplish difficult tasks in the nonproblem area. This information will be very useful to the caseworker and to the family when they begin to look for possible strategies to apply to the problem pattern area. It also communicates to the family that the worker has not already made up his/her mind about them.

Noticing Competence within the Problem Pattern Area

Starting with general strengths in nonproblem areas, a full understanding of competency is added to when the caseworker notices strengths within the problem area itself. While this might sound like a difficult technique, it actually flows quite directly out of the worker's assumption that a part of the person is not happy with the results of the problem, and would not intend for the family to experience the negative impact of the behavior. This does not mean that the family member is taking responsibility for the negative event: he/she may in fact be minimizing or even denying his/her role in the problems. However, this does not keep the person from having parallel thoughts of regret. In fact, we are quite familiar with this process of having more than one thought on a given subject. At difficult emotional moments we might have thoughts that are quite conflictual (e.g., I want to fight, I want to resolve this, I just want to leave). These thoughts are present before, during, and after emotional events. When listening for indicators that the client was trying to avoid the problem or tried to minimize his/her loss of control, the caseworker can call attention to the attempts. In a sense, it is a way to recognize the efforts the client was already making to work on the problem. The fact that it was ineffective only illustrates the challenge the worker and family face—it does not negate the prior established effort.

For instance, when the caseworker interviewed a client named John about his temper problem, the worker took considerable time to slow down the description of what happened so the specific thoughts and behaviors could be tracked and noticed as they occurred to John. At first this process was difficult for the worker because John had whipped his small son with a telephone cord, leaving large welts, and the worker had understandable reactions of disgust toward the client. The worker was encouraged to imagine that part of John also felt disgust with his actions. As the worker prodded, John described the early buildup of emotions when he tried to teach his son not to bite his sister while playing. John was able to describe how he was worried he might lose his temper and had tried to "stay cool." The caseworker went deeper into his efforts to maintain control by asking him, "How did you try to keep a lid on it, John? What did you do to keep yourself calm? Why do you try so hard to keep yourself calm?" John answered the last question with how much he loved his son and how he didn't want to repeat what his own father had done to him. He spoke tentatively, but with emotion, as he described what he had gone through, and the worker drew notice to his strong commitment and love for his son. These competencies, within the very pattern of events in which he eventually lost control and harmed his son, do not diminish the serious danger of John's actual problem behavior. However, noticing John's desire to attempt to be a good father allowed the caseworker to team up with him to meet this challenge. By noticing competence, the caseworker could bring into focus just how much John wanted and needed to change in order to reach his goals. This partnership allowed the worker to put it this way with John: "It must be hard for you to even think about what you did to your son given how much you love him and want better for him. I think I understand why we really need to come up with some good strategies for you, so that no matter what your son does, you know in your heart that you can control yourself and give him the father you always wanted." John and the caseworker were now in excellent position to agree on family goals (family discussions on rules and consequences for sharing toys) and individual goals (John works on controlling his temper in difficult situations).[1]

There is a cumulative effect of working in this manner with a family. Even when the initial contact with a family is made difficult by the family's defensiveness, the worker who is focused on partnership through competence knows that his/her efforts will eventually be rewarded. Almost all families who are leery of services will eventually join with a worker who is focused on partnership. Partnership must continue during this crucial stage of collaborating and co-constructing a care plan, and must continue consistently throughout the casework, not just as a ploy to get agreement on a case plan. Case plans that support positive change will also assist the worker in being able to gauge success because the family is more likely to share their lapses. Helping families develop case plans that make sense to them is an important ingredient in establishing a relationship that is built equally on trust and accountability.

STRATEGIES THAT WORK IN GAINING GOAL CONSENSUS

While in partnership, efforts should first be made to reach a consensus on the "big picture" before beginning work on the specific family and individual behaviors that need to change. As stated previously, this usually means understanding and recognizing the family's prior attempts to work out their problem. The purpose is to assist the family in restoring hope that they can achieve their individual and collective dreams for their family. It is necessary to build at least a temporary consensus with the family around their motivations because of the effects problem patterns have on families. As we have discussed, pervasive problems will lead to discouragement and blame. In such an environment, individual family members will defensively pull back into actions designed to protect themselves (this may include counterattacking). If the high-risk behavior in the family is to be addressed, the members will need bridging assistance in reaching a common goal to serve as a temporary umbrella under which they can learn the necessary prevention skills. Without it, the members have little alternative but to protect themselves (i.e., more of the same). We know that people are more likely to act on requests that are consistent with their wishes, experiences, desires, and attitudes. Consensus and partnership are best developed through a respectful approach that tracks problem patterns, uses the family language to describe the problems, locates those problems within a normal family context, and uses a wide range of resources to practice and experiment with change.

Building Consensus through Tracking Problem Patterns

One of the first steps in tracking patterns, gaining partnership, and gaining goal consensus is to help the family break the problem into parts so that it is not impervious to interruption: "He's hopeless," "He always . . . ," "This happens every time" are statements symptomatic of a family that is discouraged by an overwhelming pattern. Breaking the pattern down into more manageable parts allows hope to return. Goal consensus can also be thought of as a "re-visioning" process. Much like taking eyeglass lenses to have them reshaped so a clear picture of what is around may be seen, we assist families in once again visualizing their hopes and desires. Involving the person in a description of the sequence of events around an unfortunate incident, the caseworker has the opportunity to find positive intent, in addition to the harmful behavior. Many times just assisting people in making sense of their behaviors by tracking the pattern will engage them in choosing to change the behaviors.

In Chapter 5 we introduced the idea that the first step in a relapse prevention program was to recognize a pattern to the unwanted behavior. Without this step, the client is faced with preventing an unknown, unfamiliar, and unpredictable interaction. How are they to plan strategies in such a vaguely defined situation? How can they practice avoiding high-risk situations if they are not identified? How will they recognize their warning signals? How would they know when they had learned enough to keep themselves and their family members safe?[2] Once a basic pattern is recognized, the client, worker, and provider can work together on the second step: learning as much detail about the pattern as is possible. The assessment and case planning phase requires that the first step be accomplished during this phase and that Step II is at least under way. Recall Figure 5-1: Regardless of the presenting problem, tracking the sequence of interaction before, during, and after such an event is a critical tool of assessment. The interactional focus begins with locating the everyday family life event in which the unwanted behavior occurred. This is very easy to identify when the unwanted behavior is abusive because there was an event that everyone remembers and is upset about. For instance, a parent spanking a child, an overdose of medication, an act of sexual abuse, and an incident of domestic violence are easily identified moments that could be reviewed for understanding what happens when things go poorly in the family. Each of these events could be reviewed to place them back in the context of what the family was trying to accomplish just prior to a family member's loss of control. Other family events are more difficult to track, particularly when the behavior is chronic (been around for a while). Many issues of chronic neglect are in this category, and the family may have difficulty picking out any one event to illustrate the problem. In these situations, the behavior has become patterned, and so the caseworker simply asks the family to describe how "things usually go on a typical day when things don't work out so well." The reader should be reminded that in such situations the problem is not the exception; the problem has become routine and the exceptions may no longer even be noticed. In such cases, the assessment worker may have to work just as hard to elicit stories about "when things go better than usual, or even slightly better than usual."

A small flip chart[3] or large clipboard is an assessment tool that should be considered a standard tool of the caseworker. Beginning with the story about the event or example of a typical event, the assessment worker inquires about the minutiae of family life. This interview necessarily follows the interest of the worker as he/she interacts with the unfolding story. The worker is trying to literally visualize what happened and the sequence in which it occurred.[4] The sample questions in Figure 6-1 are meant only as possibilities, because each caseworker and each family event will lead the tracking of family patterns down a unique path.

What the assessment worker wants to emerge from the process of tracking patterned sequences is fourfold: (1) the recognition by family members that they indeed do have a problem pattern in a certain part of family life; (2) the recognition by at least one of the members that he/she has a personal problem pattern that might be interfering with the successful accomplishment of developmental family tasks; (3) a consensus on how to describe the developmental task that is currently challenging them; and (4) a consensus on the individual changes significant family members would want to make in order to help the family meet that task. In the case of John and his family, they reached consensus that at the family level they needed to work on a better plan to teach their children to play peaceably, and that on an individual level John would need to get much better control of his temper if he was going to be of help to his son and family. John also agreed that he was more at risk for losing his temper when he was drinking or recovering from drinking (he was hung over the morning of the beating). Although not yet ready to fully accept that drinking was a serious problem for him, he did recognize that it was a risk factor for him and that he would have to learn more about how to prevent drinking from interfering with his family life. The consensus was

Figure 6.1. Sample tracking questions (John X. case).

- How did that day start out, can you remember how you first felt when you woke up John?
- So this didn't occur until later on Saturday morning? Walk me through that morning, will you?
- So you first heard the kids arguing from the kitchen Jane? And what did you think about it?
- [To Jane] Did you notice John getting upset about the kid's noise? What did you notice?
- On a scale from 1 to 10, Jane, with 10 being the most upset you can get, how upset were you?
- At this point in the morning, John, how upset were you, on the same 1 to 10 scale?
- When you are at a 6 or 7, John, what do you feel in your body? Can you remember? How about what were you thinking? Can you remember some of that?
- So did the two of you talk about the situation starting to build up? Do you have a plan for what to do at times like this or do you kind of improvise?
- So, John, where were you in the house at this point, what happened next?
- And Jane, where were you? Had you already gone back to the kid's bedroom to get them to stop, or this when you left to go outside and cool down?
- John, you said earlier you didn't want to lose your temper. Why is that? Is it hard for you to control yourself after a certain point?
- Are you aware of what that point is before you get there because it sounds like, looking back, you already were at that point?
- What is the point, the number say, that you feel is too far for you, a 7, 8 or lower?
- Etc.

reached by grounding the assessment in the everyday life of the family and assuming they wanted more for their family. The offending family member was assisted in viewing his personal goal of responsible control of his temper as a contribution to better family life, and as something he had been trying to do anyway. The decision of whether John would leave, or whether the child would be removed, was made much easier based on the thorough understanding of the patterned events that led to the welts on the child's legs. In this case, because of the age of the child and John's current inability to keep drinking from interfering with his parenting, the child was placed in temporary custody of a family member until the prevention plans could be put in place and some history of practice could be established. Although not always the case, John was able to assist in developing a temporary safety plan for his son.

It should be noted that only the family pattern was discussed in the case above. John's personal problem pattern with anger was only recognized but not developed in any detail at all. For instance, only one or two of John's high-risk situations were identified, his warning signals only began to be identified, and he still has a lot to learn about how his lifestyle could be changed to help him avoid high-risk situations or interrupt them much earlier when they cannot be avoided. He does have some experience with escape plans as does his wife (going out to have a smoke and cool down) but they are not taken early enough and not integrated with other family members' needs. All this will need to be practiced and documented in ongoing work with a treatment provider and managed toward outcome by the ongoing caseworker. The ongoing case management issues involved in such a case will be discussed in Chapter 8 and the issues for the treatment provider will be addressed in Chapter 9.

Using the Family's Language

Tracking what actually happens in everyday family life won't do much good if workers, upon hearing the story told in the family's language, then shift to professional jargon and write the plan in deficit terms. Caseworkers who use the actual language that the family uses to describe their situations find the practice to be extremely helpful to building consensus about direction. Respecting the family's own language in case plans acknowledges their competence and implies that the resolution of the problem is also within their competence. In contrast, switching to professional language communicates that the resolution of the problem is in the hands of the professionals who understand the terms. Calling behaviors or situations by a common, familiar name used by the family helps them identify the plan as theirs and not one forced upon them. Tailoring the plan to their language also helps them stay focused on their high-risk behavior in everyday terms. Using familiar language like "roller coaster" for mood swings and "the blues" for depression would be very typical of this approach. The only exception to this approach is caution in selecting the language used for describing abusive or neglectful behavior. The caseworker would not want to minimize the abusive behavior itself or imply complicity by other family members who were victimized. Using the examples above to illustrate, it would be appropriate to say, "John will use his Avoid the Emotional Roller Coaster Plan to keep from harming his children," and it would be inappropriate to say, "John will follow his Avoid Misunderstandings with the Children Plan to keep his children from misinterpreting his actions." The former clearly places the work on John, the latter infers that it was the children who were actually at fault. This latter objective would typically arise from a less than thorough tracking of the family problem pattern. This is also a clue to the supervisor that worker assessment skills may need attention; these and other issues for supervision will be covered in Chapter 9. The direct use of family language communicates the caseworker's confidence in the family's ability to resolve the family problems utilizing current but underutilized competence.

Experimenting and Practicing

Traditional deficit model approaches have assumed that the worker/therapist had the answers and that the clients' job was not to resist his/her suggestions (i.e., the need for working with "resistive clients"). If clients didn't get results (i.e., cure) then they probably weren't doing it right, possibly even "sabotaging progress." Not much room for experimentation and practice in such a model. However, many workers have found that taking a "Let's experiment and see what works!" attitude with the family has helped their clients be more involved as well as receptive to working on the details of the activities. Since family life is viewed as a never-ending series of developmental adjustments, many so minute that they are difficult to perceive, the family's interest in trying new things out to see how they work is very useful. The caseworker's attitude also assures family members that they are the experts on what works inside their family. Workers can elicit that expertise by asking questions like: "Would you be interested in thinking about things that have worked for you in the past"? or "Let's brainstorm some possibilities and then you can pick and choose what you think most reasonable based on what already works for you all." This type of attitude and approach has helped workers explore with families tasks that have the potential for being useful. The "let's experiment" approach also helps influence between-session change. Family members can experiment by researching something about their past, previous generations, behavior overlooked, the timing of certain behavior, the conditions surrounding certain behavior, or any of these topics as they might be viewed in the future (see Time-Oriented Questions in Chapter 10). For example, having a family try an experiment where they reward every positive behavior of a certain family member (possibly themselves) is often helpful to discouraged families in their efforts to get a balanced picture of what needs to change.

Using Tipsheets on Family Education

One of the most productive techniques for developing a specific, tailored plan for a family on a specific developmental challenge is the use of a guideline or "tipsheet."[5] Once a caseworker is in partnership with a family (and as a way to build partnership), families have been open to universal tips that other families and experts have found useful. These guidelines describe general points that other families have found helpful in accomplishing the same developmental task. The purpose of using some guidelines for developing specific tasks is threefold: (1) The use of tipsheets tends to "depathologize" the struggle the family is experiencing by referencing its universality. In other words, if there is a tipsheet on it, it is hard to view as an exclusive problem of only your client family. (2) Having specific tasks to review assists the family and worker in efficiently targeting tasks that are likely to be useful, thus cutting down on the time for trial and error. (3) Finally, from a worker confidence point of view, tipsheets provide the caseworker greater confidence that the critical everyday life events are addressed in appropriate detail. Workers then have a greater sense of confidence in the reliability of the plan because they have discussed and covered recognized contingencies. For an example of a tipsheet, please see examples included in the appendix to this chapter.

Tapping the Collective Wisdom of the Family

Co-constructing a direction for the partnership may best occur if additional family members are brought into the process. So often a family in trouble is also a family estranged from its larger kin and social network. This estrangement occurs for a variety of reasons: Sometimes it is because the extended family has tried to help in the past and has been discouraged or defeated by the persistence of problems. Sometimes it is because the client family often feel their extended family are trying to run the family's lives or break them up. Sometimes it is due to physical isolation brought on by economic circumstances. The age-old wisdom of seeking help and guidance from one's elders is not always as easy and simple as it sounds, particularly in emotionally troubled times. For these reasons, workers often approach their family assessments (and therefore their case plans) with too narrow a focus to their lens. Engaging an extended family member may require additional phone calls, home visits, or mediation sessions. Workers' own attitudes about "breaking away" from their own family of origin may also influence their interest in tapping extended family resources (Bowen, 1978). In spite of all the restraints to tapping the wisdom and resources of extended family, the benefits still outweigh the costs.

The primary benefit of tapping extended family involvement is the additional safety net created for vulnerable family members when the extended family can assist in organizing the family's efforts. A number of professionals have attempted to influence the field toward a model of assessment and case planning that casts a much wider net (Waldegrave,

1990; Speck & Attneave, 1973; Landau-Stanton & Stanton, 1985). These field researchers have illustrated the power that can be generated when kin networks and even communities are brought together for the purpose of mobilizing their energy, intent, and efforts to assist a branch of their family. These family gatherings do not occur easily in most current cultures, but there is little question that extended family involvement can be extremely useful. The following guidelines suggest steps the caseworker might follow when initiating and facilitating a family group meeting.

Guidelines for Family Group Decision-Making in Child Protection Cases

Opening

- Introduce self and welcome all others to the family conference.
- Conduct an opening ritual designed by family (if they desire).
- Conduct introductions in terms of relationship to children.

Goal Consensus

- Affirm overall goal for the conference to be directly related to well-being of children.
- Affirm everyone's interest and commitment as evidenced by their presence.
- Predict that certain portions of discussion might be uncomfortable and even irritating, and ask for advice on how they want you to help that aspect.
- Affirm the appropriateness of making their own decision about what the case plan should include.
- Affirm the family's ability to make a plan that will be satisfactory to all parties (family, courts, protective services).

Overview Comments

- Explain the basic flow of the meeting and specifically explain that they will have some family planning time alone to help develop solutions.
- Explain the role of all non–family members (caseworker, facilitator, notetaker).
- Explain that everyone can ask questions of anyone presenting information at any time.
- Encourage creativity in generating solutions.
- Ask everyone for their consent to participate and get them to sign permission forms.

- Discuss again management of potential conflicts and difficult emotions. For example, "It is likely that some painful issues will come out at these meetings, if you need to take a break, go for a walk, go out to smoke or go to the restroom please do so. We know you want this to go well so I probably don't need to remind you that yelling or threatening someone is not OK and, to repeat, it is OK to take a break. If you momentarily leave, we do ask you to return to the meeting, however, so we know you are OK."
- Have the family select note keepers and any other roles they think would be helpful.

Discuss Family Strengths

- Ask the group to brainstorm family strengths. These can be written on a large flipchart. Extend the brainstorming to the entire kin network in order to collect strengths of the family system and have them recognized by family members.
- Emphasize how these strengths will be resources to them as they think of a good prevention and safety plan for the family.

Facilitate Meeting

- Invite questions from the beginning.
- Continue to explain the purpose of the meeting and the role of caseworkers.
- Continue to focus the family's planning process on family and individual objectives of the case plan.
- Read any prepared statement from family members unable to attend.
- Allow the family time alone to do their planning.
- Remind the family they may ask non–family members to sit in or come in to provide information or perspective.
- Supply flipchart, markers, drinks, snacks, etc.
- Remind the family they may ask the facilitator to assist them at any point if they are at an impasse.

HELPING CLIENTS ESTABLISH AN INITIAL SAFETY PLAN

The decision grid for an assessment worker is one of the most complex in the social services field. Engaging the family, tracking the sequence of patterned problem behavior related to the referral, anchoring that pattern of behavior in the everyday life of the family, and assessing the risk apparent in that pattern must all be done in the first interview. But there's more! The assessment worker must also assess related risk discovered during the interview, build a consensus with family regarding how to describe the problems, connect the family organizational issues to individual personal problem patterns, prioritize the issues in some way, explain the social services system to the family, and, finally, help the family establish an initial safety plan: by any standards, an extremely challenging professional task that requires thoughtful planning and structure.

One aspect of that necessary structure is the assessment worker's intention to build toward solutions by helping the family use the initial safety plan as the first step toward problem prevention. If successful in this formulation, the family (and the worker) sense that change has already begun and direction for future action has been carved out.

THINKING LONG-TERM WHILE TAKING SHORT-TERM STEPS

This concept might be best understood by considering its opposite, that is, taking short-term steps before you knew where you were headed long-term. While most of us would see the folly in heading off in a direction before a destination was determined, it is exactly that mistake that is repeated too often during the assessment phase of casework. Workers faced with large caseloads, unfinished paperwork, unpleasant surroundings, or related stresses are vulnerable to taking actions first and asking questions later. Hopefully the reader will recognize that such an approach creates more problems (and hours of work) than it solves. When the workers remind themselves to "think long-term" they are choosing to ensure that the family, and themselves, spend the necessary time to relocate the problem issues back within the everyday life of the family. This process takes some time for workers just learning the skill and trying to accomplish this during a time of family stress. However, once the worker and family can voice together a specific description of what needs to change, then an initial safety plan becomes the natural (and somewhat obvious) first step of reaching solution.

WHAT GOES INTO A GOOD INITIAL SAFETY PLAN?

The initial safety plan must concomitantly address immediate family safety and help focus the family (and intervention system) on long-range objectives. For this reason it should contain tasks that logically flow out of the situations in which risk to family members occurs. If the problem pattern is not located within the specific situations or incidents of risk, these situations can get lost in the ongoing work with the case. An example of this principle would be if risk occurred due to someone's inability to control his/her temper when disciplining his/her children, then a plan that called for "not hitting the children" would be too general and only address the behavior at the height of anger (a very high-risk time to try to control it). A better plan would call for the family to develop a short-term plan (to be expanded later) to handle disciplining their children, and for the individual who lost control to have a short-term plan to avoid the risk situations. Knowing that all good plans can go wrong, the family and the individual also need back up plans that detail what they should do if the general short-term agreements fail. This pattern of safety planning can accommodate the short-term crisis at the same time it prepares the family for working on a longer-term case plan.

An outline of such a safety plan follows:

- What is the general agreement for family safety?
- What topics or situations are likely to be most difficult?
- What is the family's plan for handling those situations?
- What is the individual's plan for avoiding those situations?
- How will the family know when to take emergency action?
- What emergency actions should be taken to ensure safety?
- How long does emergency action need to be?
- What is your agreement about what to do after emergency action?
- What will you use as a back-up plan for other settings?
- Consequences for not following the plan?
- Signatures

CONSIDERATIONS ON IMPLEMENTING A SAFETY PLAN

Building a consensus in case planning extends to the initial implementation of the case plan. In some jurisdictions, this might be considered a safety plan that is temporarily put into place before a long-term case plan can be developed. Although it is critically important to get consensus on the objectives of family change, it is equally important to ensure that the family's initial steps are likely to be implemented. If the client doesn't recognize your referral to a treatment provider as something really useful, it is doubtful they will get very excited about it. Caseworkers may underestimate the importance of the first meeting of client and community resource. Many caseworkers put a lot of effort into their case planning, feeling good about the family's willingness to participate, only to become very frustrated when the family members do not follow through with the referrals. Assessment caseworkers can underestimate the role they play in serving as a bridge between the family with a need and the person who can assist them in meeting that need. The family or family member doesn't know them, doesn't know their agency, may not know how to get there, and may have fears of what the provider might do with them. So much can go wrong in the "handing off" of a family from assessment caseworker to ongoing worker or treatment provider that special thought must be given to the technique of referral.

Personalize the Referral

Many workers personalize the referral as much as they can. For example, rather than just saying to the family "OK, you make an appointment at the mental health center," the worker instead will say, "I know a person at the mental health center who has handled similar situations. Families would always come back to me and praise him. Would you like his name to call or would you want me to call him first about your situation?" Workers, in their negotiations of case plans, are modeling behavior that would be helpful to the family. They are in essence coaching families on ways to ask for services that they need to build prevention skills.

Attend the First Session

If you think that the situation may need more help than a phone call, or if you think that your carefully crafted case plan might not be understood, it is a good investment of casework time to accompany your client on the first session of the referral. We will address these issues again in Chapter 7 on case management issues because case planning cannot really be separated from case implementation. Good plans without follow-through are wasted effort, wasted opportunity, and when dealing with people's lives, can even mean wasted lives.

SUMMARY OF THE ROLE OF ASSESSMENT IN CASE PLANNING

Assessment and case planning are really the same process, separated by degree and the need in systems to break tasks down by function. From a practitioner's point of view, however, the first moment of assessment is really an initial discussion of what might be a useful target direction for future work together. The partnership is forming during assessment, not after. Solutions and exceptions to the problem are being sought within the problem definition, not after the problem has been defined. Change is assumed to have already occurred within the family prior to assessment, not waiting for professional intervention after the problem has been thoroughly assessed. When assessment is practiced from a solution-based casework perspective, case planning becomes a refining process that records the creative thinking of the casework partnership.

NOTES

1.   The reader should assume that such objectives would have tasks designating the outcome skills appropriate to the objectives (i.e., ability to identify high-risk situations, ability to recognize warning signals, and having strategies for avoiding or interrupting high-risk times, and escaping at-risk situations if unable to avoid or interrupt them).

2.   Once a caseworker becomes aware of how case plans in the workplace can be written without regard to learning basic prevention skills, and how treatment providers can work on objectives that are nonspecific to the client's problem, a certain amount of frustration and alarm is not unusual.

3.   Portable lap or table top flip charts are available (about 18 by 24 inches) and work very well for home visits.

4.   In cases where the caseworker is also assessing possible abuse, the interview may be held with only one family member at a time so as to get the best possible information disclosed about the actual events that took place. In such cases, the assessment worker will have to be thinking about how to pull the various versions together in summary form for the family so they can have a working consensus on how to proceed (what direction the case plan should follow).

5.   The term "tipsheets" is used here to refer to a wide variety of family life education materials that break down suggestions for managing everyday life events in families. The term is meant to convey the conciseness and specificity of the advice offered regarding a given problem.

APPENDIX

Suggestions for
Controlling Anger

1 The first step is to **recognize that your "temper problem" is probably your biggest problem**, the one that makes everything else worse.

2 Once you have identified your temper as the problem, **find someone to talk to about facing up to this problem**. If you are able to do this, you will have taken a big first step toward your goal.

3 People who are successful in controlling anger say it is useful to **identify when you are most likely to lose your temper** (i.e. What kind of situations do I get worked up in?)

4 It is always helpful to **work with experts in identifying these situations,** seek counseling or a class to help you with this step.

5 Once you have figured out when you are "at risk" for your temper to sneak up on you, try to **notice what is happening inside of you right as your temper starts to rise.** These thoughts or feelings will be your early warning signals that you are headed down the "old road".

6 If you have identified your personal early warning signals, you need to **congratulate yourself** because you are well on the way to avoiding or at least limiting the effects of your temper.

7 Research has found that people who have been successful in controlling their temper all have a way to **catch the feeling early and take quick action** to avoid it getting any worse.

8 The next step is to **find out what quick action works best for you** to prevent, interrupt, or if necessary, escape an anger episode. See if the *Idea Sheet on Defeating Temper Problems* can give you some ideas.

9 Finding out what works for you always takes practice! Try to **notice small signs or indicators that you are changing**, maybe you are starting to catch it earlier, or you are walking away from potential risk situations. Tell someone about that change.

10 Finally, **CELEBRATE the courage of each small step**, they add up to one big journey!

Figure 6.A1. Suggestions for controlling anger.

Suggestions for
Setting Up Family Chores

1   Parents will want to **set a good example** by sharing the responsibility and duties involved in family life.

2   Remember to **consider age when assigning duties**. Even young children can begin to participate if the task is short and coached. As kids get older, the tasks can get harder.

3   Start by **listing all the possible things that need to be done**. Be sure to involve the children in making up the list.

4   Consider **rotating assignments of chores**, particularly ones that everyone likes or dislikes.

5   It is helpful to **decide or assign clear time frames** for completing each task.

6   Decide on **reasonable consequences and rewards** ahead of time. This discussion can include the children's suggestions as well.

7   Assume you will need to **provide some helpful reminders** (notes, lists, charts). Kids may want to help create these reminders depending on their age.

8   Don't assume kids know or should know how to do something. Parents who **teach them how to do the task**, by breaking the tasks down, have much better results.

9   When (not if) a chore does not get done, **avoid 'nagging' conversations or arguments about** it. Just remind them of the agreed upon consequences and then stick with your plan.

10   Parents will want to **practice their plan to keep calm** and in control of their emotions when working with their children. Otherwise, chores will become a real chore!

11   Celebrate small steps of progress, and celebrate often!

Figure 6.A2.   Suggestions for setting up family chores.

Suggestions for
Parenting Teenagers

1   **Set realistic rules** about curfew, where-abouts, and acceptable behavior. Make sure the rules are clear, repeated consistently and matter-of-factly.

2   Enforcing the rules will go much better if you can insure that other adult **family members are in general agreement** with the rules and will support them if necessary.

3   **Involve your teenagers in the decisions** about rules as they mature. Encourage their involvement whenever possible.

4   **Determine specific consequences** / punishment for breaking the family rules, i.e. grounding, transportation, special privileges, telephone calls, being with friends etc.

5   **Make the consequence "fit the crime".** Sometimes a small consequence that is easily enforced is better than a big consequence that may be very difficult to enforce.

6   Balance your discipline with **equal attention to praise and affection**, even during times of limit setting. Teenagers need reassurance that they are loved even when they act like they don't care (but, definitely not in front of others!)

7   Set a goal to **manage your own emotions** in difficult situations. Show your teenager that you can avoid screaming, calling names or striking out at them even when very frustrated with them.

8   Have a plan to **take care of yourself** so that your stress level doesn't become overwhelming. If you are "out of steam", you can be at risk to "blow off steam" with your teenager.

9   **Celebrate the progress** that you and your youth make. Change comes in small steps and can be overlooked if you don't stop to notice the little ways they and you are both improving.

Figure 6.A3. Suggestions for parenting teenagers.

Suggestions for
Parenting Young Children

1   **Set realistic rules** about bedtime, boundaries, and acceptable behavior. Make sure the rules are clear, repeated consistently and matter-of-factly.

2   Enforcing the rules will go much better if you can insure that other **adult family members are in general agreement** with the rules and will support them if necessary.

3   **Involve children in the decisions** about rules as they mature. Encourage their involvement when possible.

4   **Determine specific consequences**/punishment for breaking the family rules (i.e. no television, bike riding, videogames, telephone calls, being with friends etc.

5   Very **young children benefit from time out** or other immediate consequences to misbehavior like re-direction of their interests to some other less disturbing activity.

6   Balance discipline with **equal attention to praise and affection**, even during times of limit setting. Young children need reassurance that they are still loved even though they are being required to behave differently.

7   Set a goal to **manage your own emotions** in difficult situations. Show your child that you can avoid screaming, calling names or hitting them even when very frustrated with them.

8   Have a plan to **take care of yourself** so that your stress level doesn't become overwhelming. If you are "out of steam", you can be at risk to "blow off steam" with your child.

9   **Celebrate the progress** that you and your child make. Change comes in small steps and can be overlooked if you don't stop to notice the little ways they and you are improving.

Figure 6.A4.   Suggestions for parenting young children.

Part III

Management Issues

Chapter 7

The Process of Writing Objectives and Tasks

THE ADVANTAGES OF BEING SPECIFIC
AND MEASURABLE

Case planning is at the heart of casework, both successful and ineffective casework. Like any other profession, careful planning and purposeful implementation will usually result in a quality product. Also as in other professions, lack of planning or lackadaisical implementation will usually result in a poor outcome. Returning to an early analogy, few people would engage an attorney who did not plan a careful trial strategy before entering the courtroom. Even if the attorney was very experienced, few clients would say, "Just shoot from the hip and we'll see how it goes." If the attorney complained, "I hate all that paperwork, it's not really important," would you as client be impressed? Change these scenarios to those of another professional like a physician or an airplane pilot and our attitudes about the importance of careful planning and detailed implementation are even more compelling. Effective casework decisions often involve equally important issues of personal safety and well-being, e.g., the removal or return of children, the termination of parental rights, or the care of the elderly. Casework planning requires a professional commitment to thoughtful planning and detailed implementation of defined and measurable goals.

What Should be Measured?

The assessment question of what should be measured as outcome is a critical question considering the importance of the decisions that are made based upon the outcome criteria. In the past, the social services have been criticized for using measurements of progress that did not accurately assess the behaviors that were occurring in the family (Minuchin, 1984). Some objectives were not only unhelpful to the family but increased the caseworker's liability. When a worker is unable to identify with the family what behaviors need to occur in order for a child to be returned home or to avoid termination, the worker is left in a vulnerable, liable position, and the family is left confused and powerless. Previous measurements that have been used in the past were often stated in general terms like:

- compliance with court orders
- attendance at counseling
- attendance at parenting classes
- participation in a drug treatment program
- admission of wrongdoing
- minimal compliant behaviors
- finally, the presence or absence of a family member

Although each of these activities could be viewed as potentially useful, the only thing you can measure in most of them is compliance, or attendance, i.e., they showed up and "got treatment." Under such general objectives, clients and their attorneys argue that clients have substantially complied[1] with the objectives as they were written. If the family member has substantially complied (e.g., attended counseling) then the court is typically obligated to rule in favor of the client, e.g., to return the child to the home. However, it should be clear that whether someone attends classes or has received treatment does not measure whether or not the family members have learned and practiced prevention behaviors within the specific difficult situations.

A solution-based approach to relapse prevention defines more clearly the necessary skills a family must have in order for the caseworker to be able to predict safety in the home more accurately. As stated in Chapter 5, the specific and measurable prevention skills of identifying high-risk situations, recognizing early warning signals, and developing actions to avoid, interrupt, and escape harmful behaviors are measurable outcomes that represent quality casework planning.

The Case For Written, Relevant, and Measurable Plans

If we are to be honest, we must conclude that for too many caseworkers, the task of writing a case plan has become "more paperwork." Over time, these workers have divided their professional life into the "real work" they do directly with families and the "paperwork" they do back at the office to get their supervisor off their back. This separation often evolves over time due to the crisis nature of social service work, where immediate needs of people who are hurting or who are in trouble require a direct and meaningful response. In a crisis, writing down specific actions can appear to be an afterthought, not forethought. It isn't until further into the case (e.g., the family's life after the crisis subsides) that the need for a well thought out, defensible, written case plan becomes more clear.

In fact it is often when the crisis subsides and the resulting peace wears thin that the old patterns return and the worker feels frustrated because "Nothing has changed, they are back doing the same old thing." It is not unlike the discouragement the family feels when the same old problem patterns return. Without well thought out written objectives and tasks to guide relapse prevention, the old pattern is free to slip back into practice, seemingly without notice until one day the phone rings in the caseworker's office and a family member relates the frustrating news that "nothing has changed." It is then that the caseworker realizes that he/she has little to guide the next actions. Something has failed, but what? Did the caseworker have a plan more specific than attending counseling? Did the family start to follow that plan and then something kept them from success? Even a seasoned caseworker can experience confusion over what to do now, frustration with the family, and a lack of confidence that they have the ability to solve their problems, and self-doubts can even enter the worker's mind.

WHEN CASE PLANS BECOME COURT DOCUMENTS

For most mental health and social service professionals, the courtroom is not an arena in which they feel particularly competent and comfortable. This uneasiness is particularly pointed when they have to go into court over an issue of child protection:

- Do they have enough evidence to protect a child?
- Do they have enough evidence to return a child?
- Do they have evidence to plan for the future placement of a child?

Their fears may be compounded when the case they are petitioning the court about is one in which there has been a history of casework with the family and, for whatever reason, the family has new reports of problems. In these cases the casework records will be scrutinized. Even though the workers' efforts are to continue to assist families in remaining together and safe, there are times that removal will still be necessary. When a worker does not have the evidence to present to the court that behavioral changes did not occur in the family, then social services lose cases. Children are returned who shouldn't be and unfortunately some of those children do get hurt. Although the initial and primary intent of writing specific measurable case plans with the family is to assist them in developing a clear road map for finding their own solutions, it is also true that those well-written case plans will build the necessary evidence to prove the family's inability to protect their family members.

WRITING A CASE PLAN THAT IS FOCUSED ON SOLUTIONS

In Chapter 6, we discussed the role of assessment in case planning. It was noted that consensus with the family was a key component in establishing a partnership focused on change. In this chapter, we will give specific directions for constructing the written version of that consensus. Although every state, jurisdiction, and even agency typically has its own protocols and policy regarding case plans, we will offer an approach here based on the principles of solution-based casework. This example should not imply that there is only one way to write case plans, but to illustrate that the approach to writing and documenting change should be consistent with the mission, philosophy, and theory of change of those responsible for writing the case plans. The approach that will be demonstrated will further focus on the needs of social service caseworkers and their clients (adaptations for treatment providers are discussed in Chapter 9). With that as an introduction, we believe that quality case plans have the following common characteristics:

- A clearly defined overall goal for the family.
- The goals are broken down into objectives at both the family level and the individual level; they clearly define behaviors the family and its members will use instead of the harmful or unproductive behaviors.
- Each objective is broken down into detailed and sequential tasks (steps).
- Each objective is attainable.
- The tasks cover both case management issues and everyday family behavior.
- The tasks have clear descriptions of who will be involved in each step, what will be done, and when the task is to be done.

UNITING AROUND A FAMILY GOAL

The family goal is a broad statement that describes the desired outcome for the case. In developing the goal, the caseworker and the family build upon the strengths of the family. All work done should be consistent with that common goal. As we have discussed, building consensus with the family toward a common goal is critical to the casework process. The most common overall goals in social services relate to very basic family needs, (like remaining together and staying safe). The following goals are examples of the kinds of general overall goals that have been useful:

- Family will prevent abuse and remain safe together at home.
- Family will prevent neglect and remain safe together at home.
- Family members will be protected from harm.
- Family members will live independently at home without harm.
- Family will support adolescent in successful completion of court orders.
- Family will support placement of a family member with a relative.
- Family will support permanent substitute care for a family member.
- Family will support adoption as best alternative for a family member.
- Family will support activities for independence of a family member.

As the reader can see from these examples, the overall family goal provides a general direction for the family and hopefully speaks to either their motivation to keep the family together, or if that effort has failed, to see that the family members are well cared for. Case plans may start out with the goal of family reunification and need to be renegotiated (if possible) to reflect the failure of reunification efforts. Partnership is not simply a way to think about casework when the goal is reunification, but also when family members must make difficult decisions for the good of its more vulnerable members.

BREAKING DOWN THE GOAL INTO FAMILY OBJECTIVES

As discussed in Chapter 6, building consensus around family (and individual) objectives must begin with the first summary statements of the caseworker. As the caseworker tracks the sequence of family events that occurred when someone lost control (e.g., abuse) or when someone didn't adequately provide (e.g., neglect), the family's story must be responded to in such a way that problems are increasingly framed as developmental tasks. Statements such as, "So the morning routine with the little ones is a real problem area for you right now," or "So even though you have really been trying, having food in the refrigerator at the end of the month has really been difficult," allow objectives to be formalized around developmental tasks. Figure 7-1 illustrates how summary statements regarding family interaction can eventually lead to consensus around family-level objectives.

The challenge to writing good case plans becomes easier if the caseworker has helped the family progressively expand their definition of what is wrong. This expanded definition usually makes the transition from descriptions of problems with people (e.g., "He did . . . ," or "She never does . . .") toward a description of problem situations (e.g., "Mornings don't go well," or "Bedtime is a nightmare"). Situational definitions of everyday life events are representative of developmental issues in which the family struggles. Such problem definitions leave more room for people to work cooperatively on the problem without unproductive defensiveness. As stated previously, using an umbrella definition of the problem (i.e., family situations) doesn't mean the caseworker can ignore individual self-control problems that occur within those family events: it just means that individual problems will be worked on within the framework of helping resolve or improve a particular family situation. A solution-focused problem definition is not simply semantics, it can be the difference between a working partner or a contentious adversary.

For an example of a menu of family-level objectives (see Appendix to this chapter). The menu illustrated there is just one way to assist the caseworker in thinking through the possibilities for problem definition. Other taxonomies could be used, such as developmental stages based on

Figure 7.1. Summary statements on family interaction.

Summary of Family's Description	Eventual Consensus on Objective
"So it sounds like the morning routine, particularly with the little ones, is a real problem area for you all right now. That is a tough one for lots of families with kids the age of yours."	The family will use their "Get Our Morning Off to a Better Start Plan" to ensure that the children can get up and off to school without a lot of conflict.
"So even though you have really been trying, some months it has just been really hard to have food in the refrigerator at the end of the month. That must really be discouraging for you."	The family will use their "Put Our Kids Food First Plan" to ensure that their children receive enough food every day of the month.

the age of the children, e.g., beginning couple, school age objectives, or adolescent objectives.

In summary, family-level objectives serve as the umbrella description of what the partnership will be trying to accomplish to reduce risk to family members. The objectives will describe what the family will be doing in everyday life to successfully resolve the problem or meet the needs. Therefore, it must clearly relate to known incidents of risk. The objective must be behaviorally specific so that tasks to accomplish the objective will also be appropriately specific and measurable.

GOING FROM FAMILY-LEVEL OBJECTIVES
TO INDIVIDUAL-LEVEL OBJECTIVES

The *individual-level objective* represents the new behavior that the individual(s) will be exhibiting in order to participate successfully in the *family-level objective*. One way to think of the process for identifying individual-level objectives is for the caseworker to ask him/herself, "When this family has attempted to [set rules, get everyone off to work and school, toilet train, etc.], who loses self-control?" By thinking in this way, the worker will identify more readily who might get too angry, who might get too depressed, or who might drink too much. As we have discussed, families can tolerate a certain level of personal problems and still accomplish their developmental tasks. In such cases, other family members do more or move to insulate the effects of the personal problems on other family members, or in some cases the family is simply lucky in that no other outside stressors occur at the same time and the family gets through that stage without harm. But in substantiated child welfare, juvenile services, or adult protection type cases, at least one family event has gone so poorly that someone was harmed or put at serious risk. In such cases, it is a given that (1) the family had some task that did not go well (family-level objective) and (2) at least one individual in the family was unable to do what he/she needed to do to control him-/herself in a way that provided for basic needs for family members (individual-level objective).

As was the case in building consensus over the family-level objective, the same partnership is needed to evolve a definition of the problem that allows family members to take responsibility for their behavior in the family situation. It may be helpful to recall that individual-level objectives should be directly tied to family events (family-level objective) that clearly need to go better. Their construction should recognize the individual's desire to resolve the issue for the good of his or her family, and should be worded utilizing the client's own language (e.g., "I will use my 'keep cool plan' to ensure my family's safety from physical or emotional hurt)."

THE PRIMACY OF RISK-RELATED OBJECTIVES

Before discussing task construction issues, a word should be said about ensuring that the focus of casework remains on known and highly probable issues of risk. In many cases, the temptation to include "everything but the kitchen sink" on the case plan is compelling. However, such a temptation should be resisted. There is no question that many families face a long list of issues that workers who worry about vulnerable family members would like to see addressed before they "turn the case loose." But there are several reasons to narrow the focus of casework to those developmental issues and personal control issues that have shown evidence for high risk. The most important of these reasons is simply manageability. Too often an overeager case plan will either (1) overwhelm the family and they will resist any change, (2) overwhelm the family with appointments to keep and objectives to work on, (3) overwhelm the worker with solving small crises over a wide range of problems, (4) level the objectives so that critical issues are given the same weight as less significant issues, and/or (5) simply collapse over time due to lack of focus when workers or providers need to be replaced. It is not unusual for casework teams to review such cases a year or more down the line and find that no one can recall why the case was originally opened.

For these reasons, the practice of listing the most important objectives first, both at the family level and individual level, seems prudent. Second, most families, caseworkers, and treatment providers cannot effectively keep track of more than one or two family-level objectives and one or two individual-level objectives. Beyond that, the intent might be good, but the implementation is little more than wishful thinking. Unfortunately, wishful thinking is not always productive but can result in the damaging effects of diluting case focus.

BREAKING DOWN OBJECTIVES INTO
MANAGEABLE TASKS

Once the family and worker have built a consensus on the broad brush strokes of what needs to happen to keep everyone in the family safe and secure, the partnership must begin to lay out the plan's specifics of how they will reach the objectives they have set. In case planning this means tasks. Writing tasks that are specific and that indicate who will do what, when it will occur, and how the task will be measured is the next step. It should be noted that for a certain percentage of caseworkers, this step is not seen as important as what they would call their "real work with the family." These workers find task construction tedious and demanding, sometimes complaining of how the "paperwork" is interfering with their ability to do their job. Complaints such as "I didn't get into social work just to fill out a bunch of papers!" are not uncommon. While all of us share a certain amount of frustration with paperwork, we wish to make a very strong case for not simply dumping case planning "into the paperwork basket."

Tasks should be viewed as the step-by-step implementation of the objective. Tasks provide the detailed structure and guidance needed to accomplish the objectives. Tasks list the activities that are needed to obtain the objectives and thus reach the goal. The tasks typically define the steps or actions to be performed, who is responsible for implementing each activity, and, finally, when the activity is to take place. When tasks consist of a series of small steps, the family or family member find them easier to prioritize and implement. By providing and negotiating the methods for accomplishing the objective, the family have a greater opportunity to succeed, thus increasing their motivation.

Written tasks reflect the conversation between the worker and the family about what needs to happen to achieve certain objectives in the future. The successes of the tasks track the success of the case. The tasks are as much for the protection and guidance of the family as they are for the caseworker. With well-written plans (tasks), the family will not only be able to document the changes they have made to the caseworker, but will be able to present that information in a court of law, should that become necessary. Caseworkers want to feel good that their families have made the changes that were needed; they also want to feel protected themselves if future problems arise. Families want and need a record of evidence that counters their reputation for risk. The only vehicle for targeting, specifying, and measuring change is the tasks of the case plan. Also, when individuals are not actively making changes to avert risk, a well-documented and specific plan creates a real sense of accountability. This can, for example, provide evidence for the worker's recommendation, e.g., that the children should not be returned to their home or that parental rights should be terminated. For this reason, it is suggested that the hallmark of quality casework should be the worker's mastery of the case-planning process. Because many caseworkers do not view case planning as a reflection of their work with the family, we will be offering a specific structure to illustrate how one can manage tasks with a solution-based approach to casework. This structure will also be illustrated with several case plan examples over a range of presenting problems. The structure illustrated will make a distinction between tasks that help manage the case and those that specify the family's plan to make behavioral change. This distinction has been helpful to caseworkers looking for a way to organize their thinking about tasks.

Case Management Type Tasks

Although there are undoubtedly alternative models for structuring case plans and specifically task construction, from a solution-based perspective there are certain tasks that are consistent in each and every case plan. We know, for instance, that every family will need to know what situations pose the greatest risk to them, and they will need to identify some of their signals that warn them that the situation is "building up." These outcome skills are consistent across all problem patterns. We also know that they will need some kind of strategy (plan) to avoid these situations, or if that fails, then they will need to intervene in the pattern early enough to head off more serious problems. And, of course, if all efforts to avoid or intervene fail, they need a safety plan to escape the pattern, to end it abruptly, before anyone is harmed. We know that we will want to document, credential, and celebrate the changes they make in order to reinforce the new story about the family's competency. Since all these tasks are consistent across families, we refer to these as case management tasks and have provided in Figure 7-2 a template for including them on each and every case plan. Some might argue that this seems like "cookie-cutter case planning," to which a solution-based caseworker might point out that every family has to have a unique strategy to meet their unique challenges, but ensuring that every family case has a strategy is just good case management.

The template of case management tasks should be applied, at minimum, to the first family-level and individual-level objectives that reference the known issue of risk. For example, if the case was opened due to a young child wandering in the street, the first family-level objective might revolve around the family developing a better plan for supervising young children. Let's assume, for example, that the reason the parent wasn't supervising was a direct result of his/her drinking (a party was going on when the child went unsupervised). In such a case, the first individual-level objective would have to do with the parent's drinking. The case management tasks in Figure 7-2 would clearly help organize the partnership (family, caseworker, treatment provider, and court). If the parent also wanted to work on finances (feeling that it had contributed to the problem), a second family-level objective might be included but might not need all of the case management tasks spelled out. This example further illustrates the importance of staying focused on the incidents of

Figure 7.2. Template for case management tasks.

---

1. [Who] will identify their high-risk situations and warning signals with the help of [whom] within [time frame].
2. [Who] will review their safety plan with the FSW within [time frame].
3. [Who] will develop with [whom] a written detailed action plan within [time frame] to manage their high-risk situations [attach plan when ready].
4. [Who] will share the details of their plans with [whom] within [time frame].
5. [Who] will record their progress by [journaling, charting, etc.] beginning [time frame].
6. [Who] will notify [whom] at the first sign of difficulty with the plan beginning [time frame].
7. [Who] and the Family Service Worker will assess and celebrate progress [on at least a monthly basis].

---

high risk in the family. Although the family might be directed toward resources to assist them with their finances, the same level of documentation and strategizing would not need to be written in the case plan for secondary objectives.

The reader will note that case management tasks don't specify what is to be done in the everyday life of the family (e.g., what is the plan for supervision, child discipline, or the morning routine?). These represent the second type of tasks that need to be developed, either in conjunction with the caseworker or with the help of a treatment provider. For the purpose of keeping these tasks clear from case management type tasks, we will term them *action plans* for either the family (Our Plan to Keep the Kids Supervised and Safe) or a specific family member (My Keep from Drinking Plan).

Action Plan Tasks

The family members need a specific strategy for targeting their most high-risk times. They need to experiment with tasks that can prevent those times from happening, or keep them from getting out of hand if unavoidable (by interrupting or escaping the pattern). These plans for altering everyday family life need to be written, not just understood, because they will have to be studied, shared, and improved if lasting skills are to be learned. For these reasons, solution-based caseworkers find that separating the case management tasks from the family's action plan tasks has some advantages. If separate, the tasks the family chooses form a personalized plan of action that they can take with them, put on the refrigerator, discuss with a treatment provider, document its parts, or show to the court. The case management tasks help the partnership keep track of what needs to happen when and help them communicate the overall plan to others in the system of care. Figure 7-3 is offered as a suggested template for a written family action plan to prevent problem patterns.

As can be noted in the template, the everyday life tasks that would be included on this written action plan should indicate what is to be done, who will do it, and when they will do it. As discussed in Chapter 6, these tasks would grow out of discussions about what the family is already doing effectively (exceptions to the problems) or out of suggestions gained from family life education materials (tipsheets), or from discussions with treatment providers. Some agencies have taken the further step of putting such forms on duplicate paper so the original can be left with the family and the copy returned to the caseworker.

Typical tasks on such an action plan might be using an alarm clock, getting the children to bed by a certain time, or daily exercise to reduce stress and discouragement. As stated previously in Chapter 6, tasks should be written with the outcome behavior in mind. Therefore tasks such as "attend counseling" or "follow court orders" measure attendance and cooperation, not skill acquisition. The caseworker and family have to fully understand what is to be learned by attending counseling or following court orders.

Who Should Be Responsible: Caseworker or Treatment Provider?

In many agencies, public and private, the question of how much case direct casework intervention a caseworker does is an issue. Many caseworkers do not feel they have the time to do more than assess, make a referral, and then manage the case. Others either have the time, or make the time on a certain percentage of their cases, to "do the work themselves." A solution-based approach to casework does not consider one or the other better. However, if the caseworker sees him/herself as primarily a case manager, then he/she would probably want to ensure that the treatment provider follows the case plan worked out with the family. In this scenario, the caseworker would complete the case management type tasks but might only start the action plan with the family. Once started, he/she would send it with the family or family member to the treatment provider so that the treatment provider could pick up where the worker left off. This process allows for greater continuity of care, provides a vehicle for measuring consistent objectives, and keeps treatment focused on the same high-risk situations that the caseworker is worried about. More suggestions will be made on this cooperative relationship in Chapter 9, which is devoted to collaboration with treatment providers.

Figure 7.3. A suggested template for a written family action plan to prevent problem patterns.

Prevention Plan

High Risk Situations:

Warning Signals:

	Task to be Accomplished	Who?	When?
Prevention Plan			
Safety (Backup) Plan:			

Signed:	
Witnessed:	Date:

WRITING ACTION PLANS TO PREVENT RELAPSE

Because successful casework is based on the family's ability to prevent relapse, the family's written plan of action (i.e., action plan)[2] is crucially important. It is their part of the overall case plan that they will follow on a daily basis. Whether a caseworker assists in the writing of action plans or simply manages and tracks the success or failure of them, all caseworkers need to know what constitutes a quality action plan.

Referring again to Figure 7-3, we will discuss what kinds of things are best included in each section of the action plan. Since the action plan is intended to detail the specific actions a family or individual will take to avoid, interrupt, or escape their problem behavior pattern when at risk, it helps to have the risk situations detailed on the plan itself. That is why the first section of our sample action plan calls for a description of the high-risk situations. The same rationale applies to listing the warning signals directly on the plan, i.e., it keeps them in focus. As we have discussed earlier, warning signals range from recurring thoughts (e.g., "This always happens to me") to later physical sensations (e.g., raised voice, tightness in chest). The more specific the descriptions, the more useful they are to the client and those who are helping coach the plan.

The main part of the action plan should first list the actual steps the person is taking to avoid high-risk situations. These might be actions that help them keep their stress low, like exercise, religious activities, or getting enough sleep. They also might be educational in nature, for instance, they might feel that if they learned more about a specific problem they would be less likely to overreact. For still others, avoiding buildup might best be accomplished by practicing a certain line of thinking, like taking time each day to remind themselves that they are not in control of everything and of all that they have accomplished.

Next to be listed are any strategies the person might use to interrupt a pattern of buildup if he/she was not able to avoid it. This is why the person's warning signals are so important. If the person doesn't pick up on the warning signals, he/she will be unable to apply an interruption strategy.

Issues of Documenting Change

Solution-based casework is focused on creating a partnership with families to help them practice specific prevention skills to use in the specific high-risk situations they face. The learning of these skills, if documented, will help the family convince themselves, as well those concerned about them, that they have new abilities. Without documentation, they are at greater risk of slipping back into discouragement, overwhelmed by the challenges they face and the social forces seemingly arrayed against them. Documentation, in other words, is an underpinning of anchoring solutions and therefore good casework. Lack of documentation in casework is casework that is too general at best, slipshod at worst. Because each agency has unique ways to document the case management type tasks, the text will focus on methods for documenting the family action plans.

The simplest, most direct, and most detailed way of documenting change is a task chart. Task charts can be constructed colorfully on poster board like a behavioral chart for children, or more plainly and professionally as illustrated in Figure 7-3.

The advantage of the latter is it is easily reproduced and can serve to supplement a report to an interested party like schools, treatment providers, or courts. Tasks are recorded directly from the action plan down the left-hand side of the chart, and the dates of measurement are listed across the top of the chart. The chart is titled with whatever action plan it represents (family or individual), and new charts are provided as needed. It is often helpful to start the chart with the previous week. Even though the client may not have done all the tasks on the chart in the previous week, starting with the previous week's data communicates to the client that you are aware that he/she has already begun working on the problem. It also gives the client a head start on change and the chart will show greater change if some baseline data precede the new plan data. In a sense, the client becomes his/her own first audience for change.

NOTES

1.   The meaning of the term "substantially complied" is often the issue that is debated when caseworkers and families argue over the number of missed appointments or consistency in attendance. In order to settle these disputes, deals are even made based on the family attending a certain additional number of sessions.

2.   The term "action plan" is used here generically to refer to the specific plan of action the family is using. Some mental health providers might call it a treatment plan or even the family's homework. We choose this term to encourage the practice of putting this plan down on paper and defining the specific day-by-day steps in concrete measurable terms.

APPENDIX

Family Level Objectives

Adoption / Pregnancy Options
Will use their "————————" plan to assist adoption process as described in tasks.
Will provide assistance in permanency planning for best interests of child described in tasks.

Adaptation to Crisis
Will use their "————————" plan to adapt to the loss of a family member.
Will use their "————————" plan to adapt to the addition of a family member.
Will use their "————————" plan to adapt to changing circumstances in the family.
Will provide family members opportunities to discuss and respond to changing conditions in the family.

Behavior Management of Young Children
✔ Will use their "————————" plan to teach their children limits of behavior as described in tasks.
✔ Will use their "————————" plan to learn to use the toilet as described in tasks.
✔ Will use their "————————" plan to teach their children not to be aggressive as described in tasks.
Will use non-aggressive forms of discipline, without corporal punishment, as described in tasks.

Behavior Management of Adolescents
✔ Will use their "————————" plan to set family rules and consequences as described in tasks.
Will use their "————————" plan to resolve disagreements with teens as described in tasks.
Will use non-aggressive forms of discipline, without corporal punishment, as described in tasks.

Blended Family Issues
✔ Will use their "————————" plan to work cooperatively together as described in the tasks.
Will negotiate reasonable arrangements to prevent escalation of conflict and disruption.

Chores and Routines
✔ Will use their "————————" plan for (insert time of day) chores and routines as described in tasks.
Will structure (insert time of day) chores and routines to prevent conflict as described in tasks.

Home Cleanliness/Sanitation/Safety
Will use their "————————" plan to keep bugs away from the family as described in tasks.
Will use their "————————" plan to keep family bedding clean as described in the tasks.
✔ Will use their "————————" plan to keep their home hazard free as described in the tasks.
Will maintain home in a clean, sanitary, and safe condition as described in the tasks.

Hygiene (Family)
Will use their "————————" plan to teach children about personal hygiene as described in tasks.
Will insure healthy and clean family members as described in tasks.

Figure 7.A1. Family-level objectives.

Financial Stability
Will use their "————————" plan to manage family finances as described in tasks.
Will establish and maintain a family budget as described in tasks.
Will use their "————————" plan to support family member's employment as described in tasks.
Will establish a family routine to support employment.

Independent Living
Will use their "————————" plan to make progress toward independent living as described in tasks.
Will negotiate family responsibilities to insure progress on independent living as described in tasks.

Medical Care / Mental Health Care
Will use their "————————" plan to follow medical advice as described in tasks.
Will maintain proper medical and mental health care for the family as described in the tasks.

Nurturing and Stimulation
Will use their "————————" plan to insure nurturing as described in the tasks.
Will insure healthy development of the child through play, and interaction as described in tasks.

Nutrition
Will use their "————————" plan to maintain quality nutrition as described in tasks.
Will manage purchasing, and cooking of meals to insure nutrition as described in the tasks.

Physical Safety
✔ Will use their "————" plan to keep children safe from physical harm or its effects as described in the tasks.
Will arrange for personal safety for self and/or children as described in the tasks.

School Attendance
✔ Will use their "————————" plan to get kids to school on time as described in tasks.
Will manage mornings and work with school personnel to insure attendance as described in tasks.

School Performance
Will use their "————————" plan to insure school progress as described in tasks.
Will insure improved school performance in cooperation with the schools as described in tasks.

Sexual Abuse
✔ Will use their "————————" plan to help their child cope with abuse and insure safety as described in the tasks.
Will insure the removal of person causing harm to child as described in the tasks.
Will provide positive support for victims of sexual abuse as described in the tasks.

Sexually Reactive Behaviors
✔ Will use their "————————" plan to help their children become less reactive and safe from abuse as described in the tasks.
Will support child in coping with sexual reactivity as described in tasks.
Will provide supervision of child to insure safety from sexual activity as described in the tasks.

Shelter

Will use their "————————" plan to secure a safe and adequate home as described in the tasks.
Will insure that safe and secure shelter is provided to all family members as described in the tasks.

Supervision

✔ Will use their "————————" plan to insure supervision of young children as described in tasks.
✔ Will use their "————————" plan to insure supervision of teens as described in tasks.
Will provide daytime supervision/child care for family members as described in the tasks.
Will provide evening supervision/child care for family members as described in the tasks.
Will provide weekend supervision/child care for family members as described in the tasks.
Will negotiate roles and responsibilities for secure childcare at all times as described in the tasks.

Systems of Care

✔ Will use their "————————" plan to make visitation go well as described in the tasks.
Will interact positively and support child in dealing with placement as described in the tasks.
Will provide assistance in permanency plan for child as described in the tasks.

Individual Level Objectives

Alcohol/Drug

Will use the "———————" plan to keep clean and sober as described in the tasks.
✔ Will use the "———————" plan to keep alcohol or drugs from effecting their family as described in tasks.
Will maintain a sober/clean lifestyle by using coping skills as described in the tasks.
Will manage drinking in ways that protects all family members as described in the tasks.

Anger

✔ Will use the "———————" plan to prevent harmful expressions of anger as described in tasks.
Will insure the safety of the family by managing anger in safe, positive ways as described in the tasks.
Will identify personal hurdles to providing protection / supervision of children as described in tasks.
Will identify personal hurdles to providing self-protection from abusive others as described in tasks.

Criminal Behavior

Will use the "———————" plan to prevent criminal behavior as described in tasks.
Will manage behavior in ways that keep them from committing criminal acts as described in tasks.

Depression

✔ Will use the "———————" plan to manage discouragement as described in the tasks.
✔ Will use the "———————" plan to maintain quality parenting as described in the tasks.
✔ Will use the "———————" plan to keep the house clean as described in the tasks.
✔ Will use the "———————" plan to keep themselves clean as described in the tasks.
✔ Will use the "———————" plan to keep their job as described in the tasks.
✔ Will manage discouragement in ways that keep them doing necessary activities as described in tasks.

Education/School

Will use the "———————" plan to stay in school and out of trouble as described in the tasks.
Will use the "———————" plan to insure good school performance as described in the tasks.
Will attend school daily and maintain conduct / studies to insure progress as described in the tasks.

Financial

Will use the "——— ———————" plan to get and keep a job as described in the tasks.
Will use the "———————" plan to get and maintain temporary benefits as described in the tasks.
Will practice skills necessary to secure financial stability as described in the tasks.

Hygiene

Will use the "———————" plan to stay healthy and clean as described in the tasks.
Will use skills and activities to insure good personal hygiene as described in the tasks.
Will provide care to insure the personal cleanliness and hygiene of each person as described in the tasks.

Independent Living

Will use the "———————" plan to secure successful independent living as described in the tasks.
Will use the skills needed for successful independent living as described in the tasks.
Will provide care to insure independent living skills are leaned by family members as described in the tasks.

Medical / Health

Will use the "———————" plan to insure proper health care as described in the tasks.
Will use the "———————" plan to have a healthy pregnancy as described in the tasks.
Will use the "———————" plan to avoid unplanned childbirth in the future as described in tasks.
Will maintain proper medical and health care for themselves and as described in the tasks.

Self-Control

Will use the "———————" plan to insure a more cooperative behavior as described in the tasks.
Will insure cooperative behavior in following the family rules as described in the tasks.

Figure 7.A2. Individual-level objectives.

Self-Confidence

Will identify personal hurdles to providing protection / supervision of children as described in tasks.
Will identify personal hurdles to providing self-protection from abusive others as described in tasks.
Will identify personal hurdles to acquiring and maintaining gainful employment.
Will identify personal hurdles to providing financial stability for the family.

Sexual Abuse

Will use the "——————————" plan to prevent further acts of sexual abuse as described in tasks.
Will maintain a personal relapse prevention plan to prevent further sexual abuse as described in tasks.
Will insure the removal of themselves from any contact with victims as described in tasks.
Will identify personal hurdles to providing protection / supervision of children as described in tasks.
Will identify personal hurdles to providing self-protection from abusive others as described in tasks.

Systems of Care

✔ Will use the "——————————" plan to make visitation go well as described in the tasks.
Will interact positively and support child in dealing with placement as described in the tasks.
Will provide assistance in permanency plan for child as described in the tasks.

✔ = Tipsheet available for reference when co-constructing the plan with the family or individual.

Chapter 8

Solution-Based Case Management

THE CHALLENGE OF STAYING THE COURSE

Case planning is built upon the premise that everyone involved in the implementation of the case plan will "stay the course" to see it completed. "Murphy's law," a colloquial saying well-known in Western culture, particularly among those who work in larger systems of our culture, says, "If anything can possibly go wrong, it will." For those experienced in the public sector where individual responsibility (or control) is minimal at best, this saying connotes the seemingly endless ways a well-organized plan of action can come unraveled. The reasons for this tendency toward distraction are numerous: the pace of incoming cases, the multiple players involved in any one case, the competing interests in the family / client, the myriad of service provider requirements, the unpredictability of court action, and the lack of management skills and technology in the social services are all possibilities for getting off track. So it is not surprising that many in the field simply become accustomed to the lack of follow-through, the lack of collaboration, and the fickle nature of some court decisions. The overall effect, however, of this familiarity with organizational chaos is often professional anomie, even burnout. Once the sense of direction is gone, then organizing one's team becomes futile and a waste of energy. Like a vicious destructive cycle, professional burnout can lead to a sense of futility complete with self- statements like "What's the point of my doing something? No one else will do their piece," or "Why bother, no one is going to follow the plan anyway." These thoughts and feelings of futility ensure that case plans become mere paperwork to be filed away and forgotten once finally completed. The tragedy of this deconstruction of teamwork planning is that, in many systems, futility is so much a part of the system's culture that the decision not to manage isn't even noticed by others on the team. When futility becomes systemic, efforts to proactively manage and organize will be seen as naive or even "too eager." Since antiorganizational attitudes exist in other systems, it might be easier to see how problematic it would be if all contracts were viewed as mere paperwork and irrelevant to the specific issues of concern. For example, can you imagine a world in which several public and private parties set out to ensure a certain outcome (like building a highway) and the original plan and intent were not continually referenced as a guideline for decision-making?

A second issue of concern that comes up the longer a case stays open is the treatment team's relationship with the client. It is not unusual for a caseworker to start a case relationship based on partnership, only to jettison that partnership at the first sign of resistance or noncooperation. Such a shift is usually signaled by comments that imply distance and mistrust in the relationship like, "These people don't care if they get their child back" or "These people are just doing enough to get by—as soon as I'm gone it'll all start up again." It is a challenge to stay focused on the patterns of change in everyday life and not react to the parts of the clients' lives that have not changed. It is particularly hard if the caseworker has had little contact with them and only gets called back in times of crisis and problems. During such crisis times, focusing on the original case objectives may not seem relevant (e.g., "Action is needed!") and putting out the fire becomes the primary concern.

Because of the possibility, even likelihood, of a case drifting from its original objectives, this chapter has been included to provide some suggestions for reducing case wander and hopefully to ensure a greater success rate at achieving outcome goals. The chapter offers suggestions located around the major risk times for case management, such as when the family is transferred to someone else or when there are lapses or relapses in problem pattern behavior.

A REMINDER ABOUT TARGETING OUTCOME SKILLS

Before looking at how to maintain a focus on case objectives it is important to reemphasize that the original case plan must be directed toward specific behavioral prevention skills that the family members will use to prevent relapse. If the case plan targets attendance at counseling or parenting classes as an objective, then attendance is what you will be measuring. Your casework will be reduced to checking on attendance and scolding or threatening the family if they do not attend. If a crisis does occur, all you will be able to say is "Have you been going to counseling?" If they answer no you end up scolding them; and if they say, "Yes, but we missed some," you end up scolding them anyway for missing sessions. If they say, "Yes, every session," you really have nothing to say because "attendance" didn't solve the problems. If the case plan does not target the specific behavioral skills the family will need to avoid, interrupt, or escape their problem pattern, you won't be able to help them sort out where they allowed their problem pattern to escalate. Because you won't be able to help them identify when they became at risk, you won't be able to help them generate alternative responses to those situations.

The reminder therefore is that you can't manage a case plan that is not written with specific knowledge about the family members' high-risk problem patterns.

CHALLENGE 1: MAKING THE TRANSITION FROM INTAKE TO ONGOING

Many social service agencies, public and private, separate the in-take/assessment/investigation process from the ongoing work of a case once opened. This is particularly true of larger urban areas, where the number of cases and number of caseworkers allow such specialization. Although the practice does allow someone to specialize in the skills specific to intake or to ongoing, it also creates one of the first challenges to case management.

When a family is in crisis due to their own pain and hurt or due to outside intervention, the problem and its interaction pattern are poised for change. The way the family is helped to view their problem will greatly affect the resources they call upon to address the situation. In our own lives, when looking back over a time of change, it isn't unusual for us to say, "I guess I was just ready to hear it then" or "I hooked up with the right person and things just started to click." Change is mysterious some-times because most social scientists now believe it is discontinuous (Hoffman, 1981) and, for human beings, at least partially constructed out of previously existing cognitive formulations (Maturana & Varela 1980). Discontinuous change simply means that many small steps of adaptation need to accumulate before a more permanent structural change occurs. Change feels like it happens all at once but it really happens only when enough building blocks of the new behavior pattern are in place or are recognized as applicable to the situation in question, i.e., discontinuous. This formulation of change means that these building blocks may be already be in place in the person's or family's thinking and behaving but not organized in a way that is useful to the problem situation. This phe-nomenon may be familiar to you if you recall those moments in your life when you reflected on something you accomplished and said, "I guess I always knew what I needed to do, but I just didn't know how to get it started." In such situations, a plan of action hadn't crystallized, although it had been ready to for some time.

We have gone into a discussion of change because it is necessary for the first caseworker who meets with the family to know the importance of their role in problem definition. By tapping the preexisting building blocks of change, the caseworker helps the family construct a way to think about the problem that promotes real change. As we have discussed previously, when this is done in partnership with the family they are more likely to guide the worker toward a problem construction that is useful to them. Once this new construction of the problem has been recognized by the family as "a good way to think about the problem," it has tremendous organizing power.

Take, for example, the Smith family case. The intake worker and the family discussed the Smiths' very painful situation regarding physical harm done to their son by the boy's mother. After assisting the family to describe the specific sequence of events that led up to physical abuse, the caseworker was able to relocate the problem in the everyday life event of bathing. From there, the family could agree that bathing indeed was a problem and had been a problem for some time. In fact, the whole evening routine was a problem in their mind. The caseworker also helped the mother talk about how she wished she had handled the situation better, how she hadn't wanted to hurt the boy, and how she had always had an anger problem. She blamed the latter on the treatment she received from her father. They all agreed that (1) they needed a new routine for the evening hours, with particular attention to bathing, and (2) Mom needed someone to help her with her anger problem when under stress.[1] This construction of the problem was a contract the family felt would help them and they actually left the intake interview hopeful about the process. Restated in terms of change, they had known about the need to make these changes for some time and therefore it was easy to recognize the reasonableness of the plan.

The Smith's case was one of substantiated abuse and therefore was turned over to the ongoing treatment unit where the actual case plan would be written. However, the ongoing worker did not pick up on the existing problem definition. After reading the assessment, the ongoing worker recommended a parenting class and a drug assessment for both parents. The latter was required due to a suspicion about prior drug use mentioned in the assessment notes. While these tasks might be seen as useful, the family did not recognize them as meaningful or as a solution to their problems. Furthermore, the family no longer felt in partnership with the caseworker. The energy and hope connected to change was lost. Because the parents were afraid to offend or antagonize the ongoing worker, they said nothing about the new "requirements." The experience was actually not foreign to them; in fact, they recognized it as one of many in which social institutions "simply tell you what hoop to jump through, we're just a number to them." They wanted their child and wanted social services out of their lives so they were resigned to go through the routine, whether it was useful or not. As might be expected, problems in attendance at both the parenting classes and the drug assessment followed. In the parenting classes they reported that the leader didn't know their specific situation and they already knew all that stuff anyway. It made them mad to have to sit there and they just played along.

The ongoing worker checked on their attendance[2] and became concerned. The relationship between the family and caseworker became antagonistic and the worker threatened to suspend visitation at a family member's home if the parents didn't follow the case plan. The family felt threatened by the very case plan intended to assist them. This case went on in contention for twelve months before the original contract could be resurrected as a way to get some movement in the case. During that time, two different child placements were made and a year of the family's life together was wasted. The ongoing caseworker also had to spend considerable time in meetings that were unproductive. Although the original conceptualization of the problem was eventually restored, it was difficult to accomplish: difficult because the caseworker had been so focused on attendance, and then the family's resistance, that she could not state the everyday life event that was difficult for the family at the time of the abuse. Too much time and conflict had clouded that original construction of what needed to be changed.

If this were an isolated case of miscommunication then this case story would not be so disturbing. Unfortunately, one must assume that if the intake worker is not going to be the ongoing worker then the risk for losing focus on outcome objectives is extremely high. In short, Murphy's law applies. Therefore, caseworkers and their supervisors should place significant attention on ensuring that the transition from intake to ongoing is deliberate, with attention given to the details of how the problem issues will be defined. Specific suggestions follow.

Use a Common Language for Conceptualizing Change

Start with a common understanding of how to conceptualize problems in family life. Although the social sciences offer differing models that complement each other, it is important to have a coherent way to think about the assessment and case-planning process. We clearly believe that a family-centered model grounded in solution-based relapse prevention has advantages, but any consistent model is better than leaving it up to individual workers to make their own decisions about what model to work from. When a common model and common structures for applying that model are clearly reflected in all training experiences, forms, and procedures, a large agency has the potential for being more consistent and internally coherent.

Use the Initial Assessment to Build the Case Plan

Case planning is not a separate process from assessment.[3] Case planning is not an exclusive activity of the caseworker either. Case planning is the written result of a consensus that evolves about the problem and its solution, a consensus that begins to be formed in the first few minutes of the first conversation with the family about the problem situation. This means that assessment interviewers need to be trained in case planning, and not simply drilled on problem identification and substantiation.

Caseworkers who are simultaneously collecting information and helping to shape it into workable definitions allow a partnership to develop with their family clients. By focusing their assessment on the everyday developmental tasks that the family faces, the discussion is viewed by the family as relevant and hopeful. When the assessment worker summarizes the conversation to the family in such a way as to label the prevention skills needed, the family is able to recognize the practical nature of the solutions.

In the Smith family case discussed previously, the intake worker did just that. The worker summarized back to the family, "So it sounds like you are very concerned about the bathing routine. In fact, you say you could use a new plan for the whole evening routine." The mother confirmed this consensus with "I think so. Everything just seems to get crazy after dinner and we are all tired and too much falls on me." The worker then summarized the individual skill area: " And when you feel everything falls on you, your temper gets the best of you, the past sort of comes crashing in?" To which the mother replied, "Yeah, I just lose it and then I feel even worse about myself." The worker then confirmed the specific need by saying, "So some sort of temper taming help would help you on those occasions when for whatever reasons, the routine, even the new routine, just doesn't go as planned?" "Absolutely," the mother responded, while the father nodded in agreement.

This sort of summarizing of the presenting problem in a common practical language lays the groundwork for the partnership to continue when other team members help develop more specific tasks of the case plan.

Utilize the Family and Community Network

Another method for ensuring that the assessment process bridges successfully to the ongoing intervention is to include a wider network of resources to contribute ideas about what needs to happen for safety to be restored. The inclusion of family members or community members during the assessment process is not a new idea, but giving them more responsibility for decision-making is a relatively new practice. Although discussed elsewhere in this text, it is useful to note here the effect it has on transition issues. If other family members are included on the team, the likelihood of a caseworker going off on his/her own without being questioned is diminished. Additionally, family input tends to be very concrete and practical, thus increasing the likelihood of the family client being invested in the eventual case plan.

Use Face-to-Face Meetings Whenever Making a Transition

In the Smith case previously discussed, one can imagine a better transition if only one small step had been taken. If the assessment worker had arranged a meeting with the ongoing worker and the family to discuss their tentative plans, one can imagine the case taking a far different path. Many workers in public agencies will first say to this suggestion, "I don't have time to do that. There are so many other meetings I must attend." What they don't realize is the amount of time they have to spend in meetings because they don't spend a little time at key transition points to ensure that the case stays focused on outcome prevention skills. The Smith case consumed hours and hours of meetings and additional paperwork due to "not having time for meetings." Face-to-face meetings actually save time in the long run, and prevent family hardship.

Help the Client Recognize Small Steps of Change

By now, the reader should be very clear that staying focused on the case plan objectives means more than checking attendance. So what would the conversations be like if they reflected the intent of the case plan? The worker would be curious about the signs of progress on each of the specific case plan tasks. Using the Smith case again for illustration, the following questions might direct the conversation toward the client recognizing small steps of change:

- What is different about bath time that you are trying?
- Have you noticed anything that seems to work better at bath time?
- Which nights seem to be going better than others are?
- On a scale of 1 to 10 with 10 being a miracle night and 1 being how bad it used to get, what number would you give your family bath routine now?
- Have you discussed bathing and evening routines with any of your friends or relatives to get their ideas?

- What have you learned about situations that are high risk for you to lose your temper?
- Have you learned anything about your early warning signals regarding your temper?
- Give me an example of how you have interrupted your temper and kept from losing it.
- Who has started to notice that you are changing, even a little bit?

Such casework questions keep the focus on the target outcome skills that the case plan is designed to accomplish. They also have the effect of sharing in the excitement of family change. Curiosity about progress and confidence that change will occur can be very influential in problem-saturated families. These conversations also maintain the focus and the consensus on what needs to change.

CHALLENGE 2: MAKING THE TRANSITION FROM CASEWORK TO TREATMENT

This second challenge to managing case focus comes if and when the family is referred to a treatment provider. Chapter 9 is written primarily for the treatment provider audience and can be used as a common reading to facilitate community partnership meetings that address better collaboration. However, this section is written to reflect the specific steps caseworkers and their supervisors can take on their own to anticipate obstacles to case focus at the time of transition to treatment. These steps begin with understanding therapists and their work, providing them with clear statements of what the clients have agreed to accomplish, sharing specific information with them in a timely manner, and, finally, using target outcomes to guide requests for reports.

Understanding Therapy and Therapists

Given that social service and mental health professionals work with pretty much the same clients, it is somewhat surprising that each side knows so little about the other's work world. The graduate and training programs of social service caseworkers often do not address the realities of the therapist's world, and the therapist's graduate and training programs tend not to inform them about the real-life pressures the caseworker experiences. While this reading is not intended to cover all the issues inherent in the subject, there are a few key facts of therapist life that might be helpful for a caseworker to understand.

All Therapist Don't Work on Everyday Life Skills.   Mental health has a tradition of honoring diversity of theoretical approaches, but many of these approaches are not family-centered and many are not grounded in the stuff of everyday life. Most therapists are familiar with a family-centered approach and can adapt to work on specific changes in family life. Given that most referrals are to agencies, not individuals, it would be unwise for the caseworker to assume that the therapist will listen to the family and automatically hear the same things that the caseworker heard.

Therapist See Back-to-Back Clients in Their Office.   With significant pressures to make their weekly and monthly quotas of client contact hours, therapists must schedule clients back-to-back. They must also overbook clients because they know that a significant number won't show up. This means that clients will have a difficult time being seen every week, and a difficult time being seen at a time convenient to the family.

Back-to-back office clients can also lead to a little confusion about client goals. Imagine having only a few minutes, if any, between interviews. One's thoughts may still be with the previous session when the new client sits down for the next interview. It is not unusual for the therapist to not remember clients' names or anything about their problems. Therapists develop great memory skills that allow them to get focused as the person starts to talk, but it isn't always instantaneous. This is why many therapists have the habit of asking a general question at the beginning of the interview like, How is it going? The answer is often not directly related to treatment plan, but more a comment about some crisis or unpleasantness that is currently bothering the client. The therapist is there to help with problems and so often will inquire further. It doesn't take long for the conversation to be engaging, but not engaged on issues specific to the case plan. This same phenomenon occurs with caseworkers who allow themselves to get drawn into putting out fires rather than dealing with the longer-term agenda.

Therapists Do Not Get Paid for Networking or Paperwork.   Therapy has become more of a business, and therapists feel the pressure of production. Returning phone calls, filling out paperwork, and attending a meeting are all activities the therapist would like to be a part of, but most have to squeeze them in when a client doesn't show up, or when it is just critical to interagency relationships. Caseworkers should not automatically assume a lack of interest when in many cases therapists are simply trying to keep up with their workload.

Therapists Do Not Have Magic Answers or Abilities Unknown to Casework.   Because of professional turf issues between the various social service and mental health professions, myths have been built up about who is capable of doing certain specific tasks. Some caseworkers actually believe that a therapist is like the old physician model, a person to whom you don't ask questions and don't give suggestions. Most therapists do not perpetuate this myth but it nonetheless survives. In truth, there currently is tremendous turnover among agency therapists, and therefore a high number of frontline therapists are right out of school. Many are just as confused about what to do that would be useful as caseworkers. Even the most talented and experienced among them would say that they have no magic answers, and many welcome help and collaboration.

Setting Out a Clear Map for Change

Given that forces that can sometimes work against casework goals drive the everyday life of a therapist, it makes sense to assist treatment providers with the specific map that has been built in consensus with the family.

Many caseworkers react to this suggestion with concern that they don't feel it is their place to "direct" therapy. But sharing a map built with the family is an important step in preventing recurrence of destructive behavior. Therapists' first allegiance ethically is to their clients. Such an allegiance does not benefit from conflict between a caseworker and the client family. Therapists would much prefer to facilitate a cooperative agreement that keeps family members safe and social services happy than to go off on their own. Without assistance of a specific map, however, they have no choice but to go off on their own. They usually do not have the structural mechanisms to call everyone in and try to reach a consensus about change. Providing the therapist with the case plan written in everyday terms will be very much welcomed by many therapists.

Share Lapses and Progress in a Specific and Timely Manner

In large public agencies, no one can safely assume that others in the system know what you know (remember Murphy's law here). The caseworker cannot assume that the family will tell the therapist important news, either negative or positive. They may want to, but will they recognize change? Usually their antennae are set to pick up examples of the problem and not signs of the solution, so they may not recognize change without some assistance. And if they did recognize it, would they tell someone else about it? More often it is up to the helpers to serve as an initial audience for the signs of change. Calling a therapist if only to leave a message about a sign of progress will ensure that it is mentioned the next session and inquired about.

The same works for catching drift back to problem patterns. If the team is only engaged to notice a relapse (a recurrence of the presenting problem) then intervention options will be constrained to more drastic choices. If however the treatment team knows the problem pattern well enough to recognize the earliest warning signals that cycle buildup is starting, then the options for problem-solving alternative behaviors are much greater and less intrusive. However, what therapists don't know they can't work on. To maintain the partnership with the family, the caseworker and therapist will want to address full communication between team members and discuss the benefits of such an arrangement.[4]

It is clear that frequent and timely conversations between the caseworker, family, and treatment provider help keep everyone focused on the specific objectives of the case plan.

Make Specific Requests for Treatment Outcome Information

Hopefully this discussion of cooperation between treatment team members leads the reader to anticipate what sort of report needs to be requested from the treatment provider. This report usually is precipitated by an upcoming decision that has to be made and usually coincide with a court date.

In the past, when caseworkers and therapists were following a deficit model, this report would be requested by the caseworker in language based upon the decision that needed to be made rather than the skills that were to have been learned and practiced. For instance, the request might ask the treatment provider to determine if the children were safe to go home. The therapist would either not want to answer it and frustrate the caseworker or in some cases would frustrate the caseworker by giving an answer with which the caseworker disagreed.

The best request for information is one tied directly to the accomplishment of the case plan tasks. If the case plan has been written to address those skills needed to prevent recurrence of the presenting problem, than those skills are what need to be measured. Such a report can be partially written by the family client as well. Sometimes it is helpful to provide treatment providers with an outline of the areas such a report might cover. They can then work on it in conjunction with their client. The following outline is offered as a sample:

- What are the high-risk situations for this client?
- What are the client's early warning signals indicating problem buildup?
- What examples of client progress would indicate the client is now able to avoid his/her high-risk situations? What does he/she still need to work to avoid?
- What does the client understand to be the pattern of behavior that leads to problems?
- What examples of client progress would indicate the client is now

able to interrupt his/her problem patterns? What does he/she still
need to work to interrupt?
• What examples of client progress would indicate the client has practiced a safety plan to escape a high-risk situation if unable to avoid
or interrupt it?

Making specific requests of treatment providers is helpful to the provider, helpful to the family, and helpful to the court, which may have
to evaluate whether or not compliance with court orders has occurred.
Once again, it should be noted that good case management depends on
good case planning, which in turn depends on good case assessment. A
solution-based assessment that targets relapse prevention skills and is
grounded in the everyday life of the family makes everything start out
right. Then the challenge is to just keep it on track.

CHALLENGE 3:   INTEGRATING WELFARE TO WORK
OBJECTIVES

Many families will have financial concerns that have led to family
members being at risk for neglect or harm. As welfare-to-work reform
proceeds, some families will face a loss of benefits and will not be responding to the crisis. Rather than dismissing attributing financial issues
as "someone else's concern," caseworkers can and should address the
financial task as any other developmental challenge that threatens the
safety and stability of family members. This means that a family objective might be a part of the case plan (e.g., Our Family's Plan to Support
Mom's Work), and that objective might have an individual component
(e.g., My Plan to Stay Upbeat and Not Get Discouraged While Looking
for Work). In many states, welfare workers have expanded their functional role to include coaching such plans, or have actually merged organizational units with protective services. In other states, welfare departments
have developed special units to address casework considerations. In still
others, individual welfare workers can be approached to help clients
develop prevention plans and then serve as encouraging supporters to
their progress.

CHALLENGE 4:   MAKING THE MOST OF SETBACKS

Keeping the treatment team on track during and after a setback can be
a considerable challenge to good case management. Setbacks, in this context, refer to a recurrence of behavior that has been identified as high risk,

or to behavior that would indicate that a family member was lapsing back into his/her problem behavior. This covers a wide range of "crisis" behavior, and could even include relapse behavior, i.e., recurrence of the presenting problem.

The reason setbacks are such a challenge to ongoing case management is that a setback can discourage caseworkers and treatment providers so much that they react to the client family with strong emotions. Sometimes the reaction might be one of disgust born out of sense of betrayal, e.g., "I'm through with those people. They lied to me and lied to me and made me look stupid. I could care less what happens to them." Or it could be a reaction of anger born out of personal fears, e.g., "I don't want anything to do with him. He's a perp, he gives me the creeps, I don't trust him, he can rot in hell for all I care." Or sometimes the reaction can be one of deep discouragement born out of dashed hopes, e.g., "I guess they just don't care, or maybe they care but just don't know any better, but I just don't see them ever changing. They just keep going right back to the same old behavior. They get better for a while but as soon as I turn my back they are right back to the same old stuff. What do you do with people who don't care?"

Such deep personal responses to casework will be familiar to the experienced worker as well as the beginner. The emotional reactions are human responses to setbacks, responses that are understandable though completely unproductive.[5] The more objective observer (and hopefully the supervisor as we will discuss in the next section) sees the setback as something one should expect and even anticipate with family situations that have become deeply patterned and ingrained. Since the setback is actually just the family member doing what he/she usually does to get into trouble, it can be seen as an opportunity to work on the problem pattern. In fact, it could be seen as an ideal opportunity since the incident of setback is fresh and any alternative actions that might be tried could be practiced in the present. The advantage of coaching a family member through a high-risk time could even be seen as a necessary component of any relapse prevention intervention. The alternative would be to expect every client to immediately cease and desist any troublesome behavior immediately upon contact with the caseworker or provider and to initiate new behavior without practice or trials. It almost sounds ludicrous when put in those terms, and yet busy caseworkers and busy providers often slip into thinking that change is simply a function of singular desire and willpower.

So what should an ongoing caseworker do in situations of setback? First, let's divide setbacks into two categories: those in which a crisis has occurred and a safety plan has to be reworked with steps taken to ensure the safety of family members, and those in which the current safety plan is still adequate but treatment momentum and direction are threatened.

Setbacks That Require a New Safety Plan

When a setback occurs, it can take many forms. An emergency call late at night from a distraught parent, an anonymous report of possible abuse, a letter from a referral source indicating several missed appointments, or a home visit where high-risk behavior is observed or suspected. Ongoing casework situations present the case manager with some of the most complex decision trees any professional has to face. However, family member safety is a constant variable that needs to be assessed and managed regardless of the presenting situation.

The challenge during a crisis setback is to not jump too quickly to what actions need to be taken before discussing (assessing) the specific pattern of events that led up to the safety concerns. This usually means backing the story up to points earlier in the escalating situation than are typically discussed. For instance, if a "chronic neglect" client reports that she was sick and couldn't take the kid's clothes to the laundry (another school neglect report), some caseworkers may quickly jump ahead in their mind to removing the children in order "get the mother's attention." While this action may be the appropriate action to ensure child safety, it would be taken without any concrete knowledge that "lack of seriousness of consequence" was the actual pattern issue. The worker does not lose any options by first referring back to the family's plan of action to see what tasks were supposed to happen (in such situations) and what tasks did and or did not happen. This becomes a reassessment process in which the events are slowed down enough to identify the factors present at the time things stopped happening according to plan. If that moment was one in which the parent became discouraged, then obviously the parent needs a plan to overcome discouragement in such situations. Does the parent know what situations are difficult for him/her? If so, does he/she have a plan? If so, then what happened when he/she started to use it? Did he/she wait too long to use it? Was it too long because he/she didn't recognize the indicators, the warning signals? Does he/she need more details of what to do? Does he/she they need a sponsor or coach to call at such times for support?

By retracing the unfolding of events that occurred prior to being at risk, entering the high-risk situation, and then attempting to deal with the high-risk situation, the worker is able to pinpoint what went wrong. Knowing this information leads directly to helping the family and or treatment provider rework their plan of action. This same information helps the caseworker decide what changes need to occur in the safety plan. It could be that a new plan of action is developed but the discussion indicates that the client is only able to intervene very late in the destructive cycle. If this discovery is coupled with knowledge that a family member could be harmed if the plan fails, then the family can be assisted to take precautionary measures until it is safe for everyone to be together. If this involves removing a child, then it can be done within the partnership, including other family members in the process, and the client can be supported for taking the protective actions. This scenario has the outcome as removing the children in order to send a message, yet it sends a very different message to the family members.

Setbacks That Threaten Treatment Direction

Sometimes the setback can be simply losing momentum or direction on a case. It can happen with families who have a lot of little problems, few resources, or poor organizational skills of their own, or who are involved with multiple helpers. In such situations, it is hard for any focused activity to emerge for long because there is so much competition of the family's attention. Sometimes it is the caseworker's or treatment provider's attention that gets sidetracked on some issue. It could be an issue that personally triggers the caseworker's own sensibilities, like home cleanliness, or it could be an issue that is a problem but is not currently central to member safety, like whether or not a couple shares household duties equally. A member of the overall treatment team may select an issue to focus on that makes sense to him/her but could potentially detract focus from the presenting problem. This often happens when a family member, child for instance, is removed from the home and placed in a care facility or home of any kind. The placement personnel might have concerns about the child that they want addressed that, although important to them, have little to do with the child's home life.

In this situation as well, the case plan can serve as a unifying rudder to return the treatment team to what really needs to be accomplished. If new issues come up, the goal of the caseworker should be to relate them back in some way to the treatment plan objectives. This can often have the effect of simply reassuring other members of the treatment team, or it can shed light on the need to revise some aspect of the prevention plan to accommodate the new information.

Case Example. For instance, the Anderson family had as their family-level objective to develop rules and consequences for their teen daughter. On the individual level, the stepfather was to work on his anger control and the daughter was to work on her self-control. In this case, the child was staying with a foster family who worried about the child's past trauma (sexually abused eight years prior by biological father) and was arguing for sexual abuse counseling. The caseworker was concerned about getting the daughter home as soon as possible and didn't want the adolescent behavior issues to take a back seat. The caseworker chose to have a meeting with the foster parents to listen to their concerns and assure them that the trauma issues were not neglected. The caseworker asked a number of questions to both the foster family and to the child regarding how they thought the prior abuse might be affecting her current ability to be self-controlled. After it was firmly established that there was a connection, the caseworker arranged for a meeting between the child, herself, and the therapist who was helping her work on self-control. In this meeting, the prior conversations were shared and the discussion steered toward how this information might help the therapist and the client come up with a specific plan to minimize the effects of the past on her current ability to cooperate in the family. They came up with several areas they might explore. The caseworker closed that meeting with comments about how she was looking forward to seeing the written plan they were working on. Although it took the caseworker two meetings to incorporate the new ideas into the case plan, the effort not only kept the case on focus but actually sped up the work because she found a way for the information to inform the case plan.

It's often better to not keep adding on to "what needs fixing" but to simply fold new views into the existing plan. A family and a caseworker can only manage so many projects at a given time and they have to be somewhat protective when they sense an action that could defocus them. Sometimes good supervision is needed to assist the caseworker in meeting the challenges of managing ongoing casework. The following section offers some ideas on how that supervision might be helpful.

SUPERVISOR'S ROLE IN CASE MANAGEMENT

The burden of responsibility in casework raises anxiety in both workers and supervisors. Some supervisors respond to this anxiety by feeling the need to micromanage every decision of the caseworker. Other supervisors respond to the anxiety by retreating from making difficult decisions and putting off as many decisions as possible, providing little or no guidance to their team members. Although the range of supervisor styles might be represented by these two extremes, there are certainly numerous variations in between that seem to be effective. What appears to be consistent across all supervisor styles is the similarity between supervisor-caseworker interaction and caseworker-family interaction. Studies have noted this parallel process phenomenon (Liddle, Breunlin, & Swartz, 1988) and its effects on direct practice. These researchers have found that "as the supervision goes, so goes the casework."

From a solution-based casework perspective, the supervisory process needs to be based on the same tenets that undergird the casework: a working partnership, a focus on everyday life events, and promotion of skill development. Given the working environment for casework in the postmodern world, issues of time management emerge as one of several necessary prerequisites to practicing these tenets. This section will address (1) how to find the time to supervise case management, (2) how to build and maintain a partnership with workers, (3) how to help workers maintain their focus on specific situations and events, and finally (4) how to promote their acquisition of ongoing case management skills.

TAKING THE TIME TO SUPERVISE

It appears that most supervision in child protective services is what we call "hallway" supervision. Set supervisory times are relative unknowns to social service systems, with most supervisors having critical conversations while standing in someone's doorway or while walking down the hall. With the rise of cubicle office space and large open floor arrangements, workers may not even have to leave their desk to ask a question, they can just yell a question over the cubicle wall. Supervisors find themselves in a fast-action, crisis-oriented "triage"[6] type environment that operates largely on quick conversations that are primarily decision based. The return from holidays and weekends are often high-impact times that supervisors learn to dread because they know that caseworkers will be "waiting for them at the door."

In this environment, it is understandable that supervision tends toward the short, quick conversation when decisions have to be made. The caseworker asks a question regarding what action to take, the supervisor says what he/she should do. Given the parallel process, this tends to promote casework in which the family discusses a problem and the caseworker tells them what they should do. It takes time to establish a working partnership in which the ideas of the caseworker are sought and encouraged. It takes time to ask the caseworker to slow down the description of events being discussed so that a pattern of interaction might be discerned, and it takes time to ask a caseworker to discuss the exceptions to the family's problem pattern. All of these activities are critical to assisting the caseworker to do the same with the family, and many supervisors feel they just don't have that kind of time.

It is a paradox of sorts. In crisis situations, it appears that quick decisions need to be made, when in reality, quick decisions often lead to poor long-term planning and therefore more crises down the road. More crises, more quick decisions, it can be a vicious cycle. When a supervisor was asked to take the time to staff a case in which a child placement had disrupted for the fourteenth time she reported, "I don't have time to staff the case. I've got to have a new placement by four o'clock today!" Quality supervision lies in the ability to pull very valuable time out of a demanding schedule in order to work more proficiently. However, when supervisors take the time to teach workers the skills they need to stay focused on case plan management, their efforts actually reduce their crisis supervision time. Hallway conversations still occur, but they now reference longer prior conversations that went into the issues in more depth. Rather than "Where can I put this kid?" it becomes "How can I help the foster parent intervene earlier before the kid gets so worked up?" Taking the time to sit down and plan strategy does mean a little more work up front to mentor and coach casework skills. But as workers become clearer on their focus with a family, they are better prepared to weigh the enormous demands, content, and influences in casework.

Solution-based casework provides the supervisor and caseworker a common conceptual map that can guide how they organize their casework intervention. The map can keep them focused on the case plan and the prevention skills it targets. However, if the supervisor doesn't take the time to help the caseworker continually return to that map, then case management will be at risk of becoming crisis management.

MAINTAINING A PARTNERSHIP

All positive human relationships are based on trust and respect. Trust and respect in the supervisory relationship means that each party to the relationship has the ability to influence the others. Taking the time to ask about specific situations, to notice competency, to ask about problem exceptions, and to elicit potential solution strategies conveys trust and respect in the worker's ideas. In casework, we have discussed how the simple act of asking the client's opinion about what might work conveys a willingness to be influenced by the opinions of the family members. This same process occurs in the supervisory relationship when a supervisor asks the worker questions about what might work. Partnerships experiment with possibilities; they don't insist on single versions of actions to be taken.

Case Example

Oftentimes a worker (like a family) will ask a supervisor a "how to" question, when really all he/she is lacking is confidence. Take, for instance, the example of Lisa Ann, a new worker with one year of experience in social work, who has handled numerous child protection cases quite well. She has accomplished tasks, from intake to closure, extremely well. However, in her particular rural county, another worker has always handled the sexual abuse cases. Lisa Ann was assigned a sexual abuse investigation/assessment for the first time, and she was a bit over-whelmed. She had been busy and had not had any time to discuss the case with her supervisor. When going out for another interview, she caught her supervisor in the hallway and asked, "Marilyn, if the police officer and I can't get the child to talk, will she have to go back home? I couldn't stand the thought of her being fondled again!" The supervisor could have simply answered, "Oh no, we can get a court order. I'll tell you what to write the judge," and gone on to the next hallway conversa-tion. However, the supervisor heard more than one level of the question and asked, "Why don't you come into my office and sit down and catch me up on this case. I'm interested in what you have been learning." The supervisor heard that there was a content question around the legal and policy procedures of the department, but she also heard the possible anxiety that the worker was experiencing when assigned a new, unfamil-iar task. After listening to the worker discuss her anxiety about her skill level, the supervisor offered a competency-based, affirming response: "You know Lisa, in the year you have been here, I have yet to see a child that didn't connect with you. Let's talk about how you usually handle similar situations so you can feel confident and comfortable." This affir-mation not only assisted Lisa in feeling less anxious, but helped to forge a partnership in which Lisa Ann could and would share her concerns, knowing that her supervisor could see them in perspective.

MAINTAINING A FOCUS ON SPECIFIC SITUATIONS IN FAMILY LIFE

Solution-based casework is centered on helping families with difficult situations in their everyday life. In terms of problem definition, people are not the problem: what people do (or not do) in certain family situations is the problem. However, this central focus of casework is under constant threat of distraction in the real working world of caseworkers. Inundated with demands, responsibilities, and competing definitions of the prob-lem, workers (like families) often suffer from feeling like the low person on the totem pole. Since other professionals, funding sources, or even family members would rather frame the problem within a deficit model, a worker can easily be drawn away from his/her conceptualization of the problem. Crises can also fuel a lack of focus. A well-developed plan, just put into place, can be jettisoned with the news that there has been a problem relapse. Pressures from the community, the courts, the schools, or the internal bureaucracy can easily sway workers from a focus on simple everyday life tasks. With all of these pressures, the supervisor must play a critical role in helping the caseworker to keep returning to a focus on the pragmatic accomplishments of the case plan.

Supervisors can rely on two techniques to assist them in their efforts: (1) steering conversations back to everyday developmental issues and (2) assisting the worker in tracking the sequence of problem patterns.

Thinking Developmentally

Workers learn quickly what interests a supervisor. After only a few conversations in which the supervisor asks about a family, the worker can begin to anticipate what the supervisor is listening for and what information he/she values (Yankeelov & Barbee, 1998). The shaping influence of these conversations has tremendous implications for training outcome. A tremendous amount of time, money, and energy can be expended on training workers, but if the supervisor doesn't ask about it, it will not be viewed as a priority. Supervisors who ask about a family's developmental stage have workers who are thinking developmentally about family life.

One of the possible ways to help a worker think developmentally is to start every new case discussion with a genogram and a "thought" question to assembled staff. A question such as the following might be useful: "Even though we know nothing about this specific family yet, can we hypothesize what developmental issues they might be facing based upon their developmental stages?" The follow-up question to such a discussion would then be, "What specific task is this family having difficulty with?" Oftentimes, particularly when a worker is new to solution-based casework, he/she will answer something like, "The father is too strict," or "The mother is depressed." The answer illustrates that the new caseworker is not yet thinking "situationally" or simply doesn't know the context for the individual behavior. The supervisor will need to assist the worker in retracing his/her observations back to the situation in which "strictness" or "depression" creates a developmental problem, e.g., "And what is the family issue that Dad is considered too strict about?"

Tracking Problem Patterns

Another technique for staying focused on everyday family events is for supervisors to assist workers in tracking a family sequence. This approach helps the worker learn to think sequentially about family events and may also identify areas where more information is needed before specific plans can be made. Many supervisors have found that asking workers in a case consultation to "bring me up to date" on how a family is handling a specific situation is very helpful.

Workers who begin explaining their case by who is involved and how the interaction occurs are already thinking more about the patterns of behaviors, they are thinking developmentally. Alternatively, when workers begin to explain cases by history, by crises, by diagnosis, or by feelings, the supervisor is alerted that there may be an issue of focus in the case. The supervisor knows that the worker needs assistance in understanding the pattern of interaction in order to focus his/her attention.

Keeping Tasks Concrete, Specific, and Documented

A supervisor can tell if family life remains the focus of change if the written case plan tasks are specific and measurable, and have been documented. Simply asking the caseworker how the case is going is not going to assess whether or not the specific tasks are remaining in focus. Therefore, it is necessary to get the case plan out every time the supervisor talks with the worker about the case. Like a mantra, the supervisor can simply say, "Can you show me the case plan again? I'm having trouble remembering the specifics." The specific tasks can then be discussed and the question of documentation of task accomplishment can come up. For instance, the supervisor can respond to a worker comment that things are much improved with, "Wonderful, how have they recorded their accomplishments? Have they used a journal or a chart? This is wonderful, may I see them?"

Sometimes a worker may need some suggestions on how to be more concrete and specific when helping family members write their tasks. The supervisory relationship can then become a learning environment where the new skills are learned and practiced.

Asking About Exceptions

Noting exceptions in worker behavior was mentioned as a way to build partnerships with one's ongoing workers, but it is also helpful and necessary to assist workers in recognizing exceptions in the families they work with. We have discussed how this is particularly helpful when families and their workers become problem-saturated. Problem-saturated families and workers can only see how things are not working, how many problems there are, how far they have to go to achieve their goals. Their preoccupation with the problems blinds them to the significant exceptions that are occurring on a regular basis. These exceptions may be discounted unless a supervisor is there to see that they are not overlooked but given equal attention.

The supervisor can assist caseworkers by asking them to describe examples of similar situations in which the family seem able to cope with their problems. Or the supervisor can ask about pattern details that may show subtle differences in response if measured over longer periods of time.

Staying Focused on Long-Term Cases

If a case is open for a long period of time, then supervisors will want to assess their agency's role. This assessment is done not just to determine whether it is time to close the case due to the goals being reached or to intervene more intensely if they haven't. The assessment has to consider the agency's role as a variable in the family system. Supervisors will want to question themselves, i.e., "Have we become a part of the problem?" or "What is our impact on the continuing issues?"

The worker's frustrations in long-term cases can often play a part in the inability of the worker or family to maintain focus. In these situations, solution-based supervisors have made the following suggestions:

- Reestablish the partnership: Change the context from us doing the work back to the family's need to resolve their issue in a safe way.
- Credential change: Assist workers in seeing that some change has occurred. Supervisors have found that using time lines and scaling questions have assisted workers in seeing positive change.
- Return to the original event and preeminent risk. Many supervisors have found that asking, "How did we first get into this case?" has helped in getting refocused.
- Reevaluate the case plan to make sure it focuses on the family's developmental objectives and related individual objectives.

SUMMARY

Supervision is a mentoring process whose principles run parallel with good casework. Working in tandem with the worker, staying focused on everyday life events, and ensuring that tasks lead to specific skill development are key elements to successful management of ongoing casework. When caseworkers sense the organizational focus of their supervisor, they are able to recognize their own similar skills and continue to work successfully toward them.

NOTES

1.   Although the intake worker did not write a case plan, she had clearly laid the groundwork. In a future case plan, the "new evening routine" could have become the family-level objective and the "desire to control temper" could have worked as the individual-level objective.

2. Attendance was checked as opposed to checking on their progress of accomplishing tasks specific to their presenting problem situation (i.e., anger control during revised evening routine).

3. The term "assessment" is used here to refer to all initial interview meetings, whether they are called investigations, assessments, or intakes in a particular agency.

4. All of the necessary releases of information will also have to be signed.

5. One might also view the responses as isomorphic to the family's response to setback and often indicative of a caseworker who has become inducted into the family system.

6. The term "triage" refers to the hospital unit designated for prioritizing the care of emergency room patients. The unit is charged with quickly stabilizing patients that can survive until more urgent and critically ill patients can be treated.

Chapter 9

Treatment Providers' Role in Case Management

INTRODUCTION

Caseworkers and therapists have a long tradition of working together as collaterals on a case; that is to say, the two professions have worked cooperatively with the same individuals or families and have done so with professional respect for their colleagues. While this collegial relationship has been respectful, it has not typically been collaborative. Collaboration requires concurrence on outcome and a shared conceptual map regarding the steps to achieve the agreed-upon outcome. This concurrence has been difficult to reach because of the professional insulation of both professions, the diversity of theoretical orientations, and the lack of outside pressure to collaborate. As these restraints to collaboration have begun to loosen, new opportunities for service integration have emerged and have been shown to be useful (Todahl and Christensen, 1997).

Although this text has primarily addressed the role of the caseworker in the assessment, case planning, and case management process, this chapter will be directed toward treatment providers and their role in achieving collaboration. It is intended that this chapter be used as part of a shared curriculum for collaboration study groups of integrated service personnel. The chapter will review some basic concepts covered in more detail elsewhere in this text. Readers unfamiliar with solution-based casework may wish to first read Chapters 3, 4, and 5 for background information.

OUTCOME, OUTCOME, OUTCOME

Unfortunately, outcome skills have not been the focused target for collaboration between service partners in the past. Although child protection agencies and mental health agencies have historically worked with many of the same individuals and families, they were often only tangentially aware that they were working toward the same goal. Each profession has been focused on the work it personally was doing, and was consumed with the challenges that change involved. Although there have been exceptions, frequently each agency was only vaguely aware that another agency was involved and, if aware, tended to see the other agency's involvement as unrelated, unhelpful, or even as counterproductive to its own efforts. Many therapists are even trained to back away from cases where they do not have complete control, where someone else is involved and giving advice to the family.

While child welfare agencies have benefited from the services provided by the mental health agencies, and the mental health agencies have benefited from the client flow of child welfare agencies, both have had little understanding of the roles and expectations of their counterpart. While mental health counselors[1] have been expected to comply with the reporting statutes for families referred to their agency, there has been little discussion or guidance regarding the specificity of services needed to assist families with high-risk behavior. Child welfare caseworkers have tended to rely on therapists to "know what was best" for a client, thus providing them only minimal assessment or case-planning data. Since the caseworker has too often left treatment up to the therapist, outcome skills were rarely if ever discussed.

A typical and common contact between a child protective service caseworker (CW) and a mental health therapist (TH) has gone something like this:

CW: *Hello. This is Jane Doe of Social Services. I referred the Smith family to you a month ago. I was wondering, how are they doing?*

TH: *Oh yes, the Smith family, the mother and son case. Yes, actually they are doing quite well. The family has been to see me three times already. They had to reschedule one appointment but they seem to be very interested in continuing our work together.*

CW: *So they came in? That's great, I was worried they wouldn't show. That's great. I know it's early, but what do you think?*

TH: *Well, I've been very impressed with their interest in coming to counseling. You know most of these court- ordered cases are just not invested in change. The Smiths at least are coming regularly.*

CW: *Great! So what are they working on?*

TH: *Well, they are beginning to really open up and starting to communicate their feelings to each other. I've been trying to get the mother to not just yell at her son and she seems to be trying to do this more.*

CW: *That's encouraging. Is the boy still getting into trouble?*

TH: *I don't think so, at least Mom seems to think things are better. She hasn't mentioned anything anyway.*

CW: *That's good news, will you continue to see them?*
TH: *Oh yes. They should be in twice next month.*
CW: *Good. Well, let me know if something comes up. Talk to you soon.*

This was a cordial and respectful exchange, and it did provide some valuable information for the caseworker that would need to be documented, i.e., the family is attending, they have kept all but one appointment, they are scheduled to continue, and there is apparently some movement toward change. This is all valuable information to case management. Before discussing what is not conveyed in this conversation, it should be noted that often workers do not provide, ask for, or receive even this much information. Often the working assumption is that if either side doesn't hear from the other, then the assumption is "No news is good news."

However, the information gained and transmitted in this phone call is not nearly enough to assist the caseworker to be able to gauge safety or progress toward safety. For instance, the conversation doesn't reference why the case is open, who and under what conditions someone is at risk. Some of the questions the conversation could have referenced are as follows:

- What situations do you and the family consider high risk?
- Have those situations gone any differently lately?
- What is the family's current safety plan if they get into trouble?
- How will the family know when it is headed for trouble, i.e., what are their warning signals?
- What have you and the family learned about their problem pattern?
- Do they have a preliminary prevention plan sketched out?
- What should I [caseworker] be asking them about?
- What should I remind them if they call and are escalating?
- Is there something they would like me to notice and support if I see it?

The questions are so numerous due to the lack of specificity about outcome in the scenario depicted. The conversation also reflects the disadvantage the therapist is under when he or she is not provided details of the originating problem pattern. It would have been helpful for instance for the therapist to be provided details of what actually happened that caused the case to be opened. This problem pattern description would have led to a discussion of the outcome objectives, both for the family tasks with which the family is currently having difficulty and the outcome objectives for the individuals within the family. A case would not have been opened if the behavior of a family member did not put other family members at risk. The caseworker will be making decisions about whether or not the child will be able to stay with the mother based on the family's ability to accomplish those objectives and demonstrate that they have learned some specific prevention skills that will help them prevent further recurrence of the conflict problems. If the therapist isn't made aware of the target outcome skills, he/she will be working at great disadvantage.

GATHERING BASIC INFORMATION
ABOUT THE REFERRAL

Although families and therefore family situations certainly vary, there are still some common elements of case information that should accompany every case referred to a treatment provider.[2] These common elements may have to be sought and organized by the treatment provider because the information is not always provided as a matter of course. It is often helpful for the therapist to consider the caseworker as a customer or client, one whom they want to be completely satisfied with the services that are provided. Indeed, when the therapist does not adopt this attitude early on in the referral process, the mutual client may later pay for the mistake. A "service" attitude also ensures that the therapist is in a good position to get the kind of information that will be most useful to collaboration and therefor useful to the client family. A client is ill served when the therapist and worker disagree on what needs to change and what constitutes progress. If there are issues of opinion, it is better to air them early, when they can be addressed in the case plan as a win-win situation, rather than let the client get caught in the middle of a professional disagreement.

The issues the treatment provider should try to ascertain at the time of referral revolve around what happened, how it happened, how it is thought about, what plans have been made to remedy the situation, and what will constitute evidence of change.

WHAT HAPPENED?

Doesn't it seem obvious that this question should be answered at the time of a referral? After all, the family was going along without social services contact and then something happened or was discovered that led to an investigation or assessment and a case was opened. Something rather specific must have happened: someone was hit, someone wasn't fed, someone went to school with hair lice, someone ran away—i.e., something happened. Surprisingly therapists often get summary statements regarding the family that usually are based on a deficit theory of causality. For instance, the therapist might be told, "We think the mother has a drug problem," "The father is a real bad apple and she just won't leave him," or "The mother is just so negative with the child, I don't think she really loves the child or wants to be a mother." Yes, but what happened?

Knowing the event or events that led to the case being opened is critical to grounding the problems the family faces in everyday life, and makes the problems more manageable. It also provides a real-life example that is relevant to the family, for the therapist to explore the details of how the family moves from being "on the edge" to being "over the edge." Tracking the sequence of interaction around a specific interaction that led to trouble allows the therapist and family to describe their problem pattern. Without this information, the family and therapist will be unable to develop specific plans to prevent recurrence of the problem pattern. In summary, the first and most important piece of information the therapist must collect from the caseworker is what specifically happened that led to the case being opened. If caseworkers have been changed or somehow this information isn't known, then the therapist will have to search this information out. Without the referral source providing the therapist information about what actually happened (i.e., the sequence of events around the presenting problem) the therapist (using our previous example) may be stuck with a contract to cure the drug problem, get the woman to leave her man, or get the mother to truly love her children.

WHAT IS THE SAFETY PLAN?

Let's say that whatever happened has now been established and that there has been a thorough tracking of the events that led up to the problem. That problem definition should have resulted in the intake worker or caseworker setting up a *safety plan* with the family, a plan specifically based on the high-risk situation(s) the family has been facing. The safety plan should be more than just a verbal agreement with the family, it should be written with the family's input and signed by them, indicating their intention to carry it out. Ideally this safety plan would call for short-term actions that ensure the safety and well-being of all family members. By necessity, it can't be based on long-term prevention because family members will have only a beginning knowledge of their problem pattern and will have little awareness of anything but the latest warning signals. The family is still at risk because their only plan (the safety plan) is based on their current ability to intervene rather late in their buildup pattern. If therapists are not aware of the safety plan they cannot ask about it or continue to reinforce its use until earlier measures can be developed by the family members. When the therapist asks about the safety plan, the family also sees the therapist as equally concerned about safety issues. The client family takes their cues from the therapist regarding what is important to discuss in their meetings, i.e., when the therapist asks about safety the family talks about safety.

HOW HAS THE PROBLEM BEEN DEFINED
WITH THE FAMILY?

How the family thinks about the problem is critical to what they will be willing to do about it. This concept is very familiar to therapists who have typically studied interviewing techniques such as reframing or relabeling (Minuchin and Fishman, 1981). The idea is simply that the family need to think about the problem in such a way that guides them to new solutions versus the old ineffective problem solutions they keep trying. Earlier in this text, considerable attention was given to the benefits of developmental definitions of problems in the family. By helping the family identify their collective developmental problem (e.g., trying to get small children organized, or setting rules and consequences for teenagers), the family can work together on resolving their issues without overfocusing on the weaknesses of any given member. Family-level objectives, stated in the family's own terms (e.g., Our Get Organized Plan) provide commonsense targets within their everyday family life for their treatment efforts. In addition, certain individual family members need to make specific plans to change their at-risk behavior. This means individual objectives need to be written that focus their attention on this task and provide a common everyday way to talk about the problem behavior (e.g., My Keep Cool Plan or My Keep the Blues Away Plan).

If this framing of the family- and individual-level objectives has already occurred with the work of the caseworker, then the therapist will want to be "brought up to date" by the family and/or caseworker. This ideal situation allows the therapist to be educated by the family about their problems and plans and positions the therapist to continue in a consultant's role versus the role of the expert who is supposed to fix them. If the problem has not been formulated in everyday life terms, then the therapist will have to develop developmental objectives with the family and seek concurrence with the caseworker. Many therapists make the mistake of simply making their own judgments about how the problem should be defined and not realizing that their ideas are in competition with the views of so many others in the system. With disparate views about the problem, there will be disparate views about what outcome should look like. Sometimes families experience shifting views of what is expected of them, e.g., working to attend a class only to realize later that something else is expected of them. The therapist is in a key role to ensure that differences over problem definition are settled early and that the presenting difficulties remain in focus.

What Will be Considered Evidence of Change?

Concurrence on problem definition will lay the groundwork for a discussion of what change will look like when the family is successful in treatment. Unfortunately, evidence that change has occurred is often left up to mere stated opinion, rather than a documented history of accomplishing specific tasks. Although this chapter will later address the process for therapists to document change, at the time of referral it is important to clarify what the worker and the courts will be looking for as evidence of change. This can be somewhat difficult to do with a caseworker who has not thought through this question. Many times caseworkers will not want to be "pinned down" to specific behavior because they have not "pinned down" the problem definition. Nonetheless, it is an important part of the conversation to have at referral. Phrases such as "being a better mother" or "coming to terms with her prior abuse history" are rather vague answers to this question. Rather statements like "She needs to set rules and stick by them" or "She needs to take specific steps to keep her daughter safe from abuse" are much more on target.

SAMPLE DIALOGUE AT THE TIME OF REFERRAL

Because the conversations at the beginning of a referral are so important to framing how the case will proceed, a sample conversation between the referring caseworker and the therapist is provided below. In this particular instance, the caseworker has done a good job of developing a partnership, focusing on everyday life events, and has prepared the family members for the need to learn some specific prevention skill:

CW: *Hello. This is Jane Doe of Social Services. I referred the Smith family to you a week ago. I was wondering, have they come in yet?*

TH: *Oh yes, the Smith family, the mother and son case. No they haven't come in yet; actually they are scheduled for day after tomorrow. I'm glad you called. What is their situation?*

CW: *They are a court case, I am the ongoing worker and have only had the case a week or so myself; the intake worker is the one who made the referral to you actually.*

TH: *Oh. Do we know what happened?*

CW: *I talked with the intake worker and evidently the boy ran away to the neighbors after the stepfather smacked him in the mouth. The neighbor called the police, I guess the boy's lips were bleeding. When the police came they called us and we placed the boy temporarily with his grandmother, who lives just around the corner.*

TH: *Do we know much about what led up to this event? It's obvious the step-father has some problems controlling his anger, but what was happening in the family, what were they trying to do at the time, do we know? [looking for family objective]*

CW: *Well, as a matter of fact, the intake worker really did a nice job of interviewing this family. She backed them up to how the day started, etc., and got them to describe how things just kept getting more and more tense. Evidently, this is a real stubborn kid and the mom can't get him to do a lot of stuff. It was a Saturday and they were all home, all day, and she said she had been yelling at the kids all day . . .*

TH: *There is more than one kid?*

CW: *Yes, this son Michael is eight, but she has a second son, who is three, with this man. Anyway, she had been yelling at them all day and trying to keep them quiet because the father had worked late the night before. I think there also was an issue with the father drinking because no drinking was targeted on the safety plan.*

TH: *Is he an alcoholic?*

CW: *No, I don't think so, but he had had a couple of beers that day while working on his car in the backyard and the mother says he is less patient when he drinks.*

TH: *OK. So they had been arguing all day over household stuff and then the stepfather had been drinking some, and then do we know what happened next?*

CW: *Evidently Michael spit his food out at the dinner table when his mother told him to eat his greens. The stepfather just whacked him one with the back of his hand and knocked him out of the chair, split his lip, and from there on it was a real scene.*

TH: *So that's what happened. That really helps me.*

CW: *Well, I really like this intake worker. She got them to buy into this whole thing with them needing help on managing the behavior of the kids, and then she even got the stepfather to accept that he needed help with his anger so that he doesn't lose it again [how the problem is defined]. You'll see this stuff in their case plan, I sent you a copy, but I also gave them one to bring you. They are supposed to come up with a family plan they call their Teach Our Kids to Behave Plan [family-level objective] and then the stepfather is supposed to work on his Keep Cool Plan [individual-level objective]. Evidently he has always had a temper but feels he has been able to manage it. But he says he has been under a lot of stress lately, something at work, and that evidently this was a high-risk time for him. He says he just popped; I checked him out, he doesn't have any record that we could find. He seems workable to me but obviously we are pretty concerned about what he could do. There are not reports of domestic violence but who knows about that, you know?*

TH: *Right. Well, this is really very helpful. I really like the way this case has been defined and it sounds like I can just pick up where you two left off. I guess you are still going to be checking on them regularly?*

CW: *Oh yes, in fact, the case plan calls for them to have a written plan for each of their objectives within two weeks. I know that doesn't give you much time but we feel they need some sort of prevention plan in place to start working on because right now that son is still at Grandma's, and she is kind of old, if you know what I mean.*

TH: *Oh, I'm glad you mentioned that. I almost forgot to ask you what the safety plan calls for or if I'll get a copy of that? [inquiring about the safety plan]*

CW: *Absolutely. I sent you a copy but it basically says that the son will stay with the grandmother, and that no corporal punishment will be used, and that the stepfather will not drink more than one beer while around the children—that was his idea. It's a start.*

TH: *Well, again, this is really a nice referral when a case comes to me like this. Please say something to the intake worker, will you?*

CW: *Oh sure.*

TH: *And thank you as well. This is really set up well. Let me ask you about what you are thinking in terms of documenting change. We'll have some kind of plan for the family and for the stepfather within two weeks, and that will be written, and those plans will have some specific tasks that they will be doing to implement their plans. If we were to record somehow their accomplishment or nonaccomplishment of each of those tasks, would that give you the kind of information you need to make a decision about returning the boy home, etc.? [inquiring about evidence of change]*

CW: *Absolutely. In fact, you'll notice when you get the case plan that it calls for just that sort of thing. That would be great—it will also give me something to ask about when I go out to see them. I'll ask them to go over it with me each time.*

TH: *Sounds great. OK. I guess that's about it, isn't it? I'll see them in a couple of days and we will be able to get right to work I think. There is a men's group here of fathers who are working on parenting, and anger control is part of that group. He may be right for that group and if so, I'll let you know.*

CW: *Sounds perfect. Might make it easier for him to go if he had others working on the same thing. If he does, would you please let the therapist of the group know about the need for a written action plan for him, the "Keep Cool" thing?*

TH: *You bet.*

CW: *Great. I just don't want that to get lost. Hey, thanks for taking the case and I'll be in touch.*

TH: *OK. Thank you. Talk to you soon!*

Not every referral conversation will go this smoothly because in this conversation, both professionals were working from similar conceptual maps. In fact, the intake worker also was following a solution-based approach to assessment and case planning. But that is the point we hope to make here: when the assessment, casework, and treatment team all work from a conceptual model that anchors family problems in their everyday life, then the possibility for collaboration is greatly increased. Even when this occurs as in the example above, the reader will note that all parties still need to stay focused on pertinent data such as what actually happened, what the safety plan was, how the problem has been framed, and what will constitute evidence of change. Although the therapist could have started the case without any of this information (and often does), the chance of future problems in the treatment and collaboration would have gone up considerably.

Caseworker's Role in the Referral Conversation

Having and using a clear conceptual map that guides the worker to focus on what needs to happen in order to close a case is the first step to managing a case and thus managing treatment providers. Although many caseworkers do not see themselves in the role of managing treatment, they inevitably assume that role if they are not satisfied with the direction of therapy. If they don't manage on the front end of a referral, then they will be forced to make decisions when they are much more difficult, some of which may not favor the family. For instance, when the treatment does not focus on preparing the family to manage difficult situations they face in their lives, then the worker will end up holding the family accountable for the lack of change. While other alternatives may be sought to put off more drastic action, the partnership relationship with the family is inevitably weakened and the potential for adversarial relationships increases. And, of course, since the family is not focusing on acquiring necessary prevention skills, vulnerable family members are still at risk. In short, the consequences for assuming that "everything will be OK now that they are in therapy" are quite serious. The worker who is preparing to call a treatment provider regarding a referral will want to remember what information will be important for the therapist and to organize his/her thoughts so that the therapist will be able to recognize the critical elements regarding a family. There is always so much that could be said that it is important to proactively choose what is said.

Therapist's Role in the Referral Conversation

The therapist must take an active role in requesting and organizing the information that is presented regarding a case. Not every worker will organize the family's information around family developmental objectives and related individual objectives. Nor will every caseworker place importance on the details of interaction around the originating problem pattern. By respectfully asking questions that guide the conversation toward the information that is needed, the therapist is able to assist the caseworker in organizing all the possible data about the family. By further emphasizing recognizable themes that emerge from the conversation such as "so the family has difficulty with the morning routine," the therapist helps draw attention to a developmental framing of the presenting problem. This is, of course, more difficult when only one side of the conversation is working this way. However, the therapist will recognize that he/she has experience doing this with the families with 'whom he/she works, and the approach is very similar. The therapist must be listening for, and acquiring if necessary, the information that will eventually best serve the client. That information must include a description of what needs to change and what the caseworker will be looking for as evidence that change has occurred.

OFFERING SERVICES TO MIRROR FAMILY DEVELOPMENTAL NEEDS

Group and educational formats are not new to mental health. For treatment as well as economic reasons, it has always made sense to offer formats that spread therapist time over several clients and tap the strengths and resources of others with similar problems. Many of these formats have included classes in general parenting, nurturing, living with an alcoholic, and anger management. These formats can be used to further expand and specialize course offerings in family life education.

Introduce More Family Life Education Formats

From a casework perspective, services would be most useful if they were built around the specific developmental tasks that families face. The classes would be very short to ensure that family members would not have to spend a lot of unnecessary time in them and away from everything else they have to do. Obviously, many families could use more time in learning, but providers should always remember that client families are already overtaxed in their ability to meet all the needs of the family without the additional burden that treatment appointments add. Efforts should be made to develop formats that deliver specific information in as short an amount of time as reasonable and at times that are convenient to the family, not the agency. Some suggested subjects that would represent a developmental approach to family life education appear in Figure 9-1.

These minicourses are not intended to replace one-on-one coaching (therapy) but to offer an entry point that makes sense to the family,

Figure 9.1. Suggested subjects representing a developmental approach to family life education.

Family Life Topics Needed	Individual Topics Needed
• Managing mornings • Organizing the after-school hours • Making mealtimes go better • Getting young children off to bed • Toilet training 101 • Using time out effectively • Ten things that work with ADHD kids • Setting up family chores • Rules and consequences for teens • Conducting family meetings • Supervising young children • Supervising teenagers • Tips for parents of sexually reactive children • Tips for parents of physically harmed children • Keeping conflict from getting out of control • Improving school attendance • Improving school performance • Helping with homework • Making blended families work • Keeping the family clean and hazard free	• Learning to manage anger problems • Keeping discouragement from getting to you • Maintaining a sober lifestyle • Maintaining a drug-free lifestyle • Preventing harmful expressions of anger • Keeping the past from influencing our parenting • Managing discouragement and disappointment • Maintaining a clean house • Getting and keeping a job • Staying in school and out of trouble • Improving my school performance • Using good personal hygiene • Living independently • Staying healthy and happy • Having a healthy baby • Proving I am responsible and trustworthy • Resigning from an abusive lifestyle

provides them basic information that is immediately applicable to their situation, and emphasizes the universality of family stress points. These classes are then followed up by individualized work on the family's or individual's specific plan to address their difficulty (see next section).

Ensure That Treatment Produces a Product (Prevention Plan)

Critical to any reorganizing efforts made by an agency providing services to social services clients is to adopt a "produce a product" attitude to each and every family life educational service it provides. This simply means that every client in every class would produce a personal action plan to apply the lessons of the class in his/her own family situation (see Figure 9-2 for an example).

This personal product would ensure that a specific written plan for the

Figure 9.2. Example of a personal action plan.

	(The client names plan of action)	
	John's Keep Cool Plan	

High Risk Situations
- **Being tired or worn down**
- **Discussing rules with family**
- **Not being able to do what I planned on**
- **People raising their voices at me**

Early and Late Warning Signals
- **Feeling criticized**
- **Thinking that nobody cares**
- **Chest gets tight**
- **Want to hit something**

Who	What needs to be done	By When
John	Will get to bed on weeknights so that he has a least 7 hours of sleep	Daily
	Will talk about family rules during the day when they are not arguing over a specific event	Within one week
	Will keep up his exercise program so that he feels good about himself	M-W-F
	Spend some time with his Dad working on the old car instead of sleeping on Saturdays	2 weekends a month
	Will remind himself that he agreed to the rules earlier and they aren't trying to be unfair	When he feels picked upon
	Remind himself what happens if he starts to get upset and go back to his room to cool off	When his chest gets tight
	Write in his journal his thoughts so he can tell his therapist about it later	Every time he feels the old anger

client to follow would emerge from the very initial treatment efforts. It could, of course, be put into immediate practice and revised and improved upon with the aid of the ongoing therapist. Time is an important element to keep in mind for all parties in the partnership. The family is subject to court scrutiny, the worker has to make decisions regarding risk levels, and the therapist has limited time and resources available to spend with any one client family. Additionally, a prevention plan product will help the family and therapist meet the needs of the case plan and provide an ongoing format for sharing detailed information regarding documented change.

Figure 9.3. Documentation chart based on prevention plan illustrated in Figure 9.2.

John's Keep Cool Plan

	2/4	2/5	2/6	2/7	2/8	2/9	2/10	2/11	2/12	2/13	2/14
Got at least 7 hours of sleep	✓	✓		✓				✓	✓	✓	✓
Followed family rules w/o incident	✓	✓	✓			✓	✓	✓	✓		
Exercised (MWF)	✓		✓					✓		✓	
Spent time with Dad (Saturday only)						✓					
Used personal time out plan if needed				✓		✓					
Made a journal entry				✓		✓					

Document Accomplishment of Prevention
Plan Tasks

The third step that could be taken to organize service offerings to best meet the needs of social service clients is to ensure that every case plan for every client is broken down into tasks that are measured in some written way. Charting or journaling are excellent vehicles for recording and documenting the accomplishment of specific tasks within a prevention plan. For instance, if the plan calls for the parent to use time-out instead of spanking, then that task should be measured on a daily basis (i.e., number of situations on a given day that time-out was used instead of spanking). Figure 9-3 illustrates a documentation chart based on the prevention plan previously illustrated in Figure 9-2.

Documenting change is critical for the family. The family has a problem that goes beyond the one that required a case to be opened on them. That larger problem has to do with their reputation with others, the courts, the schools, the social services, and even themselves. The family have lived with this "old story" about them for a considerable amount of time and need hard data to help convince others that a "new story" about them has emerged. Service coordination meetings go remarkably more smoothly if providers and caseworkers don't have to argue about whether a family has changed certain behavior. If efforts have been made to change that behavior, they should have been recorded and documented. Although such documentation is not insurance that old behaviors won't return, it is, at the very least, a daily reminder to the family members of what tasks they have decided to implement to create change in their family. Everyday they must answer the question of whether a certain task was done. This focusing helps target the specific behaviors that will lead to relapse prevention.

OVERVIEW OF STEPS TO PREVENTION

Although this text offers a complete description to the relapse prevention process elsewhere,[3] a summary of the steps is offered here for those readers who are using only this chapter as a study guide.

These steps are used by caseworkers as a conceptual map for organizing what needs to occur for high-risk families to ensure safety and well-being for their members. Figure 9-4 illustrates this four-step process and the skills that accompany each step of the process.

The therapist will hopefully enter the family's work after the caseworker has assisted the family in an initial recognition of their problem pattern. Therapists familiar with substance abuse counseling or anger management counseling will recognize the basic elements of a relapse

Figure 9.4.   Four-step process and skills for relapse prevention.

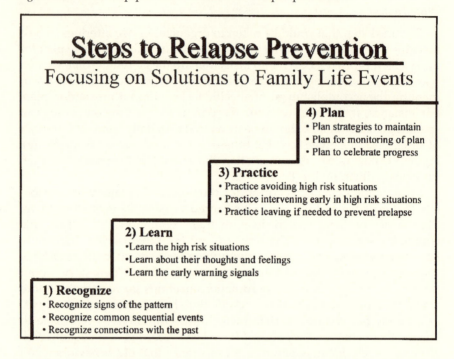

prevention model. Based in a cognitive-behavior model, the approach is meant to help clients (1) recognize that there is a pattern to their high-risk behavior, (2) learn all they can about that pattern, and then (3) start to practice small steps of alternative behavior. The final step is (4) to take everything they have learned about their pattern and develop a long-term prevention plan that will help them either avoid high-risk situations or keep them from escalating out of control. The following sections offer some advice on the therapist's role in helping their clients learn the details of their patterns, practice small steps of change, and come up with detailed written prevention plans.

HELPING CLIENTS LEARN THE DETAILS
OF THEIR PATTERNS

As therapists know very well, individuals and families who are engrossed in maladaptive behavior generally have little knowledge of their individual and collective actions, how they contribute to escalating conflict, and when they are prone to destructive behavior. Without assistance, some may be unable to recognize gradations in their emotions, or to identify the conditions in which they are prone to violence. A similar cycle can be identified with neglect: the guardian(s) may report constant fatigue and be unable to identify any events, thoughts, or feelings that led to his/her depressed state, let alone identify exceptions to his/her motivation. Therefore, developing the ability to recognize and understand that behaviors are embedded in interactional patterns is the first step in reducing recurrence of maladaptive conduct. When clients engage in a conversation that helps them to recognize key sequences, previously unnoticed adaptive and maladaptive behavior becomes obvious.

Illuminating triggering events has the advantage of obvious relevance to the family, and also begins the process of building accountability. The aim is to thoroughly diagram the vulnerable and explosive moments within the life of the family. The process of identifying and exploring specific destructive interactions in a family often creates a defensive and protective response by the family. The family and sometimes the caseworker may have a desire to place blame as a way to deal with this stress. Instead, when professionals and families engage in a disarming, solution-oriented conversation about (1) the challenges in everyday life, (2) specific high-risk behavior, and (3) how they can draw on their resources to prevent further conflict, transgressors are more apt to begin activities that lead to accepting responsibility, and fully engage in the change process.

Entrenched, nonproductive patterns can be thought of as cyclical in nature (Lane, 1997) and self-perpetuating. Assisting clients in mapping their patterned behavior (cycle work) is a powerful assessment and case-planning tool. Because cycle work is considered intrinsic to a solution-based approach to casework, it is essential that the therapist, client, and caseworker all be familiar with the tool. Although many practitioners have developed their own version of this tool, Figure 9-5 offers an example of the common elements of most.

A *triggering event* (e.g., comment, thought, act of omission) initiates an escalation of tension. This might be as simple as being spoken to with a raised voice, a critical comment, or simply being ignored. The thoughts and emotions that follow triggering events often include a sense of injustice and are frequently self-punitive (e.g., "I'll never be loved," "Why does this happen to me?" "It's not fair"). This *early buildup* phase typically involves blaming others. In high-risk situations, tension often mounts within the individual, as manifested in physical signs (e.g., muscle tension, rapid heart rate), fantasy, and the construction of excuses (*late buildup*). In problem-saturated individuals and families, the release of tension is often manifested in some sort of *harmful incident,* such as self-abuse, aggressive retribution, or a symbolic act meant to punish both self and others (e.g., sexual promiscuity). Typically, the process includes a *justi-*

Figure 9.5. The common elements of mapping clients' patterned behavior.

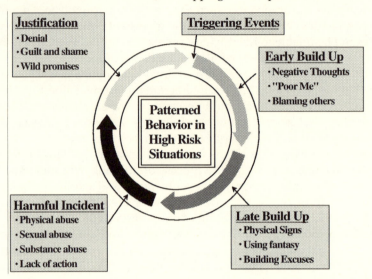

fication phase in which the individual attempts to exonerate his/her action and avoid responsibility and/or to pacify those involved by apologizing.

Assessment questions that assume change will occur are empowering and generally create a willingness to discuss the sequential details of maladaptive patterns. For instance, individuals are more apt to participate in a conversation about productive solutions when the question posed to them is "When you have dealt with similar conflict in a manner that you feel good about, what exactly did you do?" Or "If this problem you have with temper disappeared one day, how would you handle similar situations? What exactly would you do?" Therapists may be aware of other versions of questions that assume competence, anticipate change, and forecast positive outcomes. These familiar techniques will blend well with a solution-based approach to relapse prevention.

In summary, the first step in this process from a treatment point of view is to assist the family members in learning as much about the way they and their family escalate in high-stress or high-risk situations. Once they are familiar with their problem pattern, then they can begin the process of experimenting with small steps that intervene in that pattern.

HELPING CLIENTS PRACTICE SMALL STEPS OF CHANGE

An old cliché states, "Casework is hard by the yard but a cinch by the inch." Although this expression is probably common to many professions, it does seem that all things must be manageable in order to be accomplished. As the family members become increasingly aware of the interactional pattern during their high-risk situations, they will want to change their behavior. It is very empowering for families to learn the power of changing one small behavior and to find that a whole different outcome can result.

A particular key to the safe management of stressful, high-risk life events is the ability of members to intervene early in their cycle. The therapeutic relationship offers a natural practice field for such efforts. This may take different forms throughout treatment. Early on, it may take the form of a debriefing after a cycle gets out of hand. Eventually, individuals can learn to routinely recognize early warning signals in a safe manner and they are better able to develop strategies that avoid high risk or, that failing, are able to interrupt their pattern effectively. Since all problems cannot be avoided and some are too difficult to interrupt, successful individuals also need plans to escape (leave safely) when all other options have failed (a safety plan).

Avoiding High-Risk Situations.

By avoiding high-risk situations, individuals and families enter fewer dangerous sequences and are therefore less frequently at risk. This requires practicing a series of alternative actions to entrenched routines based on detailed knowledge about high-risk situations. For instance, a mother recognized that she frequently loses her temper and argues with her daughter. She moved a step closer to creating a well thought out plan when she further identified the conditions surrounding her loss of control. She realized that these arguments only occurred when she and her daughter were alone in the house, typically on weekends when she had custody, and usually only late at night when both were tired and edgy. Through trial and error, she and her daughter learned to limit those times and have something fun scheduled when they did occur. This one change eliminated most of their potential arguments.

Interrupting High-Risk Situations.

Safety also depends on a predetermined plan once in the midst of a maladaptive sequence (i.e., when plans to avoid high-risk situations have faltered). As previously stated, this skill is critical and probably the most difficult to apply since it assumes that emotions have already begun to escalate. However, when families are prepared—when they discuss ahead of time how to intervene in high-risk situations—they can agree to a strategy that will interrupt the cycle. If an interruption plan is not identified proactively, behaviors can be misinterpreted and safe de-escalation of conflict is less likely. Families and individuals will need to practice implementing their plans to see if they will work at stressful times. One couple with a history of escalating arguments decided that when they found themselves in an argument over their finances (an old high-risk situation), one could call attention to the escalating cycle by waving a white handkerchief (each had found this a funny interruption in a previous argument). This small step signaled a postponement of the discussion until each felt ready to resume it safely or drop it altogether. An agreement of this nature must be practiced and obviously does not guarantee safety, yet is an important skill that interrupts destructive processes. The couple identified this solution strategy when asked, "When have you started an argument but then did something that kept it from escalating?"

Escaping High-Risk Situations.

Since even the best plans can fail, it is essential that family members prepare for those moments when behaviors suggest emerging loss of control and interruption seems unlikely. In these situations, the thrust of the plan is safety and avoidance of otherwise imminent relapse. This may involve practicing actions such as leaving the situation or calling a designated sponsor. Escape plans are usually the first plans put into place (safety plan), and are used until other strategies that interrupt the cycle earlier are created and tested through practice.

With each of these situations, the counselor plays an important role in helping individuals and families create, practice, and refine a relapse prevention plan. Each episode informs plan revision. For instance, if the intervention plan doesn't interrupt the escalating sequence, the worker can collect detailed pattern information and try something else. Obviously, families cannot expect conflict to be completely eliminated. Rather, they must focus on reducing the intensity and duration of conflict so that destructive behavior is reduced to a level at which everyone can be safe and cared for.

HELPING CLIENTS DEVELOP RELAPSE
PREVENTION PLANS

A key contribution of the therapist is the assistance provided the client in constructing a long-term plan to prevent relapse. This is a written plan that has evolved from experimenting with what works for the family members in terms of avoiding, interrupting, or escaping high-risk situations in their lives. In essence, it gets written each meeting as new details are learned about the problem patterns and new alternatives are created.

By documenting each of the tasks of the plans, the therapist and family create a written record of their journey together and can easily and confidently share the accomplishment (or lack of it) with the caseworker, courts, or schools.

SUMMARY OF SOLUTION-BASED INTERVIEWING TECHNIQUES

Interviewing techniques that are consistent with a solution-based approach can be drawn form a wide variety of therapeutic models. The following techniques are basic to solution-based casework and therefore are easily shared in a collaborative team effort. A fuller description with examples of each technique is provided in Chapter 10.

Normalize family struggles: Normalizing the family problems as part of the normal developmental processes that all families experience.

Search for exceptions to the pattern: Searching for and identifying any exceptions to the pattern.

Externalizing the problem: Referring to the problem as if it existed outside the client or family.

Tracking the problem pattern: Slowing down the description of a problem pattern or cycle to include details of thoughts, feelings, and actions.

Influence between session change: Using the time between sessions for more observation and discovery.

Old versus new t-charts: Using flipcharts to list the characteristics of the old way of doing things so that they can be differentiated from the new ways.

Scaling questions: Asking family members to give their best estimate of where on a scale of a given variable they might fall.

Time-oriented questions: Taking clients to another moment in time to advise themselves.

Expanding the audience for change: Ensuring an ever-expanding audience for awareness of the ongoing changes in the client's cognitive and behavioral skills.

Assessing problem pattern influence: Assessing the influence the problem has on the family and what influence the family has on the problem.

Reinforcing progress through credentialing: Reinforcing change and credentialing change from the earliest moment in therapy.

Celebrating rites of passage: Choosing to recognize significant progress with celebration and ritual to assist in securing lasting change.

STRATEGIES FOR COLLABORATION

Understand Your Colleague

As a therapist you may know that many caseworkers are reluctant to talk to mental health professionals in terms of what they expect for outcomes. For years their practice has been to send an individual to counseling or, better yet, for "intensive psychotherapy," and rely almost completely on the judgment of the therapist, psychologist, or psychiatrist. There has been a belief that therapy was not in the area of competence of caseworkers and therefore not theirs to question. Although some of this is changing, the therapist should not assume that because the worker did not ask they simply do not care. Quite the contrary, they may care a great deal but are too respectful to bring up issues so as not to "invade a therapist's turf." It is therefore helpful for the therapist to extend an interest in discussing the family with the caseworker and assist the worker in organizing the information by asking questions that elicit useful information.

In rural areas, there is more opportunity to know colleagues from a particular office because of the fewer numbers and lower turnover. With scheduled professional activities together, teamwork possibilities are greatly improved. Urban teams however have found innovative avenues for breaking down the professional walls. Many caseworkers and therapists have started monthly study teams that share articles and ideas on cases. New employees are then introduced to others in the system at these study groups. Collaborative teams that get to know each other obviously have a better chance of bridging the professional distances.

Talk Early and Often

As discussed earlier, it is critical for therapists to have contact with caseworkers at the time of referral. Also discussed was the type of conversation the collaborative team should have at referral. However, the conversations should not stop there. All members of the team must resist the "no news is good news" assumption that is so prevalent in a busy professional's life. "No news" is almost always bad news because it means that the team members are not communicating their efforts, not updating progress, not examining setbacks or lapses, and not reminding themselves what the original outcome objectives were. This lack of communication, even after a case has started out correctly, not only puts collaboration at risk but also could put members of the team into an adversarial relationship. With different data, lack of a shared mission, and pressures unique to each side, the potential for developing conflictual positions is always present. Many therapists have found themselves sitting at a conference table in heated discussion with caseworkers over whether someone is "really working," "a threat to their kids," or "deserves more services." These adversarial positions cannot be totally avoided but almost always mean that the therapist and caseworker have not talked often enough about their team efforts. One side or the other has become frustrated with carrying the responsibility alone and is now mad at the family rather than the problem.

Creating an Audience for Change. How soon can progress be noted? Many therapists are cautious when answering this question, as are many caseworkers. They are waiting for the "other shoe to drop" and do not want to look foolish. These professionals are locked into a conceptual map that goes back to the disease model, i.e., the disease is not gone as long as any of its symptoms remain. Based on this old model, the professional is always on a "search and destroy mission" for signs of the disease (problem behavior). But from a solution-based approach to relapse prevention, the professional understands that the new behavior (healthy behavior) is already present in the person's life: it is just not sufficiently applied during high-risk situations. They also understand that the old behavior will also remain a potential in the person after the treatment work is done. However, it will be under more control, will be less intense, and won't last as long. The criterion changes from "present or not" to "affecting family life or not."

So when is it too early to notice change? The simple answer from a solution-based approach is that it is never too early. In fact, the therapist should assume that change has already begun before the client family came to see him/her. This might be a result of the referral, the safety plan, or often the family's own efforts to get control of the problem. Searching for solutions, the therapist inquires about change that has already occurred prior to attending counseling. Since the therapist wants to draw attention to that change, he/she may ask the client whether anyone has noticed the new behavior or attitude. The therapist assumes that the old behavior is still a significant risk for the family member, and may always be a risk for them. However, by attending to the new behavior, the therapist becomes an initial audience for the emerging new story about the client. The next critical question is, "Who else needs to know this is occurring? Does your caseworker know? Let's call him." Celebrating change need not wait until the new skill is safely acquired: an awareness of risk and encouraging progress can and should go hand in hand. Obviously, this gives the therapist and caseworker something to talk about and notice.

Share Lapses in a Specific and Timely Manner

It is not unusual in the life of a protective service case for the focus of services to digress or wander. Time alone is a risk factor in ongoing cases and it takes considerable effort just to keep everything on track. Therefore the reliance of the entire partnership on the case plan is critical. Sharing progress and difficulties in a specific and timely manner is best done with specific references to the particular tasks that were supposed to occur in the client's prevention plans.

If a client is having difficulty documenting his/her efforts around a specific task (e.g., charting the times he/she feeds the baby), then the partnership should consider that difficulty a lapse back into risk behavior and the documentation issue should trigger contact between team members. This timely response to a lapse into the old pattern is contrasted with the policy of waiting to contact team members until a true relapse has occurred. The latter tendency to wait until there is a "problem" is reactive versus preventative and results in much more intrusive remedies.

When a family is working steadily on their issues, most therapists and caseworkers assume that there is nothing to contact each other about. However, from a solution-based perspective, it would be helpful to notice and capture exactly those times (exceptions). This is a list of possible issues for workers and providers to discuss at any time:

- What topics and situations are hot for them right now?
- On what developmental issues do they seem to do OK?
- How quickly are they able to recognize that tension is building?
- Are they able to recognize any thoughts that warn them escalation is near?
- What have they decided to do in order to avoid high-risk issues?
- What seems to work for them in these high-risk times?
- What are they going to try and do if they think tension is building?
- Have they had occasion to use their safety plan?

Invite Colleagues to Meetings

In an earlier chapter, family conferencing was discussed. *Family group decision-making, family unity,* and other similar processes are gaining attention as strategies for collaboration. *Community partnership, multiple response,* and *interdisciplinary service* are a few more from the same genre. These initiatives are bringing together agencies and local entities for the purpose of better coordination and service to families in need of protective service. The co-location of services has simplified the access to services and has been one of the keys to their success.

However, most therapists and workers do not work in an integrated service setting and must take purposeful steps to work collaboratively. One of the ways therapists have found beneficial to collaboration is to encourage caseworkers to attend the first session with the family. This can help the therapy get started on the right foot, i.e., all key parties working together to reduce high risk and to form cooperative partnerships. Therapists and caseworkers who are open to these collaborative meetings will significantly enhance casework services.

NOTES

1.   The terms "counselor," "therapist," and "treatment provider" will be used interchangeably throughout this chapter to refer to someone providing treatment, counseling, or guidance to the client.

2.   Because the previous chapters have detailed case assessment and case planning, the main elements will only be summarized in this chapter for the treatment provider reader.

3.   See Chapter 5 for a complete discussion of the steps in relapse prevention.

Chapter 10

Solution-Based Interviewing Techniques

Students of practice, regardless of experience level, are often interested in the practical "nuts and bolts" of how to talk to a client family. It is not unusual for practitioners to say, "Just give me the words to actually say." While many in the field note that the words are not as important as the intent behind the words, the interest and need for specific practice in the "actual words" are nonetheless significant. While the authors certainly agree with those who argue that theoretical clarity coupled with client sensitivity and understanding will best guide practitioners to the words they need, we also have been "students of technique" and understand the benefit of hearing others piece together language that helps fulfill theory. This chapter is intended to take a step back from the conceptual map that guides a solution-based approach to assessment, case planning, and case management to place a special focus on those techniques that have emerged as useful in conducting the practice.

The techniques discussed have been drawn from the ongoing conversation within the profession, particularly from the influences of solution-focused therapy, family systems therapy, social constructivist therapy, and relapse prevention therapy. Although many of the techniques are discussed elsewhere in the text, they have been brought together and summarized in this chapter for further practice and clarification. They have been organized around the technique's most typical use and examples are provided to help the reader visualize appropriate uses. The chapter organizes technique into three categories: (1) techniques that help build a consensus about the problem, (2) techniques that enhance interest in early signs of change, and (3) techniques that help anchor change within the "new" or emerging self. The organizational grid is offered as a learning guide and not intended to represent an exclusive method for organizing the techniques or to imply that the techniques could not be used to accomplish alternative objectives. Each technique will first be defined and described and then will be placed in several scenarios to help build a context for its use. Verbatim examples will be used, occasionally repeating examples used elsewhere in the text where we viewed repetition as potentially helpful. In attempt to further locate the technique in practice, common pitfalls for the use of each technique will be discussed. The chapter concludes with a descriptive list of resources that the student of technique might wish to pursue to further their understanding and familiarity with the techniques.

TECHNIQUES THAT BUILD A CONSENSUS ABOUT THE PROBLEM

A true partnership relationship assumes that all parties agree on what the partnership is supposed to accomplish. Partnerships in which one party decides for the other what the objective is going to be are inherently unstable. While such one-sided partnerships do exist in the world and it is acknowledged that they can accomplish some things, they usually only work when there is some third-party external threat to the parties that forces them into a temporary alliance. For the sake of survival, the threatened parties will team up. However, such an alliance is usually short-lived, narrow in scope, and guarded. We review this phenomenon because many caseworkers new to solution-based casework have difficulty giving up their old habit of simply telling the family what they have to do in order to satisfy the courts. These caseworkers know that this approach has worked for them in the past, at least in many cases. Of course, the same approach also was ineffective in many more cases, caused considerable risk to family members when it didn't work, and led to highly contentious battles with still others. Some workers used to the "I know what the family needs to change" approach often think that consensus would take too long to achieve (i.e., "I don't have time to beat around the bush with these people"). Of course, they don't recall the hours and hours of their time, supervisory time, court time, and placement time that have been spent trying to manage adversarial cases. Building a consensus around the problem takes less time than arguing with someone over whose view of the problem will win out. The following techniques have been developed with this objective in mind. Conceptually, the techniques are natural extensions of the belief that the family, similar to other families at the same stage of development, is struggling to meet certain common developmental challenges. The techniques of normalizing the problem, externalizing the problem, searching for exceptions to the problem, and tracking the problem combine to help the practitioner and family build a working definition of the problem.

NORMALIZING

Description of the Technique

Normalizing the family problems as part of the normal developmental process that all families experience is at the heart of this technique. It is meant to convey to the client family that they are not alone in experiencing this trouble, that it is somewhat understandable given their stage of the family life cycle, and that since others have gone through this challenge there is hope that there is some knowledge that could be tapped to assist resolution of their struggles.

Context for Its Use

Normalization of family strife is usually the first response to the family's description of their troubles. The family is carefully studying the reaction of the worker to their story and therefore first responses can often direct the relationship toward success or contention. The technique can range from simple facial expressions that say, "I understand what you have been facing," "When it rains it pours," or "Aren't they something at this age?" to verbal expressions of the same.

Normalization language and expressions continue to shape consensus when family comments are summarized back to them for confirmation. The following are examples of summarizing comments that place the problem description within a normal context:

- So your child is at those terrible twos we all hear about, and it has been really stressing you out, as it would any mother, and you have tried lots of different things to help her but right now nothing seems to be working?
- So she came in late after curfew, and like any parent of a teenager you were concerned for her safety. So many parents feel like there is so much out there to be afraid of right now. And you tried to get that point across to her and then everything got out of hand? This is such a difficult period.
- You are caring for your mother at the same time you are trying to raise your own children? That usually leads to a lot of stress in any family. Has it in yours as well?

Common Pitfalls

The primary pitfall in the use of normalizing is the danger of normalizing abusive behavior by "explaining" it away as a normal response given the stress. Instead of normalizing the stress that put the family member at risk to do something they regret, the pitfall is to excuse the offensive behavior as a normal response:

- Wrong: It is understandable you hit your two-year-old given the stress you were under.
- Right: So many parents tell me that raising a two-year-old is so very stressful. How do you feel the stress has affected you?

EXTERNALIZING THE PROBLEM

Description of the Technique

When the practitioner refers to the problem as if it existed outside the client or family he/she is externalizing the problem. In essence, language is used to convey that the client and the worker are in partnership against the problem. One way the worker accomplishes this conceptually is to focus on that side or part of the client that wants to the overcome the problem. This does not mean that the client's behavior necessarily reflects this desire, i.e., the side of the client that wants the behavior to stop may not be very well developed at all. Nonetheless, when the worker attends to the side of the client that wants to put things right, the partnership is aided by language that externalizes the problem.

Context for Its Use

Externalization is used often as an extension of normalization. If the consensus developing early in the conversation (assessment) has been describing the difficulties of a certain life stage, it is a small step to refer to those difficulties as somewhat external to the family. Rather than saying, "You shouldn't have toilet trained her that way" (problem is within the individual), the worker can say, "So the whole toilet training thing is really testing your patience, and right now it is winning?" The latter response acknowledges the developmental nature of the problem, i.e., its universality, and frames the problem as external to the client. In essence, externalization gives the client some breathing room to save face and discuss the problem less defensively. Examples of externalizing language in different contexts are as follows:

- It sounds like you would like to be the one to put an end to this cycle of violence in your family, for the violence to end with you, to defeat it once and for all.

- This heavy weight that you describe holding you down and keeping you from being the kind of mom you always wanted to be, do you think this heavy weight is the problem? If we could somehow lift that, you could see a difference in what you could give to your children?
- You say that these troubles keep coming around and around, almost like they have your number. It is like a pattern or something (like a same-o, same-o; street language for "like the same old thing again") when you describe it, is that what we're facing?

Common Pitfalls

The two most common pitfalls are to use externalization language in ways that reduce responsibility for abusive behavior or that implicate a victim in causality. For instance, if the worker said, "So you are really a victim of miscommunication and misunderstanding," or "So her seductiveness eventually overwhelmed your self-control," the worker would be crossing the line from making a problem easier to discuss to colluding in the minimization of responsibility. The worker might respond in these situations more appropriately by saying "So sometimes your own thinking confuses you into thinking, 'This is OK'?" or "So this old problem of misreading someone else's actions sneaked up on you again . . . with tragic results this time?"

SEARCHING FOR EXCEPTIONS TO THE PATTERN

Description of the Technique

Searching for and identifying any exceptions to the problem pattern is a cornerstone technique to solution-based casework. The solution is, in fact, the exception to the problem. It is assumed that the problem behavior is experienced as all pervasive, but in fact there are many instances in which exceptions to the problem exist. The technique is simply one of asking questions that explore times when the problem doesn't occur.

Context for Its Use

Searching for exceptions usually begins early in the relationship and consensus-building stages of the casework. If practiced fairly early in the discussion, i.e., within the first telling of the story, clients get the message that the caseworker doesn't just assume negative beliefs about the family members. From an assessment point of view, the worker is curious about the difference between those times when the problem behavior occurs and those times when the family is somehow able to keep the problem from occurring. That difference can be highlighted in the case plan, so that the plan will build upon the client family's successes. Some examples of language that attempts to tease out exceptions to the problem pattern follow:

- Have you ever been in one of these difficult times and found a way to avoid this kind of trouble?
- Have you had smaller versions of this problem, but somehow avoided it getting this bad?
- When things are going well between you two, what are you usually doing, what is going on then?
- Was there ever a time when you didn't have this problem? What was different about those times?

Common Pitfalls

The most common pitfall is simply not searching for exceptions, simply forgetting that the family is not synonymous with their problems, being so consumed by an interest in the problems that they obscure the worker's ability to be curious about the rest of the family's life.

The second most common pitfall is to search for exceptions too early, before a family has been able to describe to you "how bad the situation really is." The risk in this pitfall is that the family may view the worker's attempts to understand exceptions as simple "Pollyanna" type of behavior, and may even believe that the worker can't handle hearing about the serious situation they face. This will be particularly true if the worker is younger than the client and thus "already suspect" in the client's eyes.

TRACKING THE PROBLEM PATTERN

Description of the Technique

Tracking a problem pattern is simply slowing down a description of a patterned interaction to assist the client in learning as much as possible about his/her vulnerability to behave in certain ways. The technique is used to increase clients' ability to recognize their high-risk situations, learn their early warning signals, and enhance their strategies for avoiding, interrupting, or escaping a dangerous behavioral pattern. The technique requires tactful interruption of a client's story about the problem in order to ask more and more details about the sequence of the client's thoughts, feelings, and behavioral responses during high-risk times.

Because the pattern details are very important and difficult to remember for both client and practitioner, they are typically recorded on paper or chalkboard for repeated reference.

Context for Its Use

This technique is included as a consensus builder because the time when tracking skills are used to help shape the client's understanding of their problem is early in assessment. Because clients will try to summarize their experience with the problem, important details are sacrificed for the sake of brevity. The more times a problem story is told, the more the individual will try to get to the point, i.e., I have a problem and it is very serious. Therefore the appropriate context for this technique is when the practitioner hears a client referencing a specific situation in which the problem occurred, but does not hear the critical details about the unfolding of that situation. This is not a difficult context to gauge because it occurs almost universally when the client begins to tell his/her story.

A related opportunity for using this technique occurs later in casework when the family, caseworker, and treatment provider team is fairly familiar with the problem and its pattern. The context will be one of progress in which family members have learned to increasingly avoid high-risk situations by recognizing their warning signals and taking some form of "evasive action." As has been discussed elsewhere in this text, change is not always continuous and there will be inevitable lapses in which the family members will encounter situations that are problematic or near problematic (lapses). When the practitioner hears a "summarized" description of the old problem pattern it is an ideal time to use tracking as a tool for examining the occurrence in more depth and detail. Oftentimes, by tracking the pattern in this context, the worker will be able to identify small signs of positive change that can be favorably compared to previous client experiences in similar situations.

Because this technique often requires a tactful interruption of the client's telling of his/her story, the following examples start with the client's words and then offer some possible worker language that would initiate the interviewing technique. Following these initiation examples are examples of language that can be used once a tracking conversation is under way.

Examples of Initiation Language

Example One

CL: *I don't know why I get like that, it just happens, I guess I have always been that way, and I just hate it. It is depressing and I can't change and no one likes me because . . .*

WK: *Excuse me Jane, I'm sorry to interrupt you but I was just wondering if you could remember a recent time when this problem occurred, when you felt this way? Would it be OK to discuss one of those times, to help me understand it better?*

Example Two

CL: *So we got into it and then she kicked me out of the house like I was a nobody, just some discarded piece of trash or something. She's running around all the time . . .*

WK: *So she kicked you out after that argument? Sorry for interrupting John, I was struck how awful that must have been for you. Can you back up a second and help me understand how this argument got so out of hand? It may be hard to remember, but did the day start out like that, did you know right when you got up that it was bad? Walk me through that day will you? I think we maybe could learn something.*

Examples of Ongoing Language That Explores the Pattern in More Depth

Example One

CL: *After I saw that someone had not even bothered to clean up the spilled milk I just about lost it.*

WK: *Jane, do you remember what you were thinking at the time? I know it was a while ago, but you were in the kitchen, you looked down and saw the milk on the floor, and you are saying . . .*

CL: *What am I the maid around here?*

WK: *So you are feeling really taken advantage of, like a maid in your own home. So what did you do next, do you remember? Did you totally lose it at that point or did something else happen?*

CL: *No, I didn't lose it right then. I think I went into the bathroom and closed the door to calm down. I guess I didn't totally lose it that time but I could have or would have if just one other person had come up to me and said something I would have let them have it!*

WK: *So that was a close call example. It sounds like you were successful that time in keeping the worst from happening. At least you have an "escape strategy" that will work, but you don't want the pattern to get that far along right? It is just too upsetting and when it goes that far you really could lose it. OK, so we need some early warning signals. Let's back up this incident and see what might have been earlier signals that day. Would that be helpful?*

Example Two

CL: *When I walked in the house she just started in on me and never let up. Remember feeling really trapped and all I wanted to do was just get out of there. So I called her a few choice words and got in my truck and just took off.*

WK: *And then what did you do?*

CL: *I drove around for a while until I calmed down and then went over to work on my brother's car some. I felt rotten and we still haven't talked much since.*

WK: *So you are not happy with the way things are right now, probably regretting some of the things you said I guess. And how does that compare with how you used to handle similar situations, say six months ago?*

CL: *Oh, I suppose six months ago I wouldn't have left, she would have kept in on me, and we would have gotten into it, I'd have broken something like a lamp or something.*

WK: *You mean you would have lost it much worse? So in some ways this is progress. Not enough, you don't like the way you handled it. But it does sound different, better, doesn't it?*

CL: *suppose so. I just wish she wouldn't bore in on me the way she does.*

WK: *Or that you knew of something else to do when you feel she is doing that?*

CL: *Exactly.*

WK: *Let's go over this whole incident again only let's back it up a little more. It sounds like you may want to intervene a little earlier. What was going on with you before you walked in your front door. Do you remember your mood?*

Common Pitfalls

Probably the greatest pitfall in using this technique is to simply miss the opportunity to track a particular example of the problem. Because our social customs call for summarizing unpleasantness, we often do not recognize that an event has been summarized when we hear it. When we hear that "a fight has occurred" between two people we assume that the relevant information is that "it has occurred," not how it occurred, how a context was created in which it occurred, how it was minimized, or how it was resolved. From a solution-based perspective, the details become differences that may be used to improve specific prevention skills.

The second most common pitfall is to track a sequence too quickly. Tracking requires the practitioner to continuously make comments to slow the process down; it is hard to go slow. One of the reasons this technique is almost always done with a flipchart or chalkboard is the recording takes some time and allows some extended thought about each step of the cycle or pattern. The visual spacing of information and use of diagram tools (see Figure 9-5) also provides the client and worker an opportunity to study the interactional sequence. Some examples of language that can help slow that process down are as follows:

- Whoa, I'm lost. Why did you say that then?
- I'm sorry, what were you thinking?
- Slow down, this is good information and I'm missing it.
- Tell me again what you saw when you walked in?

- You just mentioned three or four really good things, I need to get those down, you said . . .
- That's great, how did you remember to do that? Can you remember?

A final pitfall when using this technique is failing to make occasional inferences about the need for certain prevention skills or the presence of existing skills. The practitioner must remember that the clients do not organize their life stories around the skills of identifying high-risk situations, learning their early warning signals, and developing strategies to avoid, interrupt, or escape high-risk situations. Even though these skills are the structure for effective social interactions, they are only brought out of the background and into focus when they need our total attention. Clients need the practitioner's assistance in organizing what they know into some kind of coherent strategy to target these skills. Comments like the following assist the client in this focusing process:

- So, you have a strategy for *escaping your anger* when it gets really bad, but it sounds like it is unpleasant for you and has at least once been harmful to others. You need to have some ways to *pick up on earlier signals* that you are starting to lose it. Am I right?
- So you knew this discussion was going nowhere, and actually *picked up on it before you were too upset*, but you didn't know what to do about it? You didn't know how to *interrupt it or change gears*? That's great, we know what to work on then.

Through normalizing everyday family life crises, externalizing the problem, searching for exceptions, and tracking the pattern sequence, a consensus can be reached about the definition of the problem. With that foundation, the family and worker are ready to entertain the possibility of change. The worker needs tools and techniques to help capture the small signs that change is actually occurring. The skills that follow are particularly helpful with clients who are highly discouraged by the inescapability of their predicaments.

TECHNIQUES FOR CREATING INTEREST
IN SIGNS OF CHANGE

The grouping of these techniques is to point out the need for empowering clients to recognize and accept a changing self. The pervasive grasp of the old cannot be underestimated and conversely it is hard to err on the side of empowerment of the new. In practice, the techniques discussed in this section are often used in tandem with efforts to build a consensus or when anchoring change. As the student of technique becomes comfort-able and more proficient with solution-based interviewing techniques he/she will find him-/herself creatively combining them. While these creative moments are often exciting for the practitioner because of their usefulness to the client, it is usually helpful to first practice them within a structure.

BETWEEN SESSION OBSERVATION

Description of Technique

This technique is primarily one of asking clients to observe themselves in everyday life for signs of exceptions to the problem. The technique is based on the idea that clients are normally overfocused on indicators of their problem, and thus are likely to ignore examples of times when the problem is not occurring. Although the technique can be used to ask the family to learn more about the problem interaction, it is usually better for the observation to focus on exceptions to the problem. Using the time between meetings for more observation and discovery of what is happening "when things are working" often brings new and useful information to the family, caseworker, and therapist partnership, information that can give clues to possible solutions.

An example of the caseworker making such a request follows:

- You were saying that you couldn't remember a time when you and your daughter Julie were not conflictual, that it feels like there is tension all the time. I'm wondering if you would be willing to do a little observation for me, and bring back what you learn. It would be helpful if you could notice moments in which Julie was less conflic-tual, I don't mean all lovey-dovey, just less conflictual. If you could then jot those times down in a little notebook I will give you, and jot down what was going on at the time or what had just gone on in the previous hour or so. We probably need to discuss when you would do this and how to make it convenient for you, but it would be so helpful. What do you think?

Context for Its Use

This technique is useful whenever the family is overly focused on their inability to overcome the problem or are having difficulty identifying certain aspects of their behavior pattern. For instance, if the caseworker is trying to slow down and track a family event that is a "good example" of their problem cycle, and the family members are having difficulty recalling how they avoid such an interaction at other times in their family life, they can be asked to observe and study that process for a week. The mere assignment draws increased attention to the fact that there are exceptions to their problems and builds curiosity in them to discover how those times do occur.

Common Pitfalls

There are relatively few pitfalls to this technique because it is so strength oriented. However, in families where relationships have become very explosive, the assignment can become part of their old cycle and be performed in quite different ways than the caseworker had intended (e.g., the observing is viewed by others as spying). Problem-solving discussions about the possible problems that could occur will usually head off the misuse of the technique or convince the caseworker that the technique might be contraindicated with a particular family.

OLD VERSUS NEW T-CHARTS

Description of Technique

This is a visual technique effective at collecting for clients the differences between the way they used to be and the way that they are now or are becoming. These two versions of themselves are often referred to as the *old problem story* and *new emerging story*. Narrative terms such as "story" are used to connote that clients have the ability to rewrite their life story, creating new chapters that describe a new self. Within this same vein, caseworkers discuss who knows about the change, i.e., who has served as audience for the new story. The use of this technique assists the partnership in focusing on collecting examples of the new behavior and seeking larger and larger audiences for the new behavior. This process can occur with just conversation about the differences, but the addition of a visual T-chart that divides descriptions of the old from the new is very useful in dramatizing those differences and for delegating certain behaviors as either old or new. An example of a typical T-chart is shown in Figure 10-1. The chart was constructed with a person who was trying to overcome his discouragement, which can erupt in harmful anger.

Context for Its Use

A T-chart can be used whenever the practitioner wants to help draw a more dramatic distinction between behavior the client doesn't like and behavior the client desires. It is this ability to draw attention to differences that makes the technique such a powerful method for creating or enhanc-

Figure 10.1. Sample T-chart.

"Old Hot Head"	"Cool Hand Luke"
• Angry all the time • Short fuse • Drinking too much • Not exercising • Thinking about what everybody else has • Feeling sorry for myself • Sarcastic to my kids • Worried a lot	• More relaxed • Doing stuff with my kids/not dreading it • Think of all my blessings • Talk to my folks a lot more on the phone • Exercise helps, do it everyday • Using my Walk Out technique if I'm too stressed to talk • Going out with my wife

ing interest in signs of change. This same benefit can be used to educate, persuade, or confirm a treatment partner's view of the client family. Unfortunately, there are those occasions when treatment partners retain a deficit model perspective (i.e., guilty of pathology until proven healthy). Rather than arguing with members of the team, using T-charts helps acknowledge the problems (or deficits) but places those problems in a past context. In this way the deficits are acknowledged but so are the evolving skills.

Common Pitfalls

This a technique that is hard to misuse because, from the practitioner's point of view, it is really one of simply recording the client's comments and behaviors and placing them on a flipchart on the appropriate side. About the only way this technique can be misused is in for the process to be caseworker driven rather than client driven. For instance, if the worker were to label the sides of the changing self or were to generate the lists of characteristics of each side without client input then the technique would not be effective (or solution-based). This does not mean that the worker can't make tentative suggestions that ask for the client's confirmation or refutation (e.g., "You do seem more at ease when you are 'Cool Hand Luke.' Would you agree?").

SCALING QUESTIONS

Description of Technique

Scaling questions draw attention to small increments of change by encouraging individuals to estimate where on a given scale of a given variable they might fall. For instance, asking a client to rate his/her current degree of confidence using a scale of 1 to 10 (with 1 being low confidence and 10 being extremely confident) can begin a conversation that exposes even slight differences in confidence. This information provides essential clues to individual and systemic patterns by highlighting signs of change and creating options to tailoring new solutions.

Example of Scaling Questions

WK: *On a scale of 1 to 10, with 1 being the lowest and 10 being the highest: How would you rate your self-control today?*

CL: *Oh, probably about a 4.*

WK: *How would you rate it back when you started working on it?*

CL: *Oh, then? About a 2, if that.*

WK: *Really, that's like double. Can I ask you what keeps you from slipping back to a 2?*

CL: *[responds with what he is doing different]*

WK: *What about 3 months from now, if you keep the same pace of change, where do you think you'll be then?*

CL: *I could be over halfway there, I could be like a 6 or even a 7. I don't see myself ever really being a 10, but if I could stay above a 5, I'd be fine.*

WK: *How will you know that you have achieved a "stay above 5 place"? I mean what will you be doing differently when you are always a 5 or greater? Will I recognize you?*

Context for Its Use

Scaling is such a handy technique because it can be used at almost any time in a casework relationship. An argument could be made to list it as a consensus-building technique or an anchoring technique as well. However, it is listed as a technique that creates interest in signs of change because that description accurately reflects the role of the practitioner when using this technique. An air of engaged curiosity about change characterizes the use of this technique. The practitioner's interest in the minute differences engages the client's own curiosity about how change might be occurring. Rather than focusing on the negative aspects (i.e., more change is still needed), the conversation is all about teasing out what positive change is occurring or is anticipated occurring.[1]

Scaling questions can also be used to create a graph of change over time. By asking the client to gauge where he/she was in the past, is now, and hopes to be someday, the worker and client can plot a "change chart." For instance, let's assume a client responds with the following estimates of his/her state of depression: (1) the lowest point ever was a 0 and that was a month or two before starting to work on the problem, (2) about a 1.5 after first starting to work on things, (3) currently at best a 4

Figure 10.2. Curve of improvement over time on a scaling question.

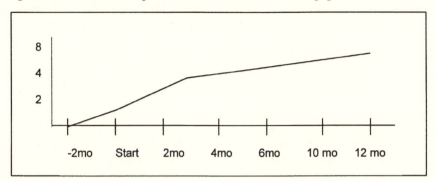

after three months of working on things, and (4) he/she hopes to some-day be able to stay at a 7 or 8 all the time. The curve in Figure 10-2 would result from such a conversation.

As can be seen by the visual impact of change on the curve, scaling can be a useful tool to help demonstrate a "trend of success" to easily discouraged clients.

Common Pitfalls

The most common pitfall of the use of scaling is for the worker to assign the values.[2] A subtle version of this is disagreeing with the client about the number chosen. The numbers can be mistaken for actual measurements rather than descriptive phrases. It is not uncommon for one person's 2 to be another person's 4. The numbers have special meaning to the individual, however, and this meaning should be respected. It is not unusual for clients to ponder small increments of difference, for instance, whether they are a 4.5 or really closer to 4.8. This should be encouraged because it offers further differences to explore and describe, thus confirming the signs of change.

TIME-ORIENTED QUESTIONS

Description of Technique

Time-oriented questions are questions that ask the client to imagine him- or herself at another moment in time and to be his or her own adviser from that perspective. Time-oriented questions are another use of language that allows the practitioner to tease out positive change, learn important values and goals that motivate, and identify subtle signs of change. Through the use of these questions, the "discouraging present" can be sidestepped to a more promising future. As was the case in the popular movie *Back to the Future*, the caseworker can take the client to the future and from that perspective have the client look back and advise him- or herself on what direction to head and what initial steps to take. The following sample questions are further examples of time-oriented questions:

- If you woke up in the morning and the problem was miraculously solved, what would be different? What is the first thing you would notice about yourself? How would you know that a miracle had occurred?[3]
- Imagine you are an old person sitting on your front porch, thinking back about this difficult period of your life. What will you say was the turning point?
- Let's say I never met you until one year from now, when all this will be behind you. What would be my first impression of you?
- How have you improved over the previous generation in this area, what have you done to keep from repeating their mistakes?
- As these changes continue in your family, what will be different about your family in one month (one year) from now?
- When will your family first notice you have changed? What will they see?

Context for Its Use

Change is always fighting against the inertia of the status quo. The purpose of all anticipatory questions is to build a context of hope and encouragement: an antidote to the stagnating experience of being overwhelmed by a problem that seems insurmountable. In a sense, the client is able to borrow confidence from the future, a skill that many clients have not learned to do on their own.

This skill is also useful to help build a consensus for change, or to anchor gains in skill development. In the former context, time-oriented questions can be used to build a vision of the future, much like a case plan would describe the future, and therefore help the partnership define the target outcome.

In the case of anchoring change, time-oriented questions allow reflection and perspective. Reflection often favors "the big picture," i.e., what's really important to the person, and can therefore serve as a measurement for signs of behavior consistent with that picture.

Common Pitfalls

The most common pitfall is phrasing the question in mundane terms that do not elicit strong values or motivations. For instance, if the question about a miracle occurring is not asked carefully (too generally) the client may respond, "I'll win the lottery and be rich and all my problems will go away. I'll be able to buy anything I want." Once a client starts that fantasy it is usually depressing to go back and discuss reality. The practitioner is at risk of saying things like, "Well, we know that will never happen, so let's focus on something more practical." This is not the stuff that dreams are made of.

The other pitfall that is not uncommon for this technique is for the worker to get too complicated or quick with imagery of the future and end up confusing the client. Jumping from the past to the future and back again can leave a client thinking the worker is a bit "too weird" for them to trust. Slowing down, simplifying the questions, and keeping them focused on the problem pattern will help the practitioner and client avoid these pitfalls.

ANCHORING CHANGE IN THE NEW SELF

Solution-based techniques are extremely flexible in their application and can be applied throughout the change process. This flexibility in application is primarily because the model views change as continuous, versus a single moment of change from dysfunction to health. Because of this flexibility, the techniques discussed in the earlier sections of this chapter can also be used to help secure or anchor change in the family.

However, three techniques are discussed specifically in this section because they share a commonality that aid in their learning. Each of the three techniques shares a focus on finding new and different forms for testing, performing, and demonstrating new skills in front of others. Their effectiveness is based on the feedback one receives when purposely performing a new skill with an expanded audience. The analogy can be made to other forms of learning in which students do not feel confident with new material until they have passed some form of test that credentials them as competent. Although their knowledge may be equal before and after the test, their confidence and ability to use their knowledge grows tremendously once they have officially passed the test. In the well-known film the *Wizard of Oz*, three of the principal characters all believe they lack a certain quality: one a brain, another a heart, the other courage. Each shows clear signs of his respective quality, yet the characters themselves do not accept or even notice this expanded version of themselves. It is not until they pass a difficult and challenging test and receive "official recognition" of their qualities that they fully embrace an altered view of their capabilities.

The following techniques have evolved with a solution-based approach to build on the need for social testing and confirmation. The techniques are (1) expanding the audience for change, (2) credentialing small steps in skill development, and (3) celebrating rites of passage.

EXPANDING THE AUDIENCE FOR CHANGE

Description of Technique

Solution-based practitioners live by the question, "Who else knows about this change?" Any effort by the practitioner to draw attention to a change in cognitive or behavior skill would be considered an effort to expand the audience of change. The audience could be as close to the client as the client him- or herself (e.g., "Does it surprise you that you were able to do that?") or could include other family members, friends, members of social circles, school or church members, or complete strangers. It even could include visualized people from the past or from the future.

Context for Its Use

The practitioner must use language to draw attention to an emerging skill, and since skill development can happen at any time in life this technique is always available for use. Understanding the context for its use requires the practitioner to have certain conceptual skills that help identify descriptions of change. In a sense, the conceptual map has to have prepared the practitioner to have a "hair trigger" for hearing elements of change. Change descriptions come from clients all the time, in almost everything they say, but unless it is heard, the practitioner will not be able to apply this technique. When the worker assumes that (1) change is already occurring but is just not being noticed and (2) that he/she must be prepared to respectfully draw it out whenever clues to its existence occur in the conversation, then the worker is prepared to recognize the context for this technique.

To assist the student of this technique with possible language to use once a context is recognized, the following "audience" questions are offered:

Helping the client become an audience for him/herself:

- So it was worse a few weeks before you came in to talk to me? Have you noticed what you have been doing to help improve the situation?

- So you are court ordered to come? Yet so many don't come at all. What does that tell you about yourself?
- Excuse me, can I ask about how you decided to lock yourself in the bathroom when you started to lose it? Isn't that different from what you have done in the past?
- Do you think your old self, the one of two years ago, would be surprised to hear what you are doing now? Would you have believed this about yourself—that you could have changed this much?

Expanding the audience to include group members:

- Has anyone in group noticed this change in you? Have they said anything that tells you they have noticed a change?
- Do you think you are ready to share this new awareness with the group members to get their reactions to what you have learned?

Expanding the audience to include family members:

- What will your family notice first when you start to make the change you are considering?
- Who in your family do you think will notice first that you have stopped reacting in the old way?
- You have accepted responsibility for what you did in here and in group—do you think you are ready to share this change with your family?

Expanding the audience to include treatment team members:

- Does your therapist know about this change in your thinking? Do they know this side of you?
- Maybe we need to collect these little changes and put them into a chart or something, some form that you could share with the others helping you in order to keep them up to date on your progress.

Common Pitfalls

In deficit models, the audience is always drawn together when there are problems (not solutions). Parents are called by the school when their children misbehave, not when they have a good day. Therapists are called when someone has shown early signs of new symptoms, not shown early signs of managing symptoms. Even case coordination conferences are called together to resolve problems rather to share successes. These are the most common pitfalls of expanding an audience for change. If the caseworker is not willing to be different he/she is vulnerable to slipping back into the practice of "no news is good news" rather than "good news is news."

REINFORCING PROGRESS THROUGH CREDENTIALING

Description of Technique

This technique describes those actions in which the practitioner chooses to reinforce change through use of dramatic "credentialing" symbols such as a diploma, certificate, or award. For instance, the client or family's skill development is acknowledged through the creation and granting of a certificate. These created symbols are tailored very specifically to the language the family has used to describe their target efforts. For instance, in the example of the young client striving to be "Cool Hand Luke" used previously to illustrate T-charts, the award might read, "To the Coolest of the Cool."

The existence or nonexistence of a difficult family situation does not overly concern a solution-focused caseworker, but how the family members handled the situation is of utmost concern. Therefore the credentials should acknowledge the family's struggle with the problem and their skill at meeting future struggles head on. Sample inquiries in which typical change can be acknowledged are offered in the following examples:

- Even though the problem is still there, was there any difference in the way you handled this event that would indicate you are starting to get this problem's number figured out?
- So it was bad, but it didn't go as far this time. Did someone recognize early warning signals and your attempt to leave the situation?
- It sounds like the argument stopped short of the intensity of the last argument. How did you all accomplish that one?
- Did anyone attempt to intervene in ways that had been discussed, even if ineffective?

These and countless other questions regarding how the family members managed their high-risk situation help to identify, acknowledge, and reinforce incremental changes.

A sample certificate follows in Figure 10-3.

Context for Use

Working from a solution-based perspective affords the caseworker an opportunity to credential change from the earliest moment in therapy.

Figure 10.3. Sample certificate.

To the
"Coolest of
the Cool"

PRESENTED TO
John Doe

In Recognition of Outstanding Effort,
Extraordinary Coolness, and Exemplary Attitude.

Teacher   Counselor   Worker

Change is not viewed as something that occurs at the end of casework: in fact, it often begins before treatment begins. Whether it is acknowledging a client's fortitude in resisting the influence of an old problem pattern or certifying expertise in defeating a current problem that has plagued a family for some time, the caseworker can move quickly to claim a solution skill and secure it before old patterns emerge to rediscourage members.

Common Pitfalls

Celebrating the end or death of problems is unrealistic and sets up clients for further discouragement if and when the problem situation recurs. Since conflict is viewed as a normal part of life in this model, it is always the management of conflict that is acknowledged and celebrated.

Because we have emphasized the partnership aspects when discussing previous techniques, it should be noted that it is not a pitfall with this technique for the caseworker to make up the certificate on his/her own. As long as it grows directly out of the conversations and language of the client, then it will have meaning to the client. In other aspects of life, certificates and awards are often given or granted based on "judged" accomplishments versus those co-created with the receiver. For this reason it actually increases the impact when there is a small element of surprise to the award. Fun and humor also help to alter the context in which the problem has been viewed. Certificates that build on an ongoing joke between the caseworker and family help "detoxify" the problem and add an expanded, helpful perspective.

CELEBRATING RITES OF PASSAGE

Description of Technique

This technique can be defined as any effort to use ritual and celebration to denote transition in social skill. Rites of passage are part of universal human culture. In every culture specific life stages are acknowledged through ceremony and ritual. These patterned social events serve to confirm the role of the individual in the group and help acknowledge and balance the "trade-offs" that occur in any transition. These transitions are often coached by individuals (e.g., shaman, guide, mentor, priest) who are trained in the dynamics of these life moments. Casework could be seen as representing a rite of passage between disharmony with self and others and harmony with self and others. Caseworkers are the shepherds of this transition and can help the client symbolize the change from an old way of being to the new way of being by celebrating the transition. Rituals in casework can range from small actions performed by clients in private to larger celebratory events conducted with the help of significant others in their social system.

The form a celebration takes can also vary. Typically celebrations do have some commonality and may involve the following steps:

- gathering all of the people the client feels should be there;
- deciding on an agenda that will help frame the event for participants;
- arranging for food and refreshments (food is always important!);
- preparing gifts to symbolize the accomplishment or future challenges;
- preparing those who will give speeches or "testimony."

Context for Its Use

Celebrating change can occur whenever change occurs, but this technique tends to work best when saved for major stage changes or transitions. A family member's graduation from treatment after struggling with the problem for years may represent a time for the family to pull together to celebrate the opportunity and to commit to further changes that may be needed in the future. Other examples might include an individual who gets his/her first job, does 'steady work for three months, or pays off his/her bills. Still others might be a favorable court order to the return of children to the home, or the closing of a case. Caseworkers should keep in mind the time they save by anchoring change through celebration versus letting it go unnoticed.

Common Pitfalls

A common pitfall when using this technique is to wait too long to employ it. Celebrating change does not mean that all problems are over, or even that risk is no longer an issue. If the practitioner delays until there is no possibility of further problems he/she risks not securing the change that has already occurred. Caseworkers may have to get over the idea that celebration with individuals who have harmed someone is not the same as condoning their behavior. Having client parties in the unit conference room may not be usual behavior for the practitioner's colleagues and therefor may dissuade them from conducting such events. Additionally the fear of looking bad in front of their colleagues might be a restraint, if the worker is worried that down the road there may be a relapse. When shifting to a solution-based casework approach, it takes a while for all staff to be comfortable with the idea that you can be firm with protection issues at the same time you extend a willingness to partner with clients for change.

REFERENCE READING SPECIFICALLY FOR TECHNIQUE

The following reference list is provided as a resource for students of technique to further pursue their understanding. The list is not exhaustive, but will afford the interested student several options for further study. It is suggested that solution-based casework technique is best learned in practice with others and shared with colleagues who are concomitantly practicing themselves. For this reason, students may wish to form study groups in which they periodically share readings, share treatment experiences, and—particularly—share stories.

Berg, I. K. (1994). *Family based services: A solution-focused approach.* New York: W. W. Norton.

Durrant, M. (1993). *Residential treatment: A cooperative, competency-based approach to therapy and program design.* New York: W. W. Norton.

de Shazer, S. (1991). *Putting difference to work.* New York: W. W. Norton.

Friedman, S. (1993). *The new language of change.* New York: Guilford.

Lane, S. (1991). The sexual abuse cycle. In G. Ryan & S. Lane (Eds.), *Juvenile sexual offending.* Lexington, MA: Lexington Books.

Miller, S., & Berg, I. K. (1995). *The miracle method: A radically new approach to problem drinking.* New York: W. W. Norton.

O'Hanlon, W., & Weiner-Davis, M. (1989). *In search of solutions: A new direction in psychotherapy.* New York: Norton.

Selekman, M. (1993). *Pathways to change: Brief therapy solutions with difficult adolescents.* New York: Guilford.

Selekman, M. (1997). *Solution-focused therapy with children.* New York: Guilford.

Way, I. F., & Speiker, S. (1997). *The cycle of offense: A framework for treating adolescent sexual offenders.* Notre Dame, IN: Jalice.

Walter, J., & Peller, J. (1992). *Becoming solution-focused in brief therapy.* New York: Brummer / Mazel.

White, M., & Epston, D. (1990). *Narrative means to therapeutic ends.* New York: W. W. Norton.

NOTES

1. The use of time in scaling questions allows a natural combination with time-oriented question, which will be discussed later in this chapter.

2. This is actually the most common pitfall for any practitioner new to solution-based casework. It is, in fact, "old hierarchical behavior" sneaking back in out of habit. The practitioner who is trying to adopt a partnership model can expect to go through a period where he/she is increasingly able to work from within the client's perspective. During that time of shifting perspective, practitioners also need encouragement that they are also showing signs of real change.

3. This question is a version of what de Shazer et al. (1986) have termed the "Miracle Question."

Chapter 11

How Staff Experience Change

This chapter describes how protection caseworkers, therapists, supervisors, social welfare workers, clients, and others have experienced moving from a traditional deficit-focused model to solution-based casework. We will detail their frustrations with "old" (i.e., deficit-focused) models, and their perceptions of the advantages of solution-based casework, challenges inherent in changing habits, successes, and suggestions for implementation. The comments in this chapter reflect the opinions of the many hundreds of social service professionals who, over a period of several years, actively participated in the development of solution-based casework. Verbatim comments in this chapter were generated through focus group discussion. Although verbatim comments were stated by one individual, they are included here since they reflect the sentiment of many.

FRUSTRATION WITH OLD MODELS

In our conversations with caseworkers, casework supervisors, therapists, and others, many expressed frustration with traditional deficit-focused models. They seemed to believe deficit-focused models are (1) prone to create adversarial relationships, (2) inordinately negative, (3) presumptuous and punitive, (4) dismissive of client competence, and that (5) "success" is narrowly defined and difficult to achieve.

Adversarial Relationships

Many experienced and inexperienced caseworkers, their supervisors, and volunteer community members stated that deficit-focused casework, which they believe emphasizes diagnostic categories and client deficits, tends to create an adversarial tension between workers and clients. They indicated that given the nature of protective service work, a certain degree of tension is inevitable. However, they believed the strain is more pronounced and more frequent than is necessary. A deficit orientation, they insisted, fosters an adversarial relationship. One community volunteer reflected the sentiment of many:

> As a representative in the community completely outside the child protection agency, my problem has been that it has become a very adversarial relationship between individual families and the agency, such that families talk about not wanting to be bothered or just saying or doing whatever is necessary to "get those people out of my life." That is not ultimately beneficial for the family.

A supervisor stated:

> With the deficit-focused model I've seen that it sets up people to lie. We go in and people are afraid to be truthful. Being a client, you are not going to tell the secrets because you are afraid you will be penalized for being truthful. People say things like he's not here or he wouldn't do that to my child . . . and they really know and they are afraid to . . . they might [otherwise] want somebody to assist them, to give them some other avenues.

Others believed that deficit-focused approaches create an adversarial relationship by adopting a rigid definition of acceptable client behavior: "The old way said you are either 100 percent or you're nothing. [It was] either-or." A supervisor pointed to the tendency to "assume the worst" about client behavior:

> The minute the mother didn't rise to the therapist's standards or expectations then everybody reverted to punitive. . . . They were very angry at her, they wanted to punish her, they wanted removal of those children. We didn't hear any information to make us believe that removal even should have been discussed.

Inordinate Negativity

Many expressed concerns about the tendency in deficit-focused models to track client deficits and largely dismiss client competencies. This negativity, they argued, makes it difficult to form a working partnership, promotes defensiveness, and perpetuates discouragement. One supervisor of supervisors seemed to reflect the sentiment of many when she suggested that emphasizing client deficits promotes dependency:

> When you look at the deficit-focused model it is all negative. It doesn't tend to look at any of the strengths. I think that served child protective services well for years and we really encouraged people to be codependent; we encouraged people to have a multitude of problems and never be able to survive on their own because it fed our own importance.

How was that encouraged (asked by the interviewer)?

> Because we focused all of our efforts in working with families on all the negatives and how overwhelming everything was, and how badly they needed the system. We didn't look at where the strengths were and we didn't [adequately] encourage them to get better and we didn't let go of them, we really basically raised families. So I think now there are many of us in protective services that do not feel like somebody died and left us in charge. We are feeling like it is not healthy for us or families or for the system to make people codependent on us and that we want to get in and work with families and build on where the positives are and get out as quickly as possible.

Others believed that an emphasis on client deficits reflects itself in the assessment process and bogs down the process of healing and recovery:

> In the past, the assessment piece was written all negative. You were trained to look for what is wrong. You were never told to look for the positives. That becomes a problem. Because if you read the case record before you go out to visit the family for the first time you are going in with a lot of preconceptions that are mostly negative. You are not looking for what did the worker do before me that didn't work. You just fall into that same pattern that the previous worker did it, which ultimately leads to failure.

In that regard another stated:

> [Working from a solution-based casework model] we wanted to talk about the positives and how to make going to treatment more convenient. How do we get her into her neighborhood, cut down the number of appointments, and work with her on what are the issues left that she still wants to work on. It was like they [therapists working from a traditional deficit-focused model] decided two years ago what the issues were and they were controlling the whole entire thing. I think the new model works very well with a family like this. It's looking at the strengths, having the mother really be a partner around the table in figuring out what are the issues, what's going on in her family, and giving her some control. That woman hadn't had any control in a blue moon.

> Another issue is that in the old system families had to be sick enough to become open and active cases. This wasn't in the best interest of families, they had to be dysfunctional enough. When you're only looking at how sick a person is, all you're able to do is triage.

Presumptuous and Punitive

Many believed that deficit-focused models are presumptuous. That is, they believe the deficit models narrowly define healthy behavior and assume clients should readily endorse the presumed wisdom of the case-worker and correct their behavior. When this does not occur punitive action is taken:

> The old way makes assumptions about how families should be. They look down at the family. They say these are the things that are wrong. The assumption is going in that first of all I have to get this person to admit they are wrong, beat themselves on the breast for having done whatever they have done, and then improve themselves. When that does not happen to the intensity in which the therapist is expecting it, then we punish the family—some kind of penance or take their kids.

This suggests that one marker of success in the deficit-focused model is client willingness to openly admit wrongdoing. However, as described in Chapter 4, the act of admitting guilt does not in itself reduce the likelihood of relapse. Admitting guilt does not naturally lead to the development of skills that target and prevent the recurrence of dangerous behavior.

Others argued that deficit-focused models assume that caseworkers and therapists, due to their expertise, should instruct clients how to live their lives differently. They believed that this arrangement disempowers clients, creates dependency, and removes the heat from the client:

> In the deficit-focused model we set ourselves up as the experts. Being the experts in that situation creates an imbalance of power. If the family or the victim was disempowered coming into the situation and then you present yourself as the expert, that further lessens the amount of power that individual has. They become dependent on you just to manage all of the crises and they are never able to move beyond all of the crises.

Dismisses Client Competence

The most commonly cited criticism of deficit-focused models was their tendency to underestimate client competence. This prevailing sentiment is reflected in this comment:

> In the past we very seldom asked the client or the family what do they see as the problem. What are the solutions that they have in mind. We should encourage them to identify some alternatives and to look into their own life. We just automatically came in there and said this is what you need to do and this is what you're going to do.

Success Is Narrowly Defined and Difficult to Achieve

Since deficit-focused models emphasize deficits and tend to narrowly define normative behavior and underestimate cultural variability, several supervisors argued that "cases go on and on, sometimes unnecessarily for years":

> If you look for problems, there will always be problems. We could never get people at a point where they were living in a two-bedroom condo in the better part of town with 2.2 children and everybody working. We are talking about redefining success because it's going to look different if we're talking about coaching and encouraging instead of punishing.

ADVANTAGES TO SOLUTION-BASED CASEWORK

Caseworkers, supervisors, therapists, social welfare employees, and community members who have practiced and observed solution-based casework believed that it offers several advantages over traditional, deficit-focused models. They believed that focusing on a specific, high-risk event leads to workable solutions; that it is efficient, empowering, and facilitates working partnerships between social workers, therapists, and clients; and that it encourages coherent planning and collaboration between professionals.

Focusing on High-Risk Events Creates Workable Solutions

Caseworkers and supervisors voiced several advantages to focusing on high-risk events and constructing relapse prevention plans around those events. One frequently mentioned advantage is that keying in on high-risk events helps clients make important distinctions between safe and unsafe handling of stressors and their surrounding circumstances. These distinctions, and the realization that there are many exceptions to their mishandling of stressors, can embolden them and set the stage for active involvement in creating workable solutions:

> I think it is very important to focus on the event. It helps them define why you're there and what the problem is. There are a thousand events, it helps you focus on the one that caused the problem. It gives them power back when you acknowledge the fact that nine times out of ten they are able to deal with it without causing any harm to anybody. But, on said day, the event caused an issue of harm to someone. So, by focusing on the event and the circumstances around it that particular day then you get to the problems that are underlying. So, families don't feel like they're just screwed up and can't do anything right, but are able to recognize where the differences are [and] what was different about that event. You can pull out that difference.

Others furthered the idea that eliciting detailed descriptions of high-risk behaviors and their surrounding circumstances is instrumental in creating workable solutions:

I think it is important when you get a report that says the mother beats the child. When you can go into that home and get at exactly what happened to create a situation where she beat him, it is focusing. And, at least the mother can say it was the straw that broke the camel's back.

I think it is real important to track the event. When you put the event on paper you allow the family members to step outside of the event and see it for themselves and see how it was a problem and what can be done to fix it.

You can focus on the real problem, instead of only what we think it is. It may be something totally different from what we think it is—it is something they have to settle. The stages and the cycle naturally focuses on the important problem.

Many professionals also believed that attending to high-risk situations is useful for them.

We need that sometimes, too, as a worker. You get a lot of insight when you back off and slow down. It gives you a clear picture.

Focusing on High-Risk Events and Solutions Is Efficient Casework Practice

Supervisors and caseworkers suggested that focusing on high-risk behaviors and their exceptions, and creating relapse prevention plans is efficient. That is, more can happen more quickly. Safety and the reduction of recidivism can be achieved in an expedient manner:

I think we move in and we move out quicker. From an agency perspective it gives you the opportunity to focus, do your business and get out sooner. From a family's perspective I think it means less intrusion for shorter periods of time.

It makes us look at how we do business. I think we have gotten real comfortable doing business for a long time the way we have. In this district, we've been cleaning up and looking at cases and reevaluating why we're involved with cases. . . . We've discovered cases that we've now cleaned up, closed out, done all the paperwork and said goodbye to families that we've been involved with for fourteen, fifteen years. My standards are rising all the time. Now, when I'm reading cases and assigning them to closure workers to go out and assess the situation we ask ourselves, "What are we doing here, should we even be involved anymore, are there other community resources to put in place?" Now, my standard is if we've been involved a year and a half to two years that's two long. Even being involved now a year and a half to two years is very inappropriate unless it is very severe and we have to move to terminate parental rights. Then a year and a half to two years is appropriate because it does take some time to do that. If it is anything less than that then we should have been able to assist the family, do our business, get focused from the beginning and be out.

Focusing on Exceptions to Problems
Is Empowering

Many have commented that focusing on exceptions to problematic behavior is empowering. Clients who may be discouraged by the apparently insurmountable stressors in their lives can become more hopeful when they begin to notice the actual frequency with which they manage high-risk moments safely:

> I think it is very important to look at strengths and not just at the problems, the exceptions about how they've handled the situation in the past that didn't lead to an incident. They get overwhelmed about the current problem and they don't think about what they did right in the past. I think it's important to review what did work before.

> [Focusing on exceptions] allows more control of their own lives. Definitely it helps the family to recognize their own inherent power. It lessens the likelihood that you get that expert involvement with the family. Agencies are less apt to see themselves as the expert with all the answers. [We] see ourselves more as conduits for change. Change that is important for the family rather than change that is important to the institution.

> The [solution-focused] questions help them to figure out their needs. I think it takes pressure off us. We don't have to have the solutions. The client or the family is encouraged to make their own solutions. It might not be what we would think would be a solution but it will work for them.

Many also suggested that a solution-based model explicitly helps clients deliberately construct their own solutions by drawing from their previous successes. This is distinct, caseworkers and supervisors have argued, from deficit- focused models, which have told clients to stop certain behaviors and instructed them how to behave differently. This approach, at best, gave the impression that clients were naive and largely unable to construct solutions:

> Instead of telling clients the endpoint, i.e., "Don't do this" and "Don't do that," you talk about what they can do. Anybody can go in and say, "Don't do this." That's the hazard we've had all along in this agency, we've taken things away from families that worked functionally. They [the client-attempted solutions] had some hazard to them, but we haven't given them anything back. [We've] taken away their map.

Some caseworkers have suggested that the process of urging clients to notice and construct their own solutions reduces the pressure workers themselves feel:

It's a relief. You don't have to own the problem since you don't have to find the solution. [With deficit-focused models], you found the solution and had to make your solution fit that family.

Focusing on Everyday Issues and Exceptions
Fosters Partnerships

Caseworkers and supervisors have often stated that detailing behaviors during high-risk situations and their exceptions reduces emphasis on client deficit and promotes hopefulness, thereby fostering working partnerships between clients and professionals:

> It's set up so that it doesn't set blame. Instead, you're looking at specific tasks and struggles, but not placing blame. It is laying it out and encouraging the family to come up with a plan for dealing with the problems.

> [Talking about exceptions and believing clients can change] gives them the chance that I would like to have if it were me. And, the future orientation says we can make some changes in the future.

> It [framing stressors in everyday terms] brings it down to normalcy. We are people too, it's not us versus them. It does put the shoe on the other foot. With this model it is easier to understand that. It has been viewed in the past as the professional and the "client."

Focusing on Relapse Prevention Plans
Fosters Collaboration

Caseworkers have expressed emerging satisfaction with how an emphasis on high-risk behaviors and relapse prevention creates detailed case plans. They have found that they are in a strengthened position both with other professionals (e.g., therapists) and the courts. For instance, caseworkers are more frequently providing direction to therapists and are more equally collaborating. Others have suggested that focusing on client resources naturally encourages community involvement:

> When you are working with other service agencies you are actually sitting down and giving directions to how far that case is going to go. When I'm sitting down with mental health, I'm saying I want you to work in this specific area and at the end of six weeks I'd like an update, i.e., did you accomplish that goal.

> It [solution-based casework] encourages workers to help families recognize resources that are within their own neighborhoods. It's bringing back the concept of community and neighborhood.

CHALLENGES INHERENT IN CHANGING HABITS

Caseworkers and supervisors described several challenges in moving from a deficit-focused practice to a practice that is based on relapse prevention and solution-focused principles. For instance, many have initially expressed concern about the apparent time demands of learning something new, e.g., "It's hard to do all this when you have so many cases." Once workers have had more exposure and experience with the model, they seem to conclude that the time spent on the "front end," i.e., creating a partnership, searching for solutions, identifying high-risk situations, and creating a relapse prevention plan, is very useful and ultimately a time saver. The most ominous challenge mentioned by caseworkers and supervisors rests in the tension that is created when caseworkers are working within a solution-based framework and other service providers (e.g., therapists, school system, legal system) are operating within deficit-focused models. One caseworker seemed to reflect the sentiment of many when she said, "You can't be discouraged because the [deficit-focused] system knocks you down. It requires practice, practice, and practice. It's worth it." Another stated, "More communication of the concepts and the procedures with the other resources is needed."

Tension between traditionally trained therapists and caseworkers has emerged and required attention. For instance, when caseworkers have more broadly defined normative behavior, elevated high-risk events, worked with parents to punctuate exceptions to problem behavior, and elicited client competencies, they have been surprised and even alarmed by therapists who rarely connect client problems to the normal, everyday stressors of family life:

> A mother had been attending therapy for a couple of years. We went to a meeting because she had missed a few sessions, although she had attended many of them—she'd been going for two years. The only thing I heard from the therapist was all negative, to the point where I was getting overwhelmed with this myself and I'm another service provider. I asked what do you see as some of the strengths. It was almost like a shock. It was, well you know, she hasn't done very well in therapy for two years. Instead of saying we need to look at what we've been doing or taking some responsibility in that, they were projecting all of that on the family. They were mad and wanted removal of the kids. When we started asking questions at least two of the kids were going for separate appointments each week and the mother was going for a separate appointment each week and they were going for a fourth appointment for family therapy. When we had a conversation with the mother she was exhausted. She was exhausted and overwhelmed and wondered when it was all going to end. It maybe started out

as positive support, but she had forgotten that. She was exhausted. This was a single parent who had children to support. It was overwhelming. Plus, there were transportation problems and she had to go across town to get to these appointments. So, the fact that she had held on for two years and made the majority of the appointments was tremendously positive.

Further, protective services have historically been used as a lever by many referring agencies. Moving from a system that is regarded as largely punitive to one that elevates partnership with families and client competencies requires effort to educate the community of the emerging distinction: "I think that it is particularly difficult because many systems within our system use child protective services to punish families."

Others have stated that implementation of solution-based casework requires a multidisciplinary conversation about success. What is successful social service intervention?

> We are talking about redefining success because it's going to look different if we're talking about coaching and encouraging instead of punishing. So, we not only have to help the family understand and participate, but also others working with the family, be it therapists or the judge or the school system. All of these other institutions have to gain a different understanding of what success is.

The courts also were frequently mentioned as being out of step with solution-based casework:

> The courts are set up as punitive and blaming. That is difficult. That is a big barrier. If you have a situation with a family where everyone is focusing on solutions, that is difficult to deal with in court because many of the guardian ad litems, county attorneys, and judges are still in that punitive mode.

> We had a child who was physically abused. Now, you take a child who was physically abused and, from the old perspective, it is natural to remove that child, have restricted visits, and place the kid in our custody for an extended period of time. That is the old [deficit-focused] way. We were going to do it differently by utilizing the extended family resources. The court said the extended family believed in whippings and corporal punishment and didn't want them involved. The abusive behavior was wrong, but they [the court] wanted to punish everybody. Initially they were not going to place the child with any family member. Eventually, though, we arranged for a family placement by arranging a plan with the mother, the teacher, the counselor, the social worker, and me [supervisor]. Everybody that was involved, including family members, took some ownership and responsibility. It was very hard initially to get the court to go for it. The

county attorney and the child's attorney was saying, "What about the risk to the child? Are you all crazy? You're going to put this child back in this home where he was beat up before?" We had to sell the idea of a family-based, solution-based, relapse prevention approach. We did our homework. We had a conference with everybody involved, the mother, the father, the grandmother, the schoolteacher, and the therapist. We had a conference and discussed what are we going to do, what is the plan when the mother needs help? This was a special needs child. We developed a plan. The grandmother was her respite and other children in the home, the sixteen-year-old and the eighteen-year-old got involved in the plan. The teacher and the mother developed a plan for regular contact. And another worker participated in setting up meetings to focus on the progress. We developed a relapse plan with the mother and father.

[Interviewer:] How did the court respond to the plan?

They were very impressed with it. But, it took a couple of court meetings to get to that.

SUCCESS STORIES

The fundamental marker of success in adult and child protective services is the safety of all involved. This includes, naturally, a safe and nurturing living environment. From a solution-based casework perspective, success is extended to include safety, nurturance, and each significant step toward a safe and nurturing environment. Therefore, establishing a partnership with a parent who heretofore had been defined as resistant or uncooperative is a success: it is movement toward the fundamental objective of safety. Likewise, when an individual who has been physically abusive begins to identify his/her high-risk situations and builds a relapse prevention plan, this is a success: it is a hopeful precursor to behavioral evidence of nonviolence. And, when tracking exceptions to the problem brings new life and a productive perspective—and in so doing emboldens discouraged professionals and families: this is success. Therefore, from a solution-based casework perspective, success is both an outcome and a process.

Caseworkers have described many successes in their efforts to apply solution-based casework. These successes, among others, have included (1) forming partnerships with clients who previously recoiled; (2) enlisting interagency cooperation; (3) fostering change when change seemed unlikely; (4) averting destructive behavior; and (5) assisting the court in proper decisions (e.g., based on evidence, or lack thereof, of relapse prevention skills).

Solution-Based Casework Has Fostered Working Partnerships.

Many workers commented on their success in forming strong, working partnerships with clients, including clients who previously were defined by others as uncooperative. They attributed this largely to (1) assuming most parents want what's best for their children, (2) emphasizing exceptions and successes, (3) emphasizing collaboration, (4) normalizing problems, and (5) staying away from a blame/fault-finding orientation:

> Others [other professionals] had been telling her what to do instead of being a partner in what to do. I share ideas. I don't tell them what they're going to do—that [telling them what to do] puts them in an adversarial role. I get in an adversarial role with some of my clients, but the majority responds to this.

> Normalizing helped, especially understanding her daily events. It helps them realize they're not the only one with a problem. And, when you make yourself more human they can see that you go through things, too. You can help them change by showing some of your own vulnerabilities.

One client who was working with a solution-based casework professional reflected the sentiment of many:

> She [the caseworker] is different [than other previous workers this client had encountered]. She said, "I want to get to know you and what you need." Others said, "This is what you have to do . . . do this and do this." She said, "What would you like to do? We can figure out a plan. We can put our heads together." She's a caseworker, she let's you know her job and sometimes even kids get taken away. I can understand the job, but it's the way she does it.

> She [the caseworker] doesn't down me. Everyone else looked at my record and just said I'm a drug user. She said I wasn't only a drug user. She said I was doing it differently. Before I had a bad attitude problem. I'd holler and scream in meetings. She helped me to sit and listen and then speak my opinion. I can talk to her. I'm doing much better. I got a job. I'm taking care of my home.

Solution-Based Case Plans Have Enlisted Cooperation and Fostered Change

Workers have frequently stated that when case plans are concrete, i.e., measurable, and when they target high-risk and relevant behaviors, progress is more likely to be noted.

The practice of noting progress has the added benefit of encouraging all involved, including discouraged professionals:

It [the case plan] is concrete so we can see progress. It helped us show the school. Before they [the school] had been complaining so much—about Mom, about her lack of cooperation—that when we began to show concrete changes they [the school] came on board. The school was able to see that a lot had changed.

Concrete and Targeted Case Plans Have Encouraged Accountability

Concrete case plans allow workers, families, and others to celebrate and note progress. On the other hand, case plans that target specific high-risk behaviors also encourage accountability. Workers and individuals can readily point to specific outcome behaviors. In high-risk situations, naturally, evidence of change is necessary—particularly evidence that one is gaining skills to avoid relapse. When case plans target specific high-risk behaviors and needed, associated skills— and when clients do not demonstrate attainment of those skills—we are left with a more solid foundation for recommending an extension of state custody, termination of parental rights, or some other appropriate action. Workers report a great deal of success in this arena:

> I have a temporary case where we identified the needs, the solutions needed, and how we'll know when it's completed. I shared this with everyone, including the court. This detail was needed to convince the court that the kids should not be returned home. The system realized the children should stay with a relative and that this would allow the mother time to take care of herself—the plan included objectives for the mother to take care of herself [e.g., drug rehabilitation].

Solution-Based Case Plans Have Enlisted Interagency Cooperation

Many workers have described their success in enlisting the cooperation of other professionals, including teachers, school counselors, school social workers, and therapists. Caseworkers reported that this success can largely be attributed to (1) their own changed attitudes about client competencies, (2) emphasis on exceptions, (3) detailed case plans that target high-risk behaviors and more readily notice progress, and (4) professionals' own observations of improved outcomes:

> The other providers are seeing our successes and now we're better able to get them to work with us. With one situation it was very hostile. Mom had burned a lot of bridges. The case plan helped everyone focus on the issues rather than on pounding Mom. There had been a lot of complaints toward Mom [by numerous professionals]. Blaming, blaming, blaming rather than looking at exceptions. When the focus turned toward solutions the attitudes of the therapists and the school changed.

[Interviewer:] What specifically happened to create the change?

Well, several things happened. When the providers saw success at school and at home, that helped a lot [they marked success with charts and a detailed case plan]. The school then helped us mark success and Mom became more involved. This helped the school and the therapist to realize Mom did want what's best. The school was then not so condescending. It was no longer an "us and them." The service meetings are now much more productive. Before Mom would just sit there and steam. Now she expresses her concerns and everyone is much more cooperative. I think they know now that Mom cares and there are exceptions to the problem.

Caseworkers have also reported that solution-based casework has helped them gain credibility with the legal system. They have found some success in building professional, more productive partnerships with attorneys and judges. This has positively influenced the service to families:

> The court was not focusing on how to get the children home and all the effort that was being done—this was a blow to Mom and all of us. We had to show it. We had to show evidence of the changes. We won the courts over and I think focusing on exceptions was a big part of it. We focused on her successes. It seemed like success built on success. Before they were against her. We've gone from terminating parental rights to I estimate this case will be closed within the year.

Helped to Foster Change When Change Seemed Unlikely

Many workers have stated that solution-based casework helped them to "rethink a case" and "get a fresh perspective." This shift in their own perspective, bolstered by the major assumptions of solution-based casework, has helped promote change in situations where productive change seemed very unlikely:

> About one and a half years ago, her parental rights were going to be terminated. She had three children committed to the state and three others in other placements. Now [about two years later], only one child is committed, two children are living with her and she has unsupervised visits with another. She has been involved in therapy and several classes.
>
> [Interviewer:] What made the difference?
>
> She had a worker who was willing to help her access services and who looked at solutions. We looked at the issues rather than blaming and criticizing. We formed a partnership, focused on concrete goals and her personal hurdles to protecting her children. We focused on exceptions and possibilities. We said, OK, maybe they [the children] won't be home on step 1, but maybe step 3. We didn't focus on the negatives of why they were taken, but instead on how we'll get the children home.

Targeted Case Plans Have Helped Bring Change to High-Risk Events

Clients have experienced success in creating plans that target high-risk events. The following client's statement represents the perspective of many clients we interviewed:

> We made a plan. The plan has helped. He [the client's son] is in order. I don't have to raise my voice like I did . . . screaming, hollering, nothing. I've followed the plan we made and it worked. I don't have any problem with him right now. I take deep breaths, I calm down, I think it through now. I see a pattern.
>
> If you sit down and get a pattern going it helps. Our old pattern was changed to a new pattern. We made up a basic plan to go by and it worked out fine. It works for my family. . . . The plan helps you notice the old way wasn't working.

IMPLEMENTING SOLUTION-BASED CASEWORK: TRAINING CONSIDERATIONS

Reducing the likelihood of neglectful and abusive behavior requires the active involvement of the community, including citizens of all persuasions and the social service, school, health care, religious, and legal communities. Solution-based casework can be one valuable component of a coordinated community effort to avert and prevent violence. Implementing solution-based casework, therefore, requires sensitivity to context, i.e., an awareness of how each vital participant can contribute to safety and relapse prevention. Naturally, endorsing a coordinated community effort has several implications for training new and experienced professionals.

This section describes several important training considerations associated with implementing solution-based casework. They include multidisciplinary training groups, a coordinated training protocol, forms that reinforce solution-based casework practice strategies, supervision, practice-based training, and training evaluation.

Multidisciplinary Training Groups

Since casework obviously does not occur in a vacuum, when a different approach to casework is implemented it has an impact on other service systems. Prosecuting attorneys, for instance, may be confused by an emphasis on "partnership" and may initially read this as a softened approach to accountability. Workers who specifically outline high-risk events and skills they believe clients need to address in counseling sessions may irritate therapists. To avoid undue tension and professional confusion, we have found it very useful to invite, for instance, nurses,

therapists, community members, community leaders, school social workers, administrators, and social welfare employees to solution-based casework caseworker training. The benefits are far-reaching. We have found
that multidisciplinary training (1) creates a mutual understanding of underlying assumptions about clients and caregiving, (2) creates a similar
and mutually understood language, (3) creates an awareness of the need
to focus casework on high-risk events, (4) creates focused plans that
target prevention and emphasize client competence and (5) helps all involved parties to better understand each other's roles and to reduce the
incidents where professionals work at cross purposes.

In our experience the creation and implementation of solution-based
casework did not begin with multidisciplinary training groups. It was,
instead, a model that emerged within casework and extended eventually
and quite naturally to include other related disciplines. Indeed, in our
experience, the impact of solution-based casework in the community led
to multidisciplinary training groups. That is, based on their encounters
with solution-based casework–trained caseworkers—and based on client
response—administrators and workers from disciplines outside protective services expressed interest in solution-based casework training.
Therefore, in implementing solution-based casework, there are many advantages to beginning with multidisciplinary training. However, we anticipate that in-house protective service training will and should readily
extend to system-wide, multidisciplinary training efforts.

Coordinated, Congruent Training Protocols

When implementing solution-based casework, and on an ongoing basis, all practice-oriented, in-house protective services training sessions
should reflect the assumptions of solution-based casework. For instance,
when workers attend a workshop on casework investigation, the trainer
should promote interviewing skills that encourage partnership, that track
high-risk sequences, and that identify exceptions to the problem. Moreover, all in-house training is an opportunity to remind workers of the
language of solution-based casework, e.g., solutions, exceptions, competence, high-risk events, relapse prevention, and tracking. As such, each
training reinforces solution-based casework assumptions and practice
skills. This requires a coordinated effort at the training and administrative
level. The benefit is practice consistency and mastery of the model for
new and experienced caseworkers.

Forms and Technology Reflect Solution-Based Casework

As is well known, the forms used in an agency often drive the service
delivery system. We encounter forms on a daily basis: they are a necessary

and somewhat irritating aspect of any work. At the same time, however, the language of the forms, as well as what is and is not included, shapes our thinking. Given that, it is to our advantage to create forms that reflect the assumptions of solution-based casework. For instance, goal sheets can be written to include a section for family- level and individual-level objectives. This increases the likelihood that workers will think about both individual and family developmental issues. Forms can also be created, for instance, to include a section titled Exceptions to the Problem. This will document important client skills and remind workers to investigate exceptions. Moreover, duplicate forms (two-page forms that make an impression on the sheet below the top sheet) that are titled High-Risk Sequence, and Relapse Prevention Plan can be carried to clients' homes. During the home visit, worker and client(s) can, in writing, track sequences, document relapse prevention plans, and then separate the duplicate. One form stays with the client and the other is placed in the case file. This saves time and creates a running record of essential information. Finally, many states are using computers to train new and experienced workers. Computer software can be written in a way to also reflect the assumptions and practice skills associated with solution-based casework.[1]

Supervision

Given the complexity of social problems, individuals, and families, and given the demands of casework itself, the supervisor is obviously a very key player in ensuring effective and safe casework practice. Naturally, for a practice model such as solution-based casework to be consistently applied and effective, it must be endorsed by all levels of the administrative hierarchy. However, the direct supervisor of frontline workers is particularly influential. The direct supervisor's attitude toward clients and his/her investment, or lack thereof, in the casework practice model is nearly always reflected in the work of his/her staff. Therefore, it essential to train direct supervisors in the practice of solution-based casework and to work very closely with them on an ongoing basis. This close relationship helps to support supervisors in the demands of their job and to grapple with practice-related questions. It is useful to conduct training at two levels: (1) separate training for direct supervisors and other administrators, and (2) joint training for supervisors and their staff. This allows for training sessions that separate issues particular to supervisors from those that are more case and practice specific.

Practice-Based Training

Training is most effective in changing practice when (1) the vision and ideas seem useful to workers, (2) the training itself is clearly presented, (3) the training is embedded in a coordinated training plan, and (4), as stated previously, when assumptions and practices permeate casework training. In addition, the opportunity to regularly apply the ideas, i.e., to practice and walk through case examples, is an essential aspect of moving the training from a hypothetical, academic discussion to a living, breathing, and relevant practice model.

Supervisors and workers need to recognize the utility of solution-based casework and to master how to apply the ideas across a wide array of problem situations and with a wide array of client personalities. To that end, solution-based training should be a supportive environment where trainees are willing to take risks, i.e., to ask difficult questions, to practice skills in the presence of colleagues, and to present difficult case situations. The use of videotape, charts, walking through a problem situation in detail, collaboratively strategizing a plan, and exercises to practice essential skills combine to make ambitious ideas practical realities.

Training Evaluation

We have found it very useful to evaluate how workers, supervisors, and others are responding to solution-based casework training. Careful evaluation of training helps trainers, administrators, supervisors, caseworkers, and others to assess what is and is not being learned and how that learning influences practice. Evaluating the training at four levels, as described by Kirkpatrick (1987), is particularly useful. Kirkpatrick's four levels of evaluation include reaction (level 1), learning (level 2), behavior (level 3), and results (level 4).

Level 1 assesses how trainees generally reacted to the training, i.e., how well they liked the presented material, its relevance for their work, training effectiveness, and trainer performance. Level 2 assesses the degree to which trainees mastered the material, including basic knowledge, skills, and attitudes. Level 3 evaluates trainee behavior. This includes an assessment of the relationship between training objectives and on-the-job behavior by trainees. Finally, level 4 evaluates the results of the training, including, for instance, client outcomes, productivity, and the degree to which the training supported organizational objectives.

In a recent evaluation of solution-based casework training (Yankeelov & Barbee, 1998), in an effort to capture knowledge gained, the evaluators administered a pretraining knowledge test and, subsequently, a posttraining, postknowledge survey. Evaluators were also able to identify participants' absolute knowledge associated with each training objective. This same study evaluated pre- and posttraining written case plans and included structured interviews with workers, supervisors, and clients. Training evaluation of this nature is particularly valuable because it helps trainers to identify training strengths, to understand how the material is being received, and to adjust accordingly. Moreover, training evaluation allows all involved to specify how their efforts and solution-based casework are useful in the effort to create working partnerships, identify high-risk behaviors, and reduce the recurrence of relapse.

NOTE

1. Information systems in Kentucky have been rewritten to reflect the concepts of a solution-based approach.

References

Adams, P., & Krauth, K. (1994). Empowering workers for empowerment-based practice. In P. Nurius & L. Gutierrez (Eds.), *Education and research for empowerment practice*. Seattle: University of Washington School of Social Work.

Adams, P., & Nelson, K. (1995). *Reinventing human services: Community and family-centered practice*. Hawthorne, NY: Aldine de Gruyter.

American Humane Association (1992). *Helping in child protective services: A competency-based casework handbook*. Englewood, CO: American Humane Society.

Aponte, H. A. (1976). Underorganization in the poor family. In P. J. Guerin (Ed.), *Family therapy: Theory and practice*, 432–448. New York: Gardner.

Areen, J. (1975). Intervention between parent and child: A reappraisal of the state's role in child neglect and abuse cases. *Georgetown Law Journal, 63*(4), 887–937.

Axinn, J., & Levin, H. (1982). *Social welfare: A history of the American response to need* (2nd ed.). New York: Harper and Row.

Bandler, B. (1963). The concept of ego-supportive psychotherapy. In H. Parad and R. Miller (Eds.), *Ego-oriented casework: Problems and perspectives*, 27–44. New York: Family Service Association of America.

Bateson, G. (1951). Information and codification: A philosophical approach. In J. Ruesch and G. Bateson (Eds.), *Communication: The social matrix of psychiatry*. New York: Norton.

Bayley, M., Seyd, R., & Tennant, A. (1989). *Local health and welfare*. Aldershot, UK: Gower.

Berg, I. K. (1994). *Family based services: A solution-focused approach*. New York: W. W. Norton.

Bowen, M. (1978). *Family therapy in clinical practice*. New York: Aronson.

Bremner, R. H. (1970). *Children and youth in America: A documentary history, 1600–1865* (Vol. 1). Cambridge, MA: Harvard University Press.

Brown, J., & Christensen, D. (1999). *Family therapy: Theory and practice* (2nd ed.). Monterey, CA: Brooks-Cole.

Burke, C. (1997). The most salient ingredient of therapeutic change: Therapists' attitude about client competency. Unpublished manuscript.

Carter, B., and McGoldrick, M. (1980). *The family life cycle*. New York: Gardner.

Carter, B., and McGoldrick, M. (1988). *The changing family life cycle: A framework for family therapy* (2nd ed.). Boston: Allyn and Bacon.

Christensen, D. N. (1997). Minimum outcome skills in the social services. Speech presented to the Kentucky Cabinet for Family and Children, Frankfort, Kentucky.

Christensen, D. N., & Todahl, J. (1999). Solution based casework: A model to prevent relapse. *Journal of Family Social Work* (forthcoming).

Daro, D. (1988). *Confronting child abuse: Research for effective program design.* New York: Free Press.

de Shazer, S. (1985). *Keys to solution in brief therapy.* New York: Norton.

de Shazer, S. (1988). *Clues: Investigating solutions in brief therapy.* New York: Norton.

de Shazer, S. (1991). *Putting difference to work.* New York: W. W. Norton.

de Shazer, S., Berg, I. K., Lipchik, E., Nunnally, E. W., Molnar, A., Gingerich, W. C., & Weiner-Davis, M. (1986). Brief therapy: Focused solution development. *Family Process, 25,* 207–221.

Dell, P. (1985). Understanding Bateson and Maturana. *Journal of Marital and Family Therapy, 11,* 1–20.

Dubois, R. (1968). *Man adapting.* New Haven, CT: Yale University Press.

Durrant, M. (1993). *Residential treatment: A cooperative, competency-based approach to therapy and program design.* New York: W. W. Norton.

Duvall, E. M. (1957). *Family development.* Philadelphia: Lippincott.

Duvall, E. M. (1971). *Family development* (4th ed.). Philadelphia: Lippincott.

Fairbairn, W. (1954). *An object-relations theory of the personality.* New York: Basic Books.

Falicov, C. J. (Ed.) (1998). *Family transitions.* New York: Guilford.

Friedman, S. (1993). *The new language of change.* New York: Guilford.

Germain, C. B. (1979). Ecology and social work. In C. B. Germain (Ed.), *Social work practice: People and environments,* 1–22. New York: Columbia University Press.

Germain, C. B., & Gitterman, A. (1996). *The life model of social work practice: Advances in theory and practice* (2nd ed.). New York: Columbia University Press.

Haley, J. (1987). *Problem-solving therapy* (2nd ed.). San Francisco: Jossey-Bass.

Hartman, A., & Laird, J. (1983). *Family-centered social work practice.* New York: Free Press.

Herr, T., Halpern, R., & Conrad, A. (1991). *Changing what counts: Rethinking the journey out of welfare.* Evanston, IL: Center for Urban Affairs and Policy Research, Northwestern University.

Hines, P. (1988). The family life cycle of poor black families. In B. Carter & M. McGoldrick (Eds.), *The changing family cycle: A framework for family therapy* (2nd ed.). New York: Gardiner.

Hoffman, L. (1981). *The foundations of family therapy.* New York: Basic Books.

Jarrett, M. (1919). The psychiatric thread running through all social case *Proceedings, National Conference on Social Welfare.*

Jenkins, A. (1990). *Invitation to responsibility: The therapeutic engagement of men who are violent and abusive.* Adelaide: Dulwich Centre Publications.

Kemp, S. P., Whittaker, J. K., & Tracy, E. M. (1997). *Person-environment practice: The social ecology of interpersonal helping.* Hawthorne, NY: Aldine de Gruyter.

Kinney, J. M., Haapala, D. A., Booth, C., & Leavitt, S. (1990). The Homebuilders model. In J. K. Whittaker, J. M. Kinney, E. Tracy, & C. Booth (Eds.), *Reaching high risk families: Intensive family preservation services in human services,* 31–64. Hawthorne, NY: Aldine de Gruyter.

Kirkpatrick, D. L. (1987). Evaluation. In R. L. Craig (Ed.), *Training and Development Handbook* (3rd ed.). New York: McGraw-Hill.

Landau-Stanton, J., & Stanton, M. D. (1985). Treating suicidal adolescents and their families. In M. Pravder Mirkin & S. Koman (Eds.), *Handbook of adolescents and family therapy*, 309–328. Hawthorne, NY: Aldine de Gruyter.

Lane, S. (1991). The sexual abuse cycle. In G. Ryan & S. Lane (Eds.), *Juvenile sexual offending*. Lexington, MA: Lexington Books.

Lane, S. (1997). The sexual abuse cycle. In G. Ryan & S. Lane (Eds.), *Juvenile sexual offending: Causes, consequences, and correction*. San Francisco: Jossey-Bass.

Lee, J. (1994). *The empowerment approach to social work practice*. New York: Columbia University Press.

Lee, P., & Kenworthy, M. (1931). *Mental hygiene and social work*. New York: Commonwealth Fund.

Liddle, H. A., Breunlin, D. C., & Swartz, R. C. (1988) Handbook of family therapy training and supervision. New York: Guilford.

Maluccio, A. N. (1981). *Promoting competence in clients: A newfold approach to social work practice*. New York: Free Press.

Marlatt, G. A., & Gordon, J. R. (1985). *Relapse prevention*. New York: Guilford.

Maturana, K., & Varela, F. (1980). *Autopsies and cognition: The realization of living*. Boston: D. Reidd.

McDaniel, S. H., Hepworth, J., & Doherty, W. J. (1992). *Medical family therapy: A biopsychosocial approach to families with health problems*. New York: Basic Books.

McGowan, B., & Meezan, W. (Eds). (1983). *Child welfare: Current dilemmas—Future directions*. Itasca, IL: F. E. Peacock.

Middleman, R., & Wood, G. (1990). *Skills for direct practice in social work*. New York: Columbia University Press.

Miller, S., & Berg, I. K. (1995). *The miracle method: A radically new approach to problem drinking*. New York: W. W. Norton.

Minuchin, S. (1974). *Families and family therapy*. Boston: Harvard University Press.

Minuchin, S. (1984). *Family kaleidoscope*. Cambridge, MA: Harvard University Press.

Minuchin, S., & Fishman, H. C. (1981). *Family therapy techniques*. Cambridge, MA: Harvard University Press.

Minuchin, S., & Nichols, M. P. (1993). *Family healing: Tales of hope and renewal from family therapy*. New York: Free Press.

Newgartin, B., & Weinstein, K. (1968). The changing American grandparents. In B. Newgartin (Ed.), *Middle age and aging*. Chicago: University of Chicago Press.

Nichols, M. P., & Schwartz, R. C. (1995). *Family therapy: Concepts and methods* (3rd ed.). Needham Heights, MA: Simon & Schuster.

Nunnally, E. W., Chilman, C. S., & Cox, F. M. (1988). Introduction to the Series. In E. W. Nunnally, C. S. Chilman, & F. M. Cox (Eds.), *Troubled relationships: Families in trouble series* (Vol. 3, 7–14). Newbury Park, CA: Sage.

O'Hanlon, W., & Weiner-Davis, M. (1989). *In search of solutions: A new direction in psychotherapy*. New York: Norton.

Olson, L., Berg, L. & Conrad, A. (1980). *High job turnover among the urban poor: The project match experience*. Evanston, IL: Center for Urban Affairs and Policy Research, Northwestern University.

Parry, A., & Doan, R. E. (1994). *Story re-visions: Narrative therapy in the postmodern world*. New York: Guilford.

Patterson, G. R., & Chamberlain, P. (1992). A functional analysis of resistance: A neobehavioral perspective. In H. Arkowitz (Ed.), *Why don't people change? New perspectives on resistance and noncompliance*. New York: Guilford Press.

Pecora, P. J., Whittaker, J. K., Maluccio, A. N., Barth, R. P, & Plotnick, R. D. (1992). *The child welfare challenge: Policy, practice, and research*. Hawthorne, NY: Aldine de Gruyter.

Peters, T. (1993). Foreword. In A. Gore, *Creating a government that works better and costs less* (ix–xxii). The report of the National Performance Review. New York: Plume.

Pithers, W. (1990). Relapse prevention with sexual aggressors: A method for maintaining therapeutic gain and enhancing external supervision. In W. L. Marshall, D. R. Laws, & H. E. Barbee (Eds.), *Handbook of sexual assault: Issues, theories and treatments of the offender*. New York: Plenum.

Pithers, W., Marques, J., Gilbat, C.. & Marlatt, A. (1983). Relapse prevention with Sexual Aggressives. In J. Green & I. Stuart (Eds.), *Sexual Aggressor*. New York: Van Nostrand Reinbold.

Reynolds, B. (1932). A changing psychology one year later. *Family, 13*, 107–111.

Richmond, M. (1917). *Social diagnosis*. New York: Russell Sage Foundation.

Richmond, M. (1930). *The long view*. New York: Russell Sage Foundation.

Robinson, V. (1930). *A changing psychology in social case work*. Chapel Hill: University of North Carolina Press.

Schorr, L. D. (1993). Keynote address. In National Association of Social Workers, *Effective strategies for increasing social program replication/adaptation: A review of the literature and summary of a seminar* (7–18). Washington, DC: NASW.

Selekman, M. (1993). *Pathways to change: Brief therapy solutions with difficult adolescents*. New York: Guilford.

Selekman, M. (1997). *Solution-focused therapy with children*. New York: Guilford.

Smale, G. G. (1995). Integrating community and individual practice: A new paradigm for practice. In P. Adams & K. Nelson (Eds.), *Reinventing human services: Community and family-centered practice*. Hawthorne, NY: Aldine de Gruyter.

Southard, E. E. (1918). The kingdom of evil: Advantages of an orderly approach in social case analysis. In *Proceedings, National Conference of Social Work*. **publisher? city? editor?**

Speck, R., & Attneave, C. (1973). *Family networks*. New York: Vintage.

Sroufe, L. A. (1978). Emotional development in infancy. In J. Osofsky (Ed.), *Handbook of infancy*. New York: Wiley.

Terkelson, K. G. (1980). Toward a theory of the family life cycle. In B. Carter & M. McGoldrick (Eds.), *The family life cycle*. New York: Gardner.

Thomas, M. P. (1972). Child abuse and neglect: Part 1. Historical overview, legal matrix, and social perspectives. *North Carolina Law Review, 50*, 293–349.

Todahl, J., & Christensen, D. N. (1997). Neighborhood Place study and consultation project: Report to the operations committee. Paper presented to the Jefferson County Public School System, Louisville, Kentucky.

von Bertalanffy, L. (1968). *General systems theory.* New York: George Braziller.

Waldegrave, C. (1990). Just therapy. *Dulwich Center Newsletter, 1,* 6–46.

Walter, J., & Peller, J. (1992). *Becoming solution-focused in brief therapy.* New York: Brummer/Mazel.

Watkins, S. A. (1990). The Mary Ellen myth: Correcting child welfare history. *Social Work, 35*(6), 500–503.

Watzlawick, P., Weakland, J., & Fisch, R. (1974). *Change: Principles of problem formation and problem resolution.* New York: Norton.

Way, I. F., & Speiker, S. (1997). *The cycle of offense: A framework for treating adolescent sexual offenders.* Notre Dame, IN: Jalice.

White, M. (1986). Negative explanation, restraint, and double description: A template for family therapy. *Family Process, 25,* 169–184.

White, M. (1988). The process of questioning: A therapy of literary merit? *Dulwich Centre Newsletter,* Winter, 8–14.

White, M., & Epston, D. (1990). *Narrative means to therapeutic ends.* New York: W. W. Norton.

Whiteside, M. F. (1982). Remarriage: A family developmental process. *Journal of Marital and Family Therapy, 8,* 59–68.

Wilson, W. (1987). *The truly disadvantaged.* Chicago: University of Chicago.

Wood, G. G., & Middleman, R. R. (1989). *The structural approach to direct practice in social work.* New York: Columbia University Press.

Yankeelov, P., & Barbee, A. (1998). Evaluation of solution based casework training for Ujima Neighborhood Place CPS workers. Paper presented to the Kentucky Cabinet for Families and Children, Frankfort, Kentucky.

Index

Action plans (*See* Guidelines)

Assessment (*See* Case planning and assessment)

Behavior, as multifactorial, 4–5

Case examples
adolescent daughter, 139
adolescent son, 39
physically abusive mother, 10, 70, 77
supervisor, caseworker's relationship with, 142

Case management, solution-based (*See also other headings under* Case *and* Casework)
assessment and case plans, integrating, 130
changes in behavior, conceptualizing, 129–130
changes in behavior, encouraging incremental, 131–132
collaboration between professionals, 132–136
family situations, maintaining focus on, 143–146
interviewing techniques (*see* Interviewing techniques, solution-based)
networks, use of, 130–131
partnerships with clients (*see* Partnerships and consensus-building)
prevention skills, need to target, 126–127
problems, conceptualizing, 127–129
referrals, 96–97
setbacks, learning from and adjusting to, 136–140, 171–172

supervisor, role of and caseworker's relationship with, 140–146
tasks, template for, 115 fig. 7.2
therapy and therapists, caseworker's dealings with, 132–136, 170–173 (*see also* Treatment providers, role in case management)
transition from casework to treatment, 132–136
transition from intake to ongoing, 127–132
welfare to work objectives, integration of, 136

Case planning and assessment (*See also* Relapse prevention; *other headings under* Case *and* Casework)
action plans and relapse prevention (*see* Guidelines)
decision-making and risk assessment, 62–63
defined, 37
developmental stages of family and, 11, 41–48
documentation, 107–108, 118–119
ecological perspective and, 5–6
family action plan, 117 fig. 7.3, 120 fig. 7.A1
family-level goals and objectives, 11, 58, 77–79, 91–94, 108–116 (*see also* Guidelines)
family life, as locus of casework (*see* Families)
individual action plan, template for, 123 fig. 7.A2
individual-level goals and objectives, 11, 77–79, 91–94, 108–116, 160–162 (*see also* Guidelines)

Casework (*cont.*)
    manageable tasks, moving from objectives to, 77–79, 112–116
    objectives, risk-related, 112
    objectives, traditional, 105–106
    objectives, under solution-based approach, 66, 106
    patterns in everyday life and (*see* Families, problems and problem patterns of)
    relapse prevention and (*see* Relapse prevention)
    responsibilities of caseworker and treatment provider, 116
    solutions to problems, need to focus on, 17–19, 108–109
    unification of, 32
Casework practice, history and recent developments in (*See also other headings under* Case *and* Casework)
    clients, strengths of and partnerships with, 31–32
    community, as a resource, 31
    evolution of, 22–25
    individual versus family, orientation toward, 23–25
    initiatives, recent, 29–33
    integration of services, 30
    objectives, 4
    psychiatric model, 24
    traditional, limitations of, 25–27
Casework, solution-based (*See also other headings under* Case *and* Casework)
    accountability, encouragement of, 211
    challenges in transition to, 207–209
    collaboration between professionals, 206, 211–212
    community involvement and, 32
    as competence-centered perspective, 7–9, 32–33
    ecological perspective, 4–6
    empowerment of clients, 205–206
    as family-centered practice, 3–4, 32 (*see also* Families)

family life cycle theory and, 9–11 (*see also* Families, life cycles and development of)
    fundamental assumptions of, 17–19, 32–33
    integration of services, 32
    organization and assessment of data, 38
    partnerships and, 32–33, 38–39, 210–212
    postmodern family and, 11–13
    prevention skills, need to target, 76
    professional training and, 213–217
    reform of casework practice, 29–33, 203–217
    rejection of deficit-focused models, 32, 199–203 (*see also* Deficit-focused models of casework)
    relapse prevention theory and, 15–17
    solution-focused family therapy and, 13–15
    solutions, efficiency of, 204, 212–213
    solutions, workability of, 203–204
    unification of assessment and planning, 32
Children, protection of, 22–25
Clients, competence of (*See also* Deficit-focused models of casework)
    as foundation for change, 7–8, 14–15, 30–32
    relapse prevention plan and, 83–86
Clients, different frameworks from which to understand, 4–5
Community
    as locus of casework practice, 30–33
    as a resource, 31
Consensus-building for a relapse prevention plan (*See also* Partnerships and consensus-building)
    as building upon partnership, 86
    initial safety plan, 94–97
    interviewing techniques (*see* Interviewing techniques, solution-based)
    referrals to treatment providers or other community resources, 97

solutions, identifying, 83–86
strategies, 86–94
Cycle work (*See* Families, problems
and problem patterns of)

Deficit-focused models of casework
adversarial relationships in, 199–200
approach to clients, as presumptuous and punitive, 201–202
defined, 7–8, 14
fragmentation of services, 26
inadequate interventions, 15–17, 25,
29, 51–53
narrow conception of success, 202–
203
negativity, 200–201
reactive services, 26–27
underestimation of client competence, 202
underutilization of client competence, 7
underutilization of community as a
resource, 27
Disease-oriented therapies (*See*
Deficit-focused models of
casework)

Ecological perspective, 4–6
Exceptions to problem patterns, as
foundations for solutions
case plans and, 79
interviewing techniques, 179–180
recognition of patterns and, 61–62
solution-based casework and, 18–
19, 31–32, 205–206
solution-focused family therapy
and, 14–15
supervisor's role in helping to identify, 145–146

Families (*See also other headings under*
Families)
collective wisdom of, 92–93
education, developmental approach
to
everyday life of, as context for assessment and case planning, 10–
11, 37–39, 48–52, 56–62

as locus for individual skill development, 37
partnerships with, 37–38
perception of, as dysfunctional, 38
routines, centrality of, 39–40
universal challenges of, 37
Families, life cycles and development
of (*See also other headings under*
Families)
case planning and, 11
developmental stages, with associated challenges, 42–48
maladaptation and discouragement,
49–50
supervisor's role and, 144
theory, 9–11, 41–42
Families, problems and problem patterns of (*See also* Relapse prevention; *other headings under*
Families)
addressing, through creation of
partnerships, 53–55
assessment and, 38–39, 48–53, 56–
62
case planning and, 76–79
clients' recognition of, 56–57
externalization of, 56
family action plan, template for, 117
fig. 7.3, 120 fig. 7.A1
family-level goals and objectives,
11, 58, 77–79, 91–94, 108–116
interviewing techniques, 176–184
maintaining focus on, 143–146
promoting clients' understanding
of, 57–61
relapse prevention plan, 17–19
supervisor's role and, 144–145
tracking, as means of consensus-
building, 87–90
treatment providers and, 159–169
Fifocal vision, 5–6

Guidelines
anger, tipsheet on avoiding, 99 fig.
6.A1
chores, tipsheet on, 100 fig. 6.A2

Guidelines (*cont.*)
  for family group decision-making
    (child protection cases), 93–94
  family-level objectives, 59 fig. 4.3,
    117 fig. 7.3, 120 fig. 7.A1
  individual-level objectives, 123 fig.
    7.A2, 161 fig. 9.2, 162 fig. 9.3
  parenting young children, tipsheet
    on, 102 fig. 6.A4
  parenting young teenagers, tipsheet
    on, 101 fig. 6.A3
  relapse prevention and, 115–116,
    118–119
  use of, in building a consensus, 91–
    92

Human services, de-centering of, 30

Interviewing techniques, solution-
    based
  change, creating client interest in
    signs of, 184–191
  change, expanding audience for,
    192–194
  consensus-building, 176–184
  credentialing, enforcing progress
    through, 194–196
  exceptions to problem patterns,
    179–180
  externalizing problems, 178–179
  normalizing problems, 177–178
  old versus new T-charts, 186–187
  recognizing problem patterns, 180–
    184
  rites of passage, celebrating, 196–
    197
  scaling questions, 187–189
  self, anchoring change in new, 191–
    197
  self-observation, 185–186
  time-oriented questions, 189–191
  and treatment providers, 169

Language, use of family's, 90–91,
    129–130
Legislation
  Child Abuse Prevention and Treat-
    ment Act, 23

parens patriae and, 22
welfare to work legislation, 28

Neighborhood Place (program), 30–32

Parens patriae, 22
Partnerships and consensus-building
    (*See also* Consensus-building for a
    relapse prevention plan)
  assessment and, 38–39
  constructivism and, 13
  interviewing techniques (*see* Inter-
    viewing techniques, solution-
    based)
  loss of cooperation and, 128–129
  as means of finding solutions, 52–
    53
  recent initiatives in casework prac-
    tice and, 31–32
  solution-based casework and, 15,
    38–39, 206
  techniques to promote, 53–56
Patch (program), 30–32
Postmodernism and constructivism
  constructivism, defined, 12–13
  contrasted with modernism, 21–22
  social work and, 11–13, 22
  as worldview, 21–22
Prevention (*See* Relapse prevention)

Relapse prevention (*See also* Case
    planning and assessment;
    Consensus-building for a relapse
    prevention plan; Treatment pro-
    viders, role in relapse prevention)
  creating a case plan, 76–79
  early warning signs, 66–67, 73–74
  escaping patterns in high-risk situa-
    tions, 75–76
  as four-step process, with associ-
    ated skills, 163–164
  high-risk situations, avoiding, 67,
    74–75
  high-risk situations, escaping pat-
    terns in, 68, 75–76
  high-risk situations, identifying, 66
  high-risk situations, interrupting
    patterns in, 67–68, 75

high-risk situations, recognizing
  patterns in, 68–73, 84–90
prevention skills, need to target,
  65–66, 76–79, 108, 126–127
reinforcing client progress, 79–80
setbacks and, 136–140
and solution-based casework, 17–19
theory of, defined, 15–17
treatment providers and (*see* Treatment providers, role in relapse
  prevention)

Solution-focused family therapy, 13–
  15
Supervisors, 140–146

Therapy and therapists (*See headings
  under* Treatment providers)
Tipsheets (*See* Guidelines)
Treatment providers, role in case
  management (*See also* Treatment
  providers, role in relapse
  prevention)
case background, need to know,
  152–153
caseworkers, as clients, 152
discontinuities between treatment
  and casework, 132–134, 149–152
family's perception of problem,
  need to know, 154–155
goal of treatment, from caseworker's perspective, 155
interviewing techniques, solution-
  based (*see* Interviewing techniques, solution-based)

referral conversation with caseworker, recommended, 155–157
referral conversation with caseworker, roles of therapist and
  caseworker in, 158–159
referral conversation with caseworker, standard, 150–151
safety plan, need to know, 153–154
Treatment providers, role in relapse
  prevention
collaboration with caseworkers,
  strategies for, 134–136, 170–173
creating a case plan, 168–169
documentation, 163
early warning signs, 164–166
family developmental needs, tailoring therapy to, 159–160
high-risk situations, avoiding, 167
high-risk situations, escaping patterns in, 168
high-risk situations, identifying,
  164–166
high-risk situations, interrupting
  patterns in, 167–168
high-risk situations, recognizing
  patterns in, 164–166
prevention, overview of steps to,
  163–164
prevention plan, 160–162

Unemployment, 28–29, 136

Welfare to work legislation, 28, 136